CONFRONTING THE HOLOCAUST

CONFRONTING THE HOLOCAUST

A Mandate for the 21st Century

Edited by

G. Jan Colijn
Marcia Sachs Littell

Studies in the Shoah

Volume XIX

University Press of America, Inc.
Lanham • New York • Oxford

University Press of America,® Inc.
4720 Boston Way
Lanham, Maryland 20706

12 Hid's Copse Rd.
Cummor Hill, Oxford OX2 9JJ

Library of Congress Cataloging-in-Publication

Confronting the Holocaust : a mandate for the 21st century / edited by
G. Jan Colijn and Marcia Sachs Littell.
p.   cm.--(Studies in the Shoah ; v. 19)
A selection of papers and plenary addresses presented at the 26th
annual Scholars' Conference on the Holocaust and the Churches,
Minneapolis, March 1996.
Includes bibliographical references.
1. Holocaust, Jewish (1939-1945)--Influence--Congresses. I. Colijn,
G. Jan. II. Littell, Marcia Sachs. III. Scholars conference on the
Holocaust and the Churches (26th : 1996 : Minneapolis, Minn.) IV.
Series.
D804.18.C66   1997   940.53'18--dc21   97-7295   CIP

ISBN 0-7618-0726-8 (cloth: alk. ppr.)

~ Dedicated to ~

YEHUDA BAUER
on the occasion of
his seventieth birthday

A WORD ABOUT KEEPING WARM

Those who have studied the Holocaust for many years, told the story to teach their contemporaries, and trained up another generation of young scholars to continue the dialogue with the past, have elected to carry a heavy weight. People - including the people of the campuses - don't want to hear the demand to remember what they would rather forget. There is a personal psychological burden too, even if the scholar is able to compare his scientific role to that of the pathologist in a medical school.

For the Holocaust continues to challenge the most cherished assumptions in our culture and our civilization. The reliability of what we have been taught about education, about the agencies of law and justice, about the behavior of persons of faith, about personal and group morality, about professional ethics - all is severely shaken. Most severe of all, the earnest confrontation with the Holocaust becomes personal. To use the vernacular, "It's cold out there!"

In surviving the excursions into the wasteland of the human spirit, and especially in daily re-committing one's self to life, no human source of energy surpasses friendship.

Yehuda Bauer has been a friend, both personal and professional since the beginnings of the Annual Scholars' Conference. Although eminent in his specialty as a scientist, as a Jewish historian writing many books and articles on the greatest single tragedy in Jewish history, he understood what many have yet to grasp: that the Holocaust is *not* "a *Jewish* affair" (only), but rather a giant question mark hanging over both our separate and our common lives in Western civilization.

As researcher and writer, as teacher and editor, as organizer and counselor - and above all as a friend - Yehuda has been indispensable. By his work and by his presence he has helped greatly to keep us warm.

-- Franklin H. Littell, Co-Founder

CONTENTS

ACKNOWLEDGEMENTS

This volume was made possible by a grant from

THE SHARON GUTMAN - CHARLES LIGHTNER
PUBLICATION FUND

with the cooperation of

THE PHILADELPHIA CENTER ON THE
HOLOCAUST, GENOCIDE AND HUMAN RIGHTS

and the

RICHARD STOCKTON COLLEGE OF NEW JERSEY

Introduction

The 26th Annual Scholars' Conference on the Holocaust and the Churches took place in Minneapolis during the first week of March 1996. The conference was founded in 1970 by Franklin H. Littell (Temple University) and Hubert G. Locke (University of Washington) as an interfaith, interdisciplinary and international organization. Devoted to remembering and learning from the Holocaust, and encouraging the participation of both educators and local communities, its mission is to promote scholarly research that examines issues raised by the "Final Solution."

The conference has grown tremendously over the years. Theologians, still grappling with the questions raised by the original intentions of the conference, have been joined by historians, social scientists, ethicists, film makers and other artists in a conference that appears to find a new voice, and continues to find new and important themes each year. Not least of these is the strong emphasis on the pedagogy of Holocaust and genocide studies as a parallel focus next to scholarly research. The burgeoning interest in the issues in the K-12 sector and the several state-wide mandates for such education now in effect simply mandate much greater attention to proper pedagogies for diverse age groups.

We were greeted in Minneapolis by one of the local hosts, Stephen Feinstein who, in sub-zero temperature, welcomed us to "... the land of the frozen chosen." The conference itself, however, took place in an atmosphere that was anything but frosty. As always, civility and politesse characterized the discourse, even when vehement disagreements occurred. Tragic events in the Middle East took place during the conference - more about this concurrence in the text itself - and the always strenuous pace of the conference and its most serious focus was further complicated by these actualities. The superb organization and the tremendous warmth with which we were received by our Minnesota hosts meant a great deal to all those in attendance.

It is of course, the norm to thank those responsible for local arrangements at the end of an introduction of any kind of proceedings. It seemed suitable to break with that tradition here and thank a number of colleagues whose organizational efforts were so pivotal: Rabbi Max A. Shapiro, 1996 Conference Chair; Karen L. Schiernan and Celeste Raspanti, Conference Coordinators; others on the Host Committee, i.e. M. Christine Athans, Marilyn Chiat, Molly Cox, Barry Cytron, Joseph Edelhert, Bill Duna, Gerda Haas, Sally Hill, Pauline Lambert, Robert Willis, Carol Wirtschafter, and Stephen Feinstein, noted earlier. In addition, we are grateful for the support of the Archdiocese of St. Paul and Minneapolis, its Commission of Ecumenism and Interreligious Affairs, the Jewish-Christian Relations Committee - Minnesota Council of Churches, the Jewish Community Relations Council, the Minneapolis Area Synod, Minneapolis Federation of Jewish Service, Minneapolis Rabbinical Association, The American Jewish Committee - Minneapolis/St. Paul chapter, and the National Conference. Each and everyone of these individuals and organizations did an outstanding job for which all scholars in attendance were most grateful. We would also be remiss in not thanking Peg Rivera and Pam Cross at the Richard Stockton College of New Jersey and Sharon Heesh of The Philadelphia Center on the Holocaust, Genocide and Human Rights for their considerable work on this volume.

Under normal circumstances, this volume of conference papers would have a broad selection of papers from the conference panels, e.g. the numerous panels on teaching the Holocaust, Post-Holocaust Christian Theologies, Christian-Jewish Relations after the Shoah, Early Christian and Medieval Roots of Jewish Persecution and newer themes, e.g. issues surrounding the so-called Second Generation. A representative companion volume such as just described will indeed be published, edited by Stephen Feinstein.

This volume, however, presents a selection of conference papers and plenary addresses made with an eye on the colleague to whom it is dedicated on the occasion of his seventieth birthday, Yehuda Bauer. It is dedicated to him because he is one of the giants in the field, one of those very few in *any* scientific field whose sheer intellectual strength, depth of insight and industry change paradigms. Yehuda Bauer's prominence among those historians associated with the "intentionalist" school of Holocaust studies hardly needs to be underscored. His public courage and his generosity in friendship set examples for us all. He will be uncomfortable with hagiography but the fact of the matter is that the field of Holocaust Studies and many of us in it owe him a debt for his strong leadership: he is a macher *and* a mensch - not necessarily a frequent combination.

Therefore, papers selected here reflect some of the themes that are of critical importance to all of us, whether in North America, Europe, Asia or elsewhere, and, we trust, will be of interest to Yehuda Bauer, e.g., the attack on the culture of remembrance by the New Right in Germany, and the dangers which social and economic tensions, in combination with xenophobia, present to democracy per se. In addition, we have included a few contributions that we knew to be of personal interest to him. We believe strongly that the quality and range of the contributions selected here constitute a fitting tribute.

We include, first of all, Yehuda Bauer's plenary address, given during the opening day of the 26th Annual Scholars' Conference. His address was given within hours of a terrorist incident in Israel, one of a series of such incidents which, besides a significant loss of life, would have a major impact on the 1996 elections in Israel -- the elections which denied Shimon Peres a continuance of his prime ministership. Professor Bauer sketched, as he has done so often, the phenomenological distinction between the destruction of European Jews and the fate of others, e.g. Gypsies and Poles, at the hands of the Nazis. He has often been misunderstood on this issue. His attempt to chart a topological landscape with analytical clarity does neither diminish personally abhorrence of the weight of the consequences to Hitler's other victims nor ignore other repeated instances of genocide in this century. Here he carefully delineates the unique ideological catalysts of Nazism, and the peculiar, unique place of Jews in our civilization, while taking issue with explanations of the Holocaust which, in his view, muddle the unique forces brought to bear *on the Jews.* Especially poignant is his painstaking effort to render the Gypsy genocide terrible in its results, but different in its causality. Drawing parallels *and* distinctions is the thankless job of historians willing to cut a wide swath on the issue of the Holocaust. Bauer's plenary address in Minneapolis was perhaps the most sure-footed way he has yet found to summarize a life's oeuvre in the span of a mere hour.

Ian Hancock's plenary address on the second day of the conference presents a different view from Bauer's but is of equal importance. Hancock provides a very thorough and authoritative account of antigypsyism in the centuries preceding ours. Entering the 1920s and 1930s, the pace of such antigypsyism inexorably increases in Germany. We are reminded of the French expression *la puissance d'une idée en marche* as German antigypsyism culminates in genocide during the war years. Especially chilling is the last part of Hancock's presentation: Rroma continue to be the prime victims of Europe's resurgent xenophobia today, victims of discrimination, violence, sterilization, deportation. It was the confluence of Hancock's masterful address and the concern among scholars, including (prominently) Bauer, that led to the statement of concern with regard to the Rroma issued on behalf of many scholars present during the last day of the conference.

John Pawlikowski's essay takes issue with Yehuda Bauer's "intentionality," which he sees echoed by others, most recently in the first volume of Steven Katz' *The Holocaust in Historical Context.* Pawlikowski, while recognizing the "sacral" dimension in the Nazi hatred of Jews and the catastrophic success of their extermination policies with respect to Europe's Jews, emphasizes additional evidence which suggests that Nazis had ominous albeit not fully realized intentions toward others, e.g., Poles and Gypsies. Yehuda Bauer likely would take issue with some of Pawlikowski's contentions. But he would and will not close the door to the exploration of new paradigms or the confrontation with another view. Hence, Pawlikowski's different views deserved inclusion.

Paul Bartrop focuses on the non-Jewish Australian attitudes toward the refugees from Nazism prior to World War II. We thought to include this contribution for the simple reason that it may interest Yehuda Bauer, perhaps intrigue him because it covers ground we presume not to be part of his usual intellectual horizons. However, there are considerably more cogent reasons to include Bartrop's essay. Of course, one must be careful to make low-rent jumps into actuality from events sixty years ago. Nevertheless, Bartrop's essay jolts the reader with an uncanny sense of recognition when the refugee and immigration issues of that time are seen through the prism of today.

There are empirically observable links between xenophobia, social and economic strain and fascism. Robert Paxton recently argued that modern strains of extremism do not fully resemble the fascism of the early part of this century but constitute "... functional equivalents in which dictatorial movements use different symbols and rhetoric but still fulfill the fascist functions of purifying, uniting, and energizing a society fearful of division and decline."[1] In the face of the recent electoral success of, for example, Le Pen in France, and in particular Haider and his Freedom Party (sic) in Austria, John Naugton recently suggested in *The Observer* that fascism "... needs two ingredients to thrive: economic hardship, preferably affecting social groups who already feel marginalized; and xenophobia."[2] The 1990s wave across Europe of economic refugees has triggered the latter, according to Naugton, and "[T]he savage cuts in welfare budgets needed to ensure that countries qualify for EMU are taking care of the former."[3] We don't intend to engage in platitudinous hand-wringing. Comparisons between those fleeing for their lives in the thirties and those fleeing economic hardship per se should, of course, be circumscribed carefully. But there can be little question that politicians riding the surf of xenophobia in Europe and elsewhere are fooling around with a pipeline that can easily lead to tragedy, bloodshed and political disaster for society at large; some do so with a pretty clear vision that such a future is exactly what they want. Bartrop's essay reminds us that the exploitation of xenophobia has very serious consequences indeed. His essay is also poignant because immigration - now of Asians - has become an issue in Australia again with fears about the "yellow race" expressed by an MP from Queensland with, apparently, substantial public support.[4]

More generally, state welfarism has, of course, been under attack for several decades, including attacks from the left.[5] The very scope of the welfare state and stresses caused by group egotism in parliamentary democracies have received attention throughout the past two decades.[6] However, as parliamentary democracies begin to dismantle the welfare state, questions arise about the viability of political order, and democracy itself. Dutch political scientist Hans Daudt already warned twenty years ago that where fundamentally different perspectives exist about the highest norms of social justice, democratic decisioning is in great danger.[7] Totalitarian or authoritarian options became more likely and we all know what that can entail for minorities.

There are some different points to be raised about Germany in particular. The tension between the German origins of the Holocaust and Germany's post-war attempts to construct a certain modicum of patriotism and national pride is still unresolved. Some years ago, the balance in Germany's emergent political culture appeared struck around a *Betroffenheitskultur* as Jacob Heilbrunn puts it, "... a culture of contrition in which every political issue is viewed through the prism of the Nazi past."[8] Following the *Historikerstreit* and generational shifts among Germany's intellectuals, Germany's political culture now appears to enter a new phase. Heilbrunn notes that the rise of the *Neue Rechte*, the new right, is on the rise in Germany, not in the political arena but among intellectuals, who wish to liberate German nationalism from history, normalize it by first normalizing the Nazi past.[9] Calls for a cohesive, national self-confidence and for a relativization of Germany's Nazi past may, of course, have grave consequences for Germany's non-German inhabitants.

Heilbrunn argues, in this regard, that there is no reason for panic. The advance of the *Neue Rechte*, he argues, is perhaps natural after 1989:

> Perhaps the Germans need to rouse rather than suppress the demon of nationalism in order to exorcise it.[10]

Heilbrunn concludes that both left and right in Germany exploit the Holocaust:

> There is an excessive preoccupation with the Holocaust in Germany, which the left, a little unwittingly, exploits for present political purposes. Some Germans experience a kind of cathartic bliss in denouncing themselves and their nationality. But the new right represents the other extreme. It too exploits the Holocaust - although in a more pernicious fashion - by scanting its importance.[11]

The issues of course are larger than another wave of historical revisionism or intellectual fashion in Germany. As Jürgen Manemann argues in this volume, the *Neue Rechte* is, for example, enamored with Carl Schmitt's central theme that democracy must be grounded in homogeneity -- a homogeneity excluding the nonhomogeneous other. That kind of homogeneity is, of course, at odds with multiculturalism.

xvii

It is also on a collision course with the anthropological realities in most European societies with their increased minorities, refugees and immigrants.

Moreover, without a cultural of remembrance, without, as Manemann puts it, "the necessity of dangerous memory," an anti-historical liberal democracy becomes a foundation of fascism because it produces an emptiness of life and because it leads to the kind of indifference to the other that made Auschwitz possible in the first place.

Some of Manemann's points are echoed in Didier Pollefeyt's contribution. Pollefeyt, too, argues that democracy is facing a difficult period. Drawing on the work of Tzvetan Todorov, Pollefeyt attempts to explore the question of what Auschwitz can teach us about the origins of human evil. Todorov's argumentation is not theological but represent the thinking of an ethicist. The central question posed is which "vision of humanity" Auschwitz compels us to believe. Is this moral catastrophe, which took place in the part of our modern Christian and humanistic world, the end of our belief in the goodness of humanity? Is not every human being capable of such racism and genocidal violence? Is it possible to rebuild ethics for humanity that is so deeply undermined by its own destructive potential? We included Pollefeyt's contribution because they are questions of great interest to Yehuda Bauer -- the person, not just the historian. Bauer alludes to his own views on the matter of good and evil just briefly in his address but we are fairly certain he will appreciate Pollefeyt's approach as well as his close and well researched reasoning.

Deborah Lipstadt's plenary address on the deniers focuses on yet another tough subject: the Holocaust denial business is a central part of the antisemitism industry. Lipstadt's contribution is a clarion call for some straight thinking about the widespread misunderstandings in the public discourse on such key concepts as freedom of speech (and not just within the American constitutional context), fair play and its pathological abuse in these post-modern times, and on the continuing importance in the academy to stand up to wrong-headed nonsense, something higher education does not always do with the requisite appetite or surefootedness. Lipstadt was, at one point, Bauer's student and she acknowledges his encouragement to focus on the Holocaust deniers. Her pugnacious presentation in Minneapolis was utterly engaging; her intellectual skills are clear in print as well.

All these contributions, from Bauer to Pollefeyt, raise fundamental questions about the direction of today's democracy, a concern which has permeated this introduction. There are corollary questions. We have just witnessed the centrifugal effects of Goldhagen's *Hitler's Willing Executioners.* The book demonized Germans, and has, of course, been criticized on scientific ground. But perhaps the most disheartening is to see, as we have, survivors carrying the book with them whenever they go because they find justification in it for their white anger not just at the Nazis, but at Germans, period. This does not bide well for German-Jewish relations. But, of course, there are positivists at work, too.

Several years ago, at the 1991 Annual Scholars Conference, a tentative and wary dialogue started between Abraham Peck, a child of Holocaust survivors and the Administrative Director of the American Jewish Archives, and Gottfried Wagner, theater and opera director, essayist and commentator, whose crusade against Bayreuth and the Nazi past of his family will enter a new phase with the 1997 publication of his autobiography *Wer nicht mit dem Wolf heult* (Kiepeneheuer & Witsch, spring 1997). This initially painful encounter has now led to the establishment of a Post-Holocaust Dialogue Group. Its statutes are as follows:

(1) We, the children of the victims and the children of the victimizers, see the Shoah/Holocaust as a unique *rift* in Western and world civilization and the starting point of a new morality in terms of thoughts, feelings and actions.

(2) We stand opposed to the repressing and silencing of any and all discussion of the Shoah/Holocaust and the continuation of any and all prejudices and hatreds resulting from the activities of our parents and grandparents both now and in the future and directly attributable to the trauma of the Shoah/Holocaust.

(3) We fully believe that the sharing of our own unique burden of this tragic past in a continuing present and future dialogue is of vital concern, independently of any religious, ideological, and/or political group. With our dialogue we give concrete evidence how our generation, and those after us, will confront the challenges presented by the Shoah/Holocaust and its ever present influences.

(4) We being our dialogue with tolerance, respect and self-critical awareness as the children of the victims and the children of the victimizers. Our mutual willingness to share our burden is coupled with our unhesitating commitment to overcome our present ignorance, prejudices, and misconceptions, and to present to those who are open and receptive a model for present and future trust and understanding.

(5) We see ourselves as an international activist organization whose avowed purpose is not only to inform others of the Shoah/Holocaust through scholarly conferences and publications, but to fight both theoretically and practically against any kind of totalitarian dogmatism religiously, politically, and ideologically. We stand for the active realization of human rights for all human beings, fully believing that we are responsible for our own actions, ever mindful of the "different other."

(6) We hope by our humanitarian actions and our scholarly work to influence governments and nation-states, thus lessening fears of present and future repetitions of the Shoah/Holocaust, striving at all times to realize our goal of a world living together in peaceful tolerance and appreciative of all diverse humanity.

Even in the face of the serious problems discussed before, positivists have not yet become an endangered species.

The last two contributions were included with Yehuda Bauer very much in mind. Elisabeth Maxwell -- in line with the calls for a culture of remembrance which underpinned the raison d'être for the two Remembering for the Future conferences she helped sponsor, and in line with earlier contributions in this volume -- makes an eloquent case for the necessity of accurate historical memory, especially as the era of Holocaust memory as a "souvenir" (the French concept of remembrance of what one has experienced) is drawing to a close. Her contribution sketches her personal journey in the confrontation with the Holocaust and therein reflects the experience of many others who have benefited, in their own confrontation with the Holocaust, from Yehuda's guidance and sagacity, and from the privileged gift that his friendship represents.

Those who have had the pleasure of spending an evening with Yehuda the musician (guitar and, as they say, vocals) accompanied by Elana Bauer (on recorder) will understand why we include the piece on camp songs by David Hirsch. Such an evening with the Bauers can run the gamut from centuries old Dutch music (Valerius) to funny Welsh ditties and plaintive Yiddish songs. The unquestionable power of music in camps has been eloquently documented in *Songs of Survival*, the film about women prisoners in a Japanese concentration camp. Here the focus is more complex: Hirsch analyses the use of music in the camps form a variety of vantage points, and he outlines the inherent contradictions in such use in a way that, we think, would earn Yehuda Bauer's approval.

Finally, there is Hubert Locke's closing address at the conference which placed the conference firmly in the context of a number of pressing actualities, some of which we have noted in this introduction.

We hope that the contributions selected will be of interest to Yehuda Bauer. They have, in fact, been selected from a vantage point on Yehuda Bauer that may well be at some odds with the views of others. Let us explain:

In Yehuda's life work, there is, of course, the relentless research productivity -- eleven books in English alone, from *The Holocaust in Historical Perspective* to *Jews for Sale,* the dozens of articles, the decade as editor of *Holocaust and Genocide Studies.* There is the foundation of the Vidal Sassoon International Center for Study of Antisemitism at Hebrew University, the editorial work also for *Yalkut Moreshet,* the main Hebrew Holocaust Studies journal. There is the academic leadership, not only in helping to organize the first Remembering for the Future conference, but at the U.S. Holocaust Memorial Museum, and now again at Yad Vashem. Despite an astonishing list of accomplishments and notwithstanding the prominence and importance of his published oeuvre, Yehuda Bauer may well be most remembered as a *teacher* (a master teacher) on, regrettably, one of the most defining episodes of our century. He sketched his (and our) work ultimately as trying to get the human orchestra to play in greater harmony. He will, we believe, be remembered one day by all those who learned from him for the clarity of that vision, and for the way his vision and his industry has helped us be guided along a path that can often seem quite stony indeed.

Thank you, therefore, Yehuda Bauer and our warmest wishes to you in your seventieth year.

G. Jan Colijn   Marcia Sachs Littell
Pomona, New Jersey   Merion Station, Pennsylvania

Notes

1. Robert O. Paxton, "The Uses of Fascism," New York Review of Books, vol. XLIII, number 19, November 28, 1996, pp. 48-52; p. 52.

2. John Naugton, "Austria seduced by the wiles of a Führer," original comment in the Observer reprinted in Manchester Guardian Weekly, vol. 155, no. 18, November 3, 1996, p. 12.

3. *Ibid.*

4. See Michael Richardson, "Australia Debates How Asian It Should Be," International Herald Tribune, November 5, 1996, p. 2.

5. See, for example, Michael Walzer, "Politics in the Welfare State. Concerning the Role of American Radicals," Dissent 15 (1968), nr. 1, reprinted in Dissent 20 (1974), pp. 290-304 [20th Anniversary Issue]; Michael Harrington, "The Welfare State and its Neoconservative Critics," Dissent 21 (1975), pp. 435-454.

6. Samuel Brittan, "The Economic Contradictions of Democracy," British Journal of Political Science (5) 1975, pp. 129-159; Robert Moss, *The Collapse of Democracy* (New Rochelle, NY: Arlington House, 1975). See also Douglas W. Rae and Hans Daudt, "The Ostrogorski Paradox. A Peculiarity of Compound Majority Decision," European Journal of Political Research 4 (1976), pp. 391-398; as cited in Hans Daudt, "De politieke toekomst van de verzorgingsstaat," in Beleid en Maatschappij, 3 (1976), pp. 175-189, reprinted in Hans Daudt, *Echte Politicologie* (Amsterdam: Bert Bakker, 1995), p. 318-341.

7. Hans Daudt, op. cit.

8. See Jacob Heilbrunn, "Germany's New Right," Foreign Affairs, November/December 1996, volume 75, no. 6, pp. 80-98; p. 82.

9. *Ibid.,* pp. 88-89.

10. *Ibid.,* p. 97.

11. *Ibid.,* pp. 97-98.

Chapter 1

THE TRAUMA OF THE HOLOCAUST: SOME HISTORICAL PERSPECTIVES

Yehuda Bauer

Thank you very much. This is the second time that I am attending the Scholars' Conference, the first time was twenty six years ago in 1970 and somebody is getting older. It can't be Hubert Locke, so it must be me.

Before I get into trouble as usual by making a lot of people angry, let me start in a very Jewish way, and say that before I speak, I would like to say a few words. I want to say something about Peretz Gans. He was born in Fulda in Germany in 1939. His name was Fritz Gans then. His parents managed to escape to France just before the outbreak of World War II, but the Nazis caught up with them. The parents gave the little boy to a Jewish orphanage. They tried to hide. They were discovered and they died in Auschwitz and Fritz, later Peretz Gans, was taken by foster parents over the Pyrenean border into Spain. When he was four years, in 1943, he boarded a ship called the Guinea, a Portuguese ship, and they arrived in Palestine. He was brought up in the Benshemen Agricultural School and then he joined Kibbutz Shoval where I was a member for forty-one years, and he was one of my charges. He married a lovely girl from Egypt. They had a son. When the parents left the Kibbutz after a number of years, the son came back to the Kibbutz. And then, one week ago, Peretz Gans boarded bus number 18 in Jerusalem and he was the man who sat next to the suicide bomber. When it happened, nothing was left of him except for one small finger of one of his hands. So, they took that finger to his house and they checked the finger prints against the finger prints of Peretz in his home. And, when the burial took place, they buried the finger of

Peretz Gans. Peretz was a carpenter by trade - a very practical man. A very practical man, who had quite a lot of the typical Israeli cynicism about him, hiding, as is usual with us, other things. And I am sure that he would be most surprised and a bit cynical if he knew that I was going to memorialize him by a speech in Minneapolis, but that is what I am doing. Let us remember Peretz Gans.

About twenty odd years ago, Robert Alter, a great professor of literature in California, wrote an article in Commentary magazine in which he said that we always have to remember the Holocaust, it always has to be with us, we must never forget it. But, we have to move onto other things. He discovered what every Jewish Holocaust scholar should know, that the Holocaust (or for that matter the State of Israel) is not the same thing as Jewish identity. Those are different things. The Holocaust, Israel all that are part of Jewish identity. Let us go beyond that, he said, and let us say that we have got enough of it. Let's move to other things. We have to be positive. Elie Wiesel said many times that he feared that, when the generation of the Holocaust survivors passes on, who is going to remember the Holocaust? Nobody will know. Nobody will understand. Well, maybe it will become part of the liturgy, but not beyond that. And, it will be basically not only forgotten, but turned into kitsch.

I think that they are both right and wrong. They were right because, yes, today in the United States of America, the Jewish communities are beginning to distance themselves from the memorialization of the Holocaust in everyday life. Budgets are for things, local things, including memorial centers or statues, and so on. I see and hear that wherever I go in this great country of yours. And, what you have instead, are two days a year. The 9th or 10th of November, the Kristallnacht Memorial, and the memorial day of the Holocaust in April, whenever the Hebrew date falls on the general calendar. So, for two days, yes, we "do" the Holocaust. Don't we? Great speeches. Wonderful speeches. And we cry and we promise we will never forget. Do I have to remind you that you will never forget your grandparents? If you have lost your parents, do I have to remind you that you should never forget your parents? If you say, I will never forget it, it means that you want to forget, but that there is something holding you back. You can't afford to ignore it publicly. And then there is that wonderful museum in Washington, with a terrific exhibit. A wonderful exhibit. Well, we created that museum in Washington, didn't we? So, off we go to Washington to "do" the Holocaust thing and then we can forget about it. And, if you can't go to Washington, then you have a local

Holocaust museum somewhere. Sometimes more than one. So, you have done your thing and the rest of the year, well, you've got other things to do.

But, they were wrong because the non-Jewish world is memorializing the Holocaust, for instance in a suburb of Hiroshima. There is a center for Holocaust studies and they are building an Auschwitz museum there. In Shanghai they teach Holocaust studies. In communist China. And people are drawn to this. It is not, as Franklin Littell so rightly said, out of morbid interest. Maybe there is something of that too, yes. But there is more to it than that. What is there? What draws the non-Jewish world into this? And, if it is drawn, then, as always, my people, the Jewish people, will copy the non-Jews in memorializing the Holocaust. It won't be forgotten. It can't, because the non-Jewish world will never forget it. Why?

The universities in this country are an excellent example. Franklin Littell has said that one of the safest things to do with Holocaust studies, if you don't want to deal with them, is to push them into Jewish studies programs, where they will become a Jewish problem dealt with on a sectarian basis, and nobody will be bothered by the general implications of the Holocaust. It is an "out" for the non-Jews who don't want to deal with this. For the Christians who want to deny responsibility, it is easy to leave it as a Jewish affair. But that does not work: increasingly the Holocaust is taught in general studies, in sociology, literature, psychology, and history or whatever. It does not have to be called a course in Holocaust studies. Sometimes it is called something else. But Holocaust is taught in these courses, and there are hundreds and hundreds of them here in the United States of America. The numbers are growing. Let me give you a personal example: I had a hundred and thirty kids in my two classes at Richard Stockton College in New Jersey. I think about twelve of them were Jewish, because Jewish students think they know all about it, therefore they don't have to take the course. As a result, I had non-Jewish kids, who were eager to know more about it. Why? I have some answers, whose correctness I cannot prove, because there are no experimental studies I can quote; it is a question of interpretation, of my opinion, of my hypothesis.

The most important thing is the uniqueness of the destruction of the Jewish people in Europe. The number of pages that have been written on this question of uniqueness can fill libraries. But I am coming back to it because it is the essential question, the essential point. Let me put it this way: why on earth, if you want to study the dark side of humanity, should you study the Holocaust, and not the murder of the Tutsis in Rwanda, or the Cambodian experience, or Biafra, or the millions of other victims just in this century, not to speak of past ages. Why not deal with the terrible genocide of the Gypsies? Or with the American Indians, not only in North America but throughout the American continent? Why not study the genocide of the Polish people under the Nazis? Why study the Jews? Why is this the center of the discussion? Did the survivors lead into that? No; as a group that was affected, they wanted to memorialize, and look what happened. A memorial was built in the center of the capital of this nation, to memorialize an event that took place thousands of miles away to people to whom the United States had no legal or political obligation whatsoever.

Now, moral obligation is something else again, because we owe moral obligations to people toward whom we do not have a political obligation. But then, why not memorialize in Washington the two million Indian peasants who died of starvation in 1942, while the Holocaust was going on in Europe? The Washington Holocaust museum is the only one in the world that had to announce - please, don't come, we are full. I have never heard of a museum like that.

The uniqueness of the Holocaust lies in the motivation of the murderers. It meant a global, not a local attack, as in literally all the other cases of genocide, on a targeted group - not on German, Polish, French, or Italian Jews, but on all Jews, everywhere. And, what was attacked bore no relation to any reality -- the target was the "international Jewish conspiracy," a purely imaginary construct. Nor was the genocidal project a side issue for the Nazis. It was at the center of their ideology. And then, it was a purely ideological issue, not a concrete one, not one of land. Nor was it a question of power. It was not even a question of nationalism. The Jews did not interfere with the aims of German nationalists. The Armenian genocide in Turkey, by comparison, was motivated by a desire to remove a foreign non-Muslim, non-Turkish element in the heart land of Turkey in order to create a Pan-Turkic empire ruled by the young Turks in World War I. But, Jews did not have any land, and contrary to legend, they did not control the German economy. They owned department stores, but heavy industry, transportation, politics -- no. It was an attack that had no real basis in political science terms, no economic, political or military background. It was purely ideological. Do you know what that means? Have you asked yourselves why did World War II start? The German economy was thriving. It had emerged from the crisis of the 1930s.

The German industrialists did not want war. The German military did not want war. So, why did it break out? The trite answer is that Hitler wanted it, and the next question is -- why did he want it? And, was he the only one? There was an elite of the Nazi party of which Hitler was the head and that elite, that ideological elite, exercising a dictatorship over a tremendously civilized and developed country, wanted an ideological war for two reasons. First of all, to establish the empire of the Germanic peoples of the Aryan race in Europe, and by controlling Europe control the world; they said it explicitly. And, secondly, they could not achieve that, they thought, without destroying "international Jewry" which was behind all their main enemies: the Bolshevik Russians and the capitalist Americans, and the French democrats, and ultimately the British as well. What does that mean? Many people have said that something like thirty-five million died in World War II. I think that figure is much too low. I don't know the real figure. I don't think anyone knows it. But, let's say thirty-five million. Then, what I mean is that thirty-five million people died for ideology. Pure ideology. No real reason. And, part of that ideology, in other words, part of the reason for the outbreak of World War II and the attendant tragedies in their tens of millions that accompanied it, was due to antisemitism. It was due to the desire to eliminate the Jewish people. A people that was seen in a completely delusionary way, as satan incarnate. The perpetrators were part of a population that had been brought up on Christian traditions where you had the elements of a Manichean world view, of a duality of God and Satan. It was based on a tremendously old tradition. No, Christian antisemitism did not produce the Holocaust. Christian antisemitism never argued for the physical annihilation of Jews. But, Christian antisemitism forms the background from which a secular, anti-Christian antisemitism arose to murder the Jews.

That means that it was the Nazi regime that was unique in history, and we don't pay enough attention to that. If the argument for the uniqueness of the Holocaust is correct and I think it is absolutely true, then, that means that the regime that posited this kind of an ideology was unique in the world and it is unique because it was a rebellion against the civilization from which is sprang. The Nazis were illegitimate heirs of Jean Jacques Rousseau, of the French Enlightenment generally, of western philosophy, especially of course of German philosophy. They were the illegitimate sons of the greatest philosophical schools that were produced in the last few hundred years, and they rebelled against them. They wanted to go back to a pagan world, beautiful, naturalistic, where natural hierarchies based on the supremacy of the strong would be established, because strong equalled good, powerful equalled civilized. Their world did have a kind of a God, the merciless God of nature, the brutal God of races, the oppressive God of hierarchies. The Nazis wanted to go back to what they thought, wrongly, were the Greek origins of European culture. They wanted to build. They wanted to settle the East in their image, removing those whose land they would take; they wanted to build Germanic cities; they wanted to have wonderful Germanic architecture. And what remained of it after it was all over, in 1946 and 1947? Did they build anything? Did they produce anything? Well, yes they produced one lasting memorial, one great achievement of the Nazi empire did remain -- Auschwitz. That was the great cultural achievement of the Nazi regime.

That is unique. Not only in western history. It is historically unique, I know of no other example like that. Unique means without precedent. Unique does not mean it cannot be repeated. Soviet Communism, with which Nazism is often compared, with all its murder and brutality and camps and God knows what else, tried to achieve a kind of humanistic, egalitarian utopia, also based on ideas that originated in the Enlightenment. The Nazis were very conscious of the fact that that was not what they wanted to do. They wanted to break with all that. Conscience, Hitler is reported to have said, was a Jewish invention and had to be abolished. A doctoral student of mine recently wrote a Ph.D. called *Unusual Bureaucrats* about the group around Adolf Eichmann. These people were not the types of ordinary postal clerks, as Hannah Arendt tried to describe them, when she wrote about the "banality of evil." Not only is there never anything banal about evil, but the group around Eichmann were organized, well educated murderers with a developed consciousness of what they were doing and a deep nationalistic and antisemitic, national-socialist conviction. They were unusual bureaucrats.

This lead me to another aspects of the problem. I find it most disconcerting that some of my most valued colleagues and friends say: "We don't know. We will never understand. We will never be able to fathom Nazism because we can never really understand the Holocaust." The many serious historians and commentators who argue like that seem to me to live in a never-never world, in a cloud of abstractions. I intensely dislike these mystifications. If you don't understand murder, what do you understand? Half of the history of the human race is about murder. It is all around you. If you don't understand it, it is because you don't want to, because it is too near to our skins, because we all have the potential capacity to being brutal murderers but, thank God, we sublimate it, and attend conferences instead. If you don't understand murder, you don't understand yourself, and the community of which you are a part; or the history you deal with.

People may take issue with Rudolph J. Rummel of Honolulu who wrote a book called *Democide,*[1] and who argues that between 1900 and 1987 some one hundred and fifty-nine million civilians (he does not include soldiers in his calculations), were murdered by governments or quasi-governmental organizations. People may question the accuracy of his figures or question his methodology but does it really matter whether he is wrong by ten or twenty million one way or the other? His is an analysis of our humanity. In the light of findings like that I would say that anyone who argues that they do not understand the Holocaust are terribly wrong. Of course we understand the Holocaust, in principle at least. We cannot feel what the survivors feel, nor are the survivors keen that we should. But we can empathize with them, because they feel pain, and humans know pain, even if there is no comparison at all between the "normal" pain we feel and their pain. As far as the murderers are concerned, we can understand them because we all have the potential for murder within us. Human history is replete with murder, mass murder and brutality of all kinds. If we do not understand that, what do we understand? People talk about "man's inhumanity to man." What kind of language is that? Were the Nazis really inhuman? Surely our whole problem is that they were very human indeed. If they had been inhuman it would be very easy for us. They would be creatures from another world, and we would not be like them. We could claim that we would never have done this. But we protest much too loudly. The Nazis were beasts? Come on! That is an insult to the animals. Animals don't do things like that. It is only the human animal that destroys its own kind.

I don't know whether there is a God or a Satan outside of me. I have my great doubts. But I am absolutely certain that there is a God and a Satan inside of me, so, that there *is* in a way, a God and a Satan. We are indeed capable of being close to one of these extremes. That is basically what we are discussing at this conference. Ours is not an ivory tower project. Our project is found in the streets. Our project is to try and find out what happened the last time round. It then widens to include not only the Holocaust (as though that were not enough) but all genocides, of which the Holocaust was a very unique, extreme case. Our purpose should to try, and maybe there is one millionth of a chance, possibly to influence the powers that be; maybe humans can improve their performance in the future, and, I will come back to this later.

There is another reason to concentration on the Holocaust, namely the Jews. The Jews are a very peculiar people - I don't have to tell you, many of you belong to that group. Jews, they say, are just like every one else only more so. One of the reasons may be that they are the heirs to a culture that is crucially important to what we call, maybe wrongly, Western civilization, which is spreading, albeit in a terribly superficial and often very damaging way, all over the globe. The Greeks and Romans were one pillar of that civilization, but they are no longer around. The Italian the Greek peoples of today no longer speak the original languages, and they do not have the same belief systems - there is no direct continuity of the cultures. But my two granddaughters now read something that was written thousands of years ago, in the original. It is a continuing civilization.

If your basic culture is English, or English-American, just try to read Chaucer without a dictionary, and Chaucer wrote only about five hundred years ago. The Jews are no better than others, nor are they worse, but they are culturally different. They have been carrying a very ancient tradition on their shoulders, longer than most other groups. And, as you know, they fight each other like cats and dogs about what the interpretation of that tradition is. But the tradition is there, and it has crucially influenced the civilization against which the Nazis rebelled. If you look at Europe some two hundred years ago: what was the book in people's home, if they had any book at all? It was the Christian Bible, and that was composed of the Old Testament, or the Hebrew Scriptures, and the New Testament, and both of them were largely written by Jews. So, when the Nazis attacked the civilization they came from it was not unnatural that they should attack the Jews. They attacked the one group that symbolized, better perhaps than others, the civilization against which they were rebelling. That is part of the explanation for the uniqueness of the Holocaust.

Some people then come and propose all kinds of peculiar theories to explain the Holocaust. Zygmunt Bauman, in his *Modernity and the Holocaust*,[2] says that the Holocaust is not result of antisemitism, because antisemitism has been around for ages, and only in our century did the Holocaust occur, so that antisemitism is no explanation. So, the

Nazis loved the Jews, but killed them nevertheless? Also, and this is quite true, many of the murderers had had no thorough antisemitic education, or had a record of being antisemitic in the past. But this can be easily explained by describing the consensus in Nazified society, which saw the Jew as *the* enemy of the regime who had to be eliminated. No deep convictions were necessarily involved on the part of the actual murderers, but of course they did exist, and very much so, among the leadership that directed things. As to Bauman's main argument about the longevity of antisemitic ideologies, he does not see the difference between the non-genocidal, though often very violent, Christian antisemitism, and the modern genocidal variety that built upon the Christian antisemitic foundations and was yet very different from it. If we take Bauman's theory to its logical conclusion, we would have to conclude that the Nazis murdered the Jews although they really had nothing against them, which is not very convincing. Bauman himself then retreats from his extreme position and argues that antisemitism was a necessary, but not a sufficient reason for the Holocaust to occur - well, no one I have read has ever argued anything else. But his main explanation is that modernity (whatever that means, and he does not define it) did it. Now, I understand that there was modernity in America, Britain, France, Russia and so on, too, so why did it happen in Germany? Why not in Fascist Italy, which also was modern, and allied to Germany?

The explanation may well be that the Nazi genocidal project succeeded because of the identification of large masses of the population not with the genocidal intentions, but with the regime as such, and with its charismatic leader. I suspect that if the consensus had been to eliminate all people wearing earrings, they would have done that too; but there were very important historical reasons, as I have tried to show, why the Jews were targeted, and not others. The central role of the bureaucracy has of course been brilliantly described by Raul Hilberg. That this was the result of modernity cannot be in doubt, but again, the same basic system was in place in America, Britain, France and elsewhere. The Nazi bureaucrats, as Hilberg has shown, organized trains transporting Jews to their deaths in exactly the same way, and by the same procedures, as they organized children's outings to summer camps. But, neither Bauman nor Hilberg can explain why they sent Jews to death camps rather than German children to summer camps. Bureaucracy by itself does not explain anything, because someone instructs the bureaucrat to do the one thing rather than the other. Once a consensus is achieved, the bureaucrat shows drive and initiative of his own; or else, the bureaucrat is himself an ideologue who chooses to further and develop the consensus of which he is a part. But then the explanation is not modernity, but ideology.

Arnold J. Mayer wrote a book called *Why Did The Heavens Not Darken?*[3] in which he says that the Nazi project was directed against Marxism (perhaps because of Mayer's general neo-Marxist stand), and that the Nazi movement's main preoccupation was directed against Communism. The Jews sort of got caught up with it. Of course, some of them were Marxist. Mayer totally ignores a tremendous volume of documentation that shows quite clearly that in the Nazis' eyes Communism, and Marxism generally, was a Jewish invention, and that the Communists and Social-Democrats were tools in the hands of the Jews, instruments of Judaism which tried to achieve world domination. But Mayer's theory is very typical, he is running away from the Jewish uniqueness issue, and from the issue of the uniqueness of the Holocaust. Why? I think that because like members of any minority (Mayer himself is a survivor from Luxembourg) people like that lie with a deep sense of insecurity, and it is much easier to hide among the crowd and say, no, it wasn't I they were after, but a much wider and different category of people. We Jews were not the main target, the main target was Marxism, and the Jews were murdered as a kind of afterthought.

Then there are people, and they are increasing in numbers, who argue that Holocaust is the name of what happened to Jews, Gypsies and the German handicapped in what the Nazis euphemistically called "euthanasia." I do not doubt that the murder of Gypsies was one of the worst horrors the Nazis committed. We don't even know how many Gypsies were murdered. The figures run from a low 200,000 to a high of 810,000.

> In sheer demonic cold-blooded brutality the tragedy of the Romanies is one of the most terrible indictments of the Nazis. The fact that their fate is hardly ever mentioned and that the mutilated Romany nation continues to be vilified and persecuted to this day should put all their host nations to shame.

I wrote this fourteen years ago. However, one has to say that the policy of the Nazis towards the Gypsies was different from that towards the Jews. Undoubtedly, they approached both groups from the same basic racist point of view. But they approached everyone from a racist point of view. Poles, French, Italians, and Germans as well, were examined from this same warped perspective. An SS officer could not marry an Italian woman without special permission because Italians were of a lower race. But we know that they approached all these groups differently; their racism was not "egalitarian," the whole purpose was to differentiate and discriminate. The Jews were different from all the others, from that same racist perspective; they were not a race at all, actually; they were an anti-race, a satanic invasion of humanity.

I have been upbraided by my Romany friends, more than once, for quoting the Nazis and saying that the Nazis saw in the Gypsies a minor irritant. Well, what could I do? That is what they thought them to be. But that is they, not I or, I hope, we. The tragedy is that we don't relate to the fact that a whole people with a language and a basically oral culture and tradition of great interest was the victim of mass murder. The paradox is that the only "real Aryans" in Europe were the Gypsies. These people were dehumanized by being treated as a minor irritant and murdered, chiefly insofar as they were organized in wandering groups. In Germany, Austria and the Protectorate of Bohemia and Moravia, in the heartland of the German Reich, every Gypsy was involved. Elsewhere we still have not sufficient information. The old book by Donald Kenrick and Grattan Puxon[4] is not satisfactory anymore. We have to do much more research. But we do know that on July 13, 1943, an order was circulated in the Ostland (the Baltic region and some parts of present Belarus) originating from Himmler, that all wandering Gypsies should be treated like Jews, and all sedentary ones like the local population. Hitler himself does not deal with the fate of the Gypsies, neither in his books nor in his speeches or recorded conversations.

I am telling my Romany friends not to tag their story onto the Jewish one. You have an important tradition of your own which was attacked and largely destroyed by the Nazis; your fate after the war is worse than that of the Jews because Gypsies are still, as I have said, racially discriminated against, persecuted and vilified. Which is the reason why, as long as I was the editor of Holocaust and Genocide Studies, I invited articles on the terrible genocide of the Gypsies. But the Gypsies were not seen by the Nazis as their the main enemies, they were not at the center of Nazi ideology. They were not the people who represented or symbolized to the Nazis everything the Nazis were fighting against. There are, to be sure, parallels between Jews and Gypsies; both were basically non-European peoples who, in a sense, were wandering nations.

There is much to discover; but the motivation for the Holocaust and for the murder of Gypsies was radically different. I think I was the first person to publish, in English, a testimony of a Gypsy survivor of Auschwitz, in order to show that from the point of view of personal tragedy, of suffering, there was no difference whatever between Jews and Gypsies. But there is a vast difference between the Holocaust, which for the Nazis was the central issue in their war against humanity, and the partial genocide of a group they saw as a marginal, hereditarily asocial and criminal element, the Gypsies.

As far as the handicapped go, there is no doubt that the experience gathered by the Nazis in murdering handicapped Germans (and of course Jews as well) was the technical forerunner and formed the precedent for the mass killing of the Jews by gassing. But the handicapped were, from the Nazi point of view, an internal racial problem, a problem of internal racial cleansing, if you will. How can you compare that with their main ideological preoccupation, the Jews?

The fate of the Jews was unlike that of the Poles, who also suffered a genocidal attack - three million Poles were either killed or died as a result of the events of the war. The Nazis wanted to destroy, to eliminate the Polish nation as a nation. They had no plans - in fact they rejected them explicitly - to murder all Polish individuals. They needed them as slaves.

The Holocaust has parallels with all these and many other cases, but the differences are crucial. One of the elements of similarity is the fact that all these cases led to a series of communal traumata. And the Jews, like so many others, exhibit a tremendous difficulty in dealing with these traumata. This should not come as a surprise, because it has a very important, tragic source. People, survivors and others, ask: what did close to six million Jews die for? They desperately want to be able to say that the deaths of their loved ones had a meaning. I am sorry, it had none, none whatsoever. The only meaning the mass dying could have had was the meaning it had for the Nazis. They knew what they were doing, they had a purpose, for them it had meaning. And the terrible truth is that close to six million innocent people were murdered for somebody else's ideology. In a way, so were the Gypsies, and the Poles, and the Armenians before them. That does not mean that we do not give meaning to the murder after the fact. We must do that, because otherwise we are unable to cope with it. This is very legitimate, but we must recognize that it is a *post facto* meaning that we are providing. Sure, there were many Jews during the Holocaust who wanted to give a meaning to their suffering and who went to their deaths for the religious Sanctification of the Name of God, *Kiddush Hashem*, as it is known in Hebrew. There were many others who in their deaths tried to sanctify other beliefs - socialism, Zionism or whatever it was. That was what they were dying for, in their own minds. But the Nazis were not interested in what the Jews believed, and those were not the reasons for which they murdered their victims. They murdered them because they had been born to Jewish grandparents.

Then you have a universalist kind of interpretation, which usually flies in the face of facts. In the Israeli culture we have the secular, liberal so-called "new historians," a group which you may not have heard about. If so, you are lucky. There is for instance a book by Tom Segev called *The Seventh Million*, which you can find in every bookstore in this country. The book tries to provide an answer to the question who "really" was responsible for the murder of the Jews. We all know the Nazis did it, but that, for Segev, is a trite answer. It was the Jewish leadership during the war that is the real culprit. The Jewish leaders in Palestine and in America could have saved the Jews and they did not. They are responsible. Well, one can objectively and seriously argue, with perfect hindsight, about what they did wrong, and what they did right. But there is a tradition quoting an old Hebrew proverb, *Mipnei Hata'einu,* which means "for our sins." Because of our sins we were exiled from our country. All the tragedies in Jewish history are explained by some Jewish fault. This is perfectly understandable, because how else could you explain that God's chosen people were abandoned by God to a great deal of suffering? They had to accuse themselves, because if they explained the events rationally, if they analyzed the real causes which lay not with themselves but with the world around them that would not let them live their traditions the way they wanted, they would have had to despair: so much of the world was against them! So they explained to themselves that the reason was that they had not obeyed the Law properly. This is the basic stance of many orthodox Jewish interpreters of the Holocaust, but here we find that the secular, liberal, cosmopolitan Jewish post-modernists and non-Zionists such as Segev adopt the traditional Jewish position: we are responsible; well, not quite "we," but rather the non-deceased Jewish leadership during the Holocaust. I think this is something very peculiarly Jewish.

In the United States, a New York professor by the name of Seymour Finger organized - quite a few years ago - a committee to investigate the responsibility of the American Jewish leadership for not rescuing the

Jews of Europe.[5] And, surprise, surprise, they found the leadership guilty. I find in all this something very interesting, namely internalization of antisemitic stereotypes by the victim group, by the Jews. The Jews in the free world during World War II are presented as politically very powerful, and of course controlling vast funds. There are antisemitic images, and they bear absolutely no relation to the facts -- the Jews were politically powerless, because of course they could not very well oppose the Roosevelt administration which was conducting the war against the Germans. You just read the correspondence of the State Department, or the British Foreign Office, and see what they say about the Jews. Powerful? My foot! They were viewed as an irksome burden, to be pitied at best. And their funds, during war-time, were very limited. American Jews never had crucial financial power. The big banks and the big industries were not only in non-Jewish hands, but were often controlled by American businessmen who did not like Jews at all. The Segevs and their orthodox brethren, assume that the Jews were powerful, they could have rescued, and they did not. Why? Because they were sinners (say the orthodox), or they were useless schlemiels wedded to Zionist nationalism and cared only about establishing a Jewish state in Palestine, which of course is a terrible sin (Segev and the post-Zionists, or post-modernists in Israel), so they abandoned the European Jews.

Yes, there are balanced accounts - by David S. Wyman,[6] Henry Feingold,[7] and a number of others for the United States, or Dina Porat[8] and others for wartime Palestine, and these do not fall into the opposite mistake of writing hagiographies about how wonderful these wartime leaders were.

Then you have some of our orthodox brethren. Why did the Holocaust happen? Because God willed it. Nothing is explicable except as the work of God. So, he must have had a good reason. And, from the vantage point of orthodoxy, the answers seem pretty obvious: God punished the Jews because many of them abandoned religion, converted, or became Reform Jews who abandoned orthodoxy. Some of the ultra-orthodox say the reason must have been because the Zionists wanted to go to Palestine instead of waiting for the messiah to lead them there; others say the opposite -- because ultra-orthodox leaders refused to go to Palestine and opposed the Zionists. Take your pick and make your choice. All these are, in these almost crazy illogicalities, in my view, the outcomes of a massive collective trauma, and one has to empathize with it.

This leads me to another aberration, which is the flip side of universalism, namely Jewish sectarianism. Some Jews say: yes, we are a group disappointed with so-called civilized humanity. The whole world was against us. This is what Israel's ex-Premier, Yitzhak Shamir, often says. Again, one has to empathize with this approach; after all, there were many who were indeed against us. But we don't have to put everyone into this category. Whole nations behaved, as a generalization (to which there were exceptions, of course), in a neighborly, sympathetic way - the Bulgarians, the Danes, the Norwegians, the Belgians, the Italians, quite a proportion of the French. Sectarianism also is a precocious, ethnically exclusive turning inward, the result, one has to remember, of very grim experiences with quite a number of anti-Jewish societies. It sometimes goes to the extreme of denying that the Holocaust had anything to do with general Nazi policies, with the development of the international situation, with internal German pressures of an economic and social kind, or even with the overall racial policies of the Nazi; even a denial that the Holocaust was indeed a form of genocide, different and unique, but a genocide nonetheless. Such interpretations would take the Holocaust out of history and paradoxically, make it irrelevant, because if it is not part of human history, there are no lessons, conclusions, and so on to be drawn from it, indeed there is no point in dealing with it at all. But when you argue for the uniqueness of the Holocaust, you must compare it with other tragedies, such as the Armenian, the Gypsy, the Tutsi or the Cambodian disasters, in our century or in ages past. Sectarianism also means that you see the Holocaust as a Jewish thing only -- goyim, keep out. Such interpreters refuse to see concerned gentiles, concerned Christians, as their natural allies. The whole aspect of the Holocaust being a warning to all of humanity, in other words the legitimate universalist aspect of important features, is ignored. What happened once, can happen again, to anyone, by anyone - not perhaps in the same form, but in similar forms. That is a crucial lesson one can learn, and exclusivist, self-defeating sectarianism leads us away from it.

Here I want to deal with another dangerous mistake: there is a tendency among Jews and non-Jews alike to see the Jews as a suffering people. There is a "wonderful" Christian tradition that says that the suffering of the Jews is their most important contribution to humanity since Jesus. They have to suffer because they did not recognize Jesus as the Messiah -- which of course is an exact parallel to the Jewish orthodox who say that God punished the Jews for their transgressions -

Reform, assimilation (including conversion to Christianity by a proportion of Jews), Zionism, or anti-Zionism. All these worthies, Christian theologians or Jewish interpreters, know exactly what God had in mind, and that indeed Auschwitz was part of God's plan. A plan for exactly what, one may ask? The suffering of the Jews is hailed as proof for the truth, supposedly, of Christianity - a nonsensical, anti-humanistic, anti-moral proposition, which by the way is not only ideologically disgusting, but also historically false: the history of the Jews is *not* the history of their persecutions. In most countries, for most of the time, Jews were not molested; sometimes they suffered, they were tolerated, sometimes treated with indifference, sometimes invited and welcomed and treated with respect and good-neighborliness and yes, periodically persecuted, evicted, murdered. As Salo Baron, doyen of twentieth-century Jewish historians has said, the lachrymose interpretation of Jewish history is erroneous. Jewish history is the history of a lively, fascinating people who produced material and spiritual goods, had wonderfully complex social organizations, contributed to themselves and others, were and are part of a developing, vibrant civilization. Christian theology about Jews still needs a great deal of self-criticism.

I would like to conclude by coming back to what I said earlier: we here should have a practical agenda, which I would see almost as a kind of Kantian imperative. If we can contribute a tiny little iota to the perhaps remote possibility that genocide might either be diminished or even made to disappear in some future, then we are duty bound to do that. I now speak as an academic: academics are not totally helpless. They can make a difference. They educate, well, some of them try to, a very high proportion of young people, here in America as well as in many countries of the world. We do have some impact. We could, if we wanted to, try and form groups that would see what can be done to influence politicians. There are such groups here in the United States, only recently formed. And I am not running down the politicians, some of my best friends are politicians, but you have to admit that they are a problem. We have to treat them with the sympathy and kindness they deserve and perhaps try and help them along a little bit. We ought to show them what their predecessors' policies led to. We disagree amongst each other, but that is fine -- let them see the different options we present as to how to improve on the present and the past. For this venture the study of the Holocaust is essential; it is the extreme case, not of suffering, because that is the same in all these mass murders, but of a social malady affecting humanity. In doing this essentially political work, we will remember the millions of Jewish victims, and together with them all the others who were victims of genocides and mass murders, and they cannot even be counted. They were, all of them, people like ourselves. We are like them, and we cannot afford not to deal with every individual and every group as contributors to a general orchestra of humanity in which all these individual cultures and civilizations will play their smaller or larger instruments. Perhaps, playing different tunes, they will harmonize the overall symphony of mankind. This is, to be sure, utopian, but we should at least try. How to do that -- well, that is not my brief tonight, but we should begin to agonize over that.

Thank you.

Notes

1. Rudolph J. Rummel, *Democide*, New Brunswick: Transaction Publisher, 1992.

2. Zygmunt Bauman, *Modernity and the Holocaust*, Ithaca, New York: Cornell University Press, 1991.

3. Arnold J. Mayer, *Why Did the Heavens Not Darken*, New York: Patheon, 1989.

4. Donald Kendrick and Grattan Puxon, *The Destiny of Europe's Gypsies,* New York: Basic Books, 1972.

5. Seymour M. Finger, *American Jewry During the Holocaust*, New York: Holmes and Meyer, 1984.

6. David S. Wyman, *The Abandonment of the Jews*, New York: Pantheon, 1984.

7. Henry Feingold, *Politics of Rescue*, New Brunswick: Rutgers U. Press, 1970.

8. Dina Porat, *The Blue and Yellow Stars of David*, Cambridge: Harvard University Press, 1990.

Chapter 2

THE ROOTS OF ANTIGYPSYISM: TO THE HOLOCAUST AND AFTER[1]

Ian Hancock

"Di zelbike zun vos farvayst di layvnt, farshvartst oykh'm Tsigayner." ("The same sun that whitens the linen also turns the Gypsy black.")

Yiddish Proverb

"One exhibit [at the Holocaust Museum at Buchenwald] quotes SS chief Heinrich Himmler on December 8th, 1938, as calling for the 'final solution of the Gypsy question,' and cites his order of December 16th, 1942, to have all Gypsies remaining in Europe deported to Auschwitz."

Sheldon Rantz (1995:11)

While Holocaust scholars are rapidly adding to their knowledge of the details of the fate of the Romani people in Hitler's Germany, and while it is now generally acknowledged that together with Jews, the Romani victims were the only ethnic/racial population selected for total annihilation according to the genocidal policy of the Final Solution[2] (Friedlander, 1995;[3] Hancock, 1996), far less has been written about the *reasons* for the Nazi policy of ethnic cleansing as it was directed at that population. Tenenbaum, who forty years ago defined the Final Solution as the "physical extermination of Jews and Gypsies in the great death camps," (1956:373) nevertheless called the German persecution of Gypsies "one of the major mysteries of Nazi racialism" (1956:399).

Earlier discussions of the Third Reich have usually assumed that the so-called *Zigeuner* were merely regarded as asocials, misfits in the Nazi's new spartan order, and were targeted on those grounds alone (see e.g. Bauer, 1980:45; 1994:441); but an examination of the historical roots of antigypsyism in Germany (what Tenenbaum refers to as Hitler's "gypsomania") demonstrates very clearly that the notion that Rroma were a racial threat to national stability extends to the time of their initial entry into that country in the early 1400s. Elsewhere I have provided a chronology of the Holocaust as it relates to Sinti and Rroma[4] (Hancock, 1989), where a list of some of the events in Germany's history which preceded it is also included. In the present essay the focus is on the pre-1933 period in more detail, and also to examine the reasons for anti-gypsyism, since it is here that we can find the origins of Hitler's policy of extermination as it affected Rroma and Sinti; but I will also demonstrate that it is for exactly the same reasons that the Romani people in Europe are today the most vilified and discriminated against of all ethnic or national populations, and the most victimized by racist violence and discriminatory governmental policies.

The Historical Roots of Antigypsyism

Reasons for the institutionalized prejudice against the Romani people may be traced to a number of factors:

a)   The association of the first Rroma in Europe with the encroachment of the Asiatic invaders and of Islam, reflected in a number of contemporary exonyms applied to Romani populations, such as *Saracens, Tatars, Gypsies* (from "*Egyptians*"), *Turks, Heathens,* &c. Rroma, who entered Europe following the holy wars which resulted from the occupation of the Byzantine Empire by the Muslims, were everywhere regarded as being a part of the western infringement of Islam, and were persecuted as a result. The Ottomans not only posed a threat to the Christian establishment and had occupied the Holy Land, but they had also blocked off routes to the East, thereby also affecting trade and the European economy.

b)   The association in medieval Christian doctrine of light with purity and darkness with sin. The earliest church records documenting the arrival of Rroma alluded to the darkness of their complexion - more so the case seven hundred years ago than today - and the inherent evil which that supposedly demonstrated. "The conviction that blackness denotes inferiority and evil [was] well rooted in the western mind. The nearly black skins of many Gypsies marked them out to be victims of this prejudice" (Kenrick & Puxon, 1972:19). Hobson expands upon this (1965:338):... "Association with darkness and dirt is a convenient hook on which to hang certain projections, especially if [the target] is a relatively unknown visitor from a far-off country with a strange culture, or if he threatens important economic and other social, vested interests. He is also clearly 'not me.' While the association between darkness and evil is a purely metaphorical one, its effects have been devastating." Philip Mason (1968:61) has emphasized that "hardly any white man has overcome the confusion between biological accident and symbolic metaphor."

The persona of the Rrom as non-white, non-Christian outsider became incorporated into Christian European folklore, which served to justify and encourage the prejudice against him. Like Asahuerus, the Jew doomed to wander through eternity because he refused to allow Jesus to rest on his way to Calvary, Rroma were accused of forging the nails with which Christ was crucified. And while Jews were accused of drinking the blood of Christian babies in hidden rites to which no outsider was privy, Rroma were likewise charged with stealing and even eating those babies. Parallelling even more closely the Asahuerus myth is the belief that the original sin of the Rroma was their refusal to give Mary and the baby Jesus shelter during their flight from King Herod into Egypt (Scheier, 1925, vol. II, p. 77).

c) Romani culture, called *Rromanija* or *Rromanipe*, does not encourage close social relationships with non-Romani populations,[5] who are referred to as *gadže* in Romani and sometimes *gentiles* in English. Such an exclusivist society can create an assumption on the part of those who are excluded that it is furtive, and must therefore be hiding something. A common accusation in medieval Germany, for instance, was that Rroma were spies, a charge which was also repeated by the Nazis many times. The maintenance of cultural and/or religious restrictions which keep outsiders at a distance must certainly be seen as a factor, historically, in both antigypsyism and antisemitism.

d) Because of laws forbidding Rroma to settle anywhere, various means of livelihood had to be relied upon which could be easily and quickly gathered up when it became necessary to move out of an area. One such was fortune-telling, but this only helped reinforce the image of mystery and exoticism which was growing in the European mind. Rroma in turn exploited this image as a means of protection, since one is less likely to show hostility towards a person whom one believes to have some measure of control over, or knowledge of, one's destiny. The fact that Rroma are, fundamentally, an Asian population in Europe, speaking an Asian language which serves as the vehicle of a culture and world-view rooted in Asia, has also created conflict. Fortune-telling is a highly regarded profession in India, but drew no such respect in Europe; begging is likewise viewed very differently in Hindu and Islamic society, but has no such special status in Europe.

e)   The fact that as Okely has pointed out, "outsiders have projected onto Gypsies their own repressed fantasies and longings for disorder" (1983:232; see also Sibley, 1981:195-196), and have at the same time used those imagined characteristics of the "gypsy" as a yardstick by which to measure the boundaries of their own identities. Thus an individual's occasional urge to challenge the system, or to perpetrate some anti-social act, or even his subconscious fascination with anarchy, as psychologists know are not likely ever to be realized by that individual, but which can be experienced vicariously or subliminally by being projected onto the "outlaw" Romani population. This phenomenon is reflected repeatedly in the media as well as in works of fiction. Use of the word "Gypsy" for an image rather than for an individual occurred recently in an article concerning a case of alleged poisoning in California: the detective involved was quoted as saying "this guy is definitely a Gypsy ... the Gypsy was Angela Tene" (Nicoll, 1995:25). It is highly unlikely that he would have said "this guy is definitely a Jew ... the Jew was Angela Tene," since the ethnicity or race of a suspect is immaterial to the details of a case. It can only have been included, therefore, if it were believed that some link existed between criminality and genetic identity. In press coverage, the race of a suspected criminal who is a person of color is often provided, though as a rule omitted where the suspect is white; in the European papers, such information may even appear in the articles' headlines as well (*cf.* Hancock, 1978:145-162).

While racially based arguments were codified and used by the Nazis as justification for the extermination of Jews and Rroma, an added factor condemned the Jews of Europe as well: their supposed economic strength, which was used as an antisemitic argument long before Hitler came to power.

The Holocaust forever altered the structure of society in much of the area, and particularly in Poland, the Czech lands, and Hungary, where the Jews had played an important cultural as well as an economic role. At the other end of society the Gypsies were equally savaged by the Nazi death machine (Walters, 1988:271).

f)   The fact that Rroma have no military, political, economic and particularly territorial strength, and no nation state to speak for them, ensures that they are an ideal target for scapegoatism. Beck (1985:103) has made this point succinctly in referring to the situation of Rroma in Romania:

> Romania's German-speaking populations have received support from the West German state. Magyars are supported by the Hungarian state, and Jews by Israel. Groups such as the [Rroma] do not have such an advantage. Lacking a protective state, they have no one to turn to when discrimination is inflicted upon them as a group. Unlike ethnic groups represented by states, [Rroma] are not recognized as having a history that could legitimize them.

Non-territoriality is having its most extreme repercussions in post-communist Europe, where Rroma now find themselves outsiders in everybody's ethnic territory. While the American press does not acknowledge it, the Romani minority in Bosnia and Serbia is being systematically eradicated, while in Slovakia, France, Germany and elsewhere, programs of deportation and banishment are routinely in effect. Further to Beck's observation on scapegoatism, it has been argued, by e.g. Kenedi, that there is a need in all societies to select groups to blame its ills upon, and those least able to defend themselves, such as Rroma, provide the most likely candidates.

g)   The fact that, since the 19th Century, a literary "gypsy," (always written with a lower-case "g") has emerged, which is presented as the epitome of freedom: freedom from responsibility, freedom from moral constraints, freedom from the requirements of hygiene, freedom from nine-to-five routine. This has remained unchallenged by the Romani community because of the traditional lack of access to the means necessary to combat stereotyping, and thus there has grown in the popular mind an image which combines fascination with resentment, even with repulsion. As Janos Kenedi has noted (1986:14), because of their reliance in large measure upon literary and poorly-researched sources for their background information on Rroma, "the mass media, in a veiled and often less-veiled form, goad opinion in an anti-Gypsy direction." This fictionalized image originates in the idealizing of the western European Romani populations during the period of the industrial revolution, when they came to symbolize in literature an earlier idyllic, rural way of life. This coincided with European concepts of the "noble savage," and the realization that there were heathen populations in the heart of civilization in desperate need of Christian salvation. The early Victorian period saw the appearance of several works on missionary activity amongst Rroma (Mayall, 1988).

h)   The need to keep the gentile population at arm's length has also prevented investigators from gaining too intimate an acquaintance with the Romani world, which has led to highly embellished and stereotyped published accounts. These in turn have kept alive the "otherness" and distance of Rroma, both of which factors have helped sustain a literary or fantasy image, and which have worked very effectively against Romani issues being taken seriously. Most recently a review article dealing with an outsider's introduction to the Romani community described how two investigators, one of whom was "terrified" and the other armed with "a deck of cards and a packet of cigarettes" steeled themselves and intrepidly *"went in"* (Smith, 1995:18).

In sum, then, we can seek the historical basis of anti-Romani prejudice in a number of areas, in particular racism, religious intolerance, outsider status and the fact that Rroma maintain an exclusivist or separatist culture. In large part too, the literary image of the "gypsy" blurs the distinction between the real and the imagined population, so that even factual reports of antigypsyism seldom receive the concern they deserve. How many historical treatments of the 20th Century Armenian genocide, for example, have mentioned, even as a footnote, the fact that nearly all of the Armenian Gypsies (the *Lom*) were destroyed by the Turks and the Kurds? All of these factors underlie the problems which face the Romani population throughout the world today.

Anti-Rroma Attitudes in Pre-20th Century Germany

Rroma were first documented in German-speaking Europe in 1407; the first anti-Gypsy law was issued in 1416, the beginning of centuries of legal discrimination. Bischoff (1827:3) wrote that

in Germany, the greatest number of decrees of banishment were published against them ... this unhappy people was persecuted, strung up without exception as thieves and robbers when caught and, guilty or innocent, destroyed by the thousands.

By 1417 commentaries on their frightening physical appearance were beginning to be recorded; Hermann Cornerus wrote of the Rroma's "very ugly" and "black" faces, and likened them to the Tatars (*in* Eccard, 1723), while in 1435 the Roman Catholic monk Rufus of Lübeck wrote disparagingly of their dark skin and black hair (Grautoff, 1872). The first accusations of their being spies, carriers of the plague and traitors to Christendom were made in 1496 and again in 1497, and yet again in 1498. In 1500, all Rroma were banished from Germany on pain of death by Maximilian I, while German citizens were told that killing Rroma was not a punishable offense. In 1543, in a diatribe directed at both Jews and Rroma, Martin Luther recommended that Jews be rounded up and put into stables "like Gypsies," in order to be reminded of their lowly status in German society (Gilbert, 1985:19). In 1566, King Ferdinand reaffirmed the expulsion order of Maximilian; two years later, Pope Pius the Fifth banished all Rroma from the realm of the Holy Roman Church. In 1659, the mass murder of Rroma was reported in a pogrom near Neudorf, outside of Dresden; in 1709, a German law was passed for the arrest of Rroma simply because of what they were, to be deported to the American colonies, or to be used as galley slaves. In the following year, King Frederick I condemned all males to forced labor, and began a program of removing Romani children from their families in order to separate them permanently from their ethnic identity.

In 1721, Emperor Karl VI ordered the extermination of all Rroma everywhere, 220 years before the same directive was issued by Hitler. In 1725, King Frederick William I condemned all Rroma of eighteen years and over to be hanged. At the end of that century, Heinrich Grellmann published his groundbreaking treatise which established the Indian origin of the Romani people but claimed that, in doing his research among them, he felt "a clear repugnancy, like a biologist dissecting some nauseating, crawling thing in the interest of science." Ten years after that, in 1793, anti-Romani racism received further establishment sanction, this time from the Church, when the Lutheran minister Martinus Zippel declared that "Gypsies in a well-ordered state in the present day, are like vermin on an animal's body" (Biester, 1793:110). Acknowledgement of the physical and social differences of the Rroma were gradually being incorporated into German scholarly and ecclesiastical attitudes.

In his *Addresses to the German Nation* (1808), Johann Fichte wrote that the German "race" had been selected by God himself for preeminence among the world's peoples; two years later, the German nationalist Jahn wrote that "a state without *Volk* is a soulless artifice, while a *Volk* without a state is nothing, a bodiless, airless phantom, like the Gypsies and the Jews." Once again, the fact of non-territoriality marked both Rroma and Jews as asocials, populations who didn't fit in. In 1819, Hartwig von Hundt-Radowsky compared Rroma and Jews, and wrote about their shared propensity for stealing babies (Wippermann, 1986:57). Like the charge of cannibalism which was sometimes made, the accusation of child-stealing is psychologically a very powerful one, human beings instinctively reacting with fear or loathing. In 1830, using the same techniques employed in the previous century, the Nordhausen city council attempted to bring about the eventual eradication of the Romani population by taking children away from their parents for permanent placement with non-Gypsies. One must ask who were the real child-stealers, given the prevalence of the stereotype of the *Gypsy* in this role.

In 1835, Theodor Tetzner referred in print to Rroma as "the excrement of humanity" (Hehemann, 1987: 99, 116, 127, and Wippermann, 1986:57-58). In 1848, Colin de Plancy wrote that Rroma were in fact Jews "intermarried with Christian vagrants," while in 1850, Robert Knox, in his *Races of Men* described Rroma as the "refuse of the human race." Five years after that, in 1855, Gobineau (who also wrote about Gypsies) published his book *Essai sur l'inégalité des races humaines*, which argued that human beings could be ranked into higher and lower races, with the white "Aryans", and particularly the Nordic people within them, placed at the very top: "Aryans were the cream of mankind," Gobineau believed, "and the Germans, the cream of the cream - a race of princes" (Tenenbaum, 1956:9). This had particular impact upon the development of German philosophical and political thinking. A decree issued in the Duchy of Baden in that same year warned the citizens that

> in recent times, Gypsies, especially those from Alsace, have frequently been re-entering and travelling about with their families, purportedly to engage in trade but mostly for the purposes of begging or other illegal activities.

In 1863, Richard Liebich wrote about the "criminal practices" of the Rroma, and described them as *worthless life*, a phrase which was repeated by R. Kulemann six years later, and which was to have ominous significance in the 20th Century (Hehemann, 1987:127). The opinions of these scholars started to have repercussions at the highest administrative levels, for just one year later, on November 18th, 1870, Imperial Chancellor Otto von Bismarck circulated a brief demanding the "complete prohibition of foreign Gypsies crossing the German border," and which stated further that when arrested, they were to be "transported by the closest route to their country of origin." He also demanded in the same circular that Rroma in Germany be asked to show documentary proof of citizenship, and that if this were not forthcoming, they be denied travelling passes (Mihalik & Kreutzkamp, 1990:123). When Alsace and Lorraine were annexed by the German Empire in 1871, each was made responsible for the control of Rroma at the borders into other areas of the new Reich (Fings, 1990:250). Charles Darwin, also writing in 1871,

> employed unmistakably racial terms when he noted "the uniform appearance in various parts of the world of Gypsies and Jews" ... which contrast[ed] sharply with all the virtues represented by the territorially settled and "culturally advanced" Nordic Aryan race. (Fox, 1995:7).

Basing his ideas on Darwin, Cesare Lombroso published his influential work *L'uomo deliquente* in 1876, which contained a lengthy chapter on the genetically criminal character of the Rroma, whom he described as "a living example of a whole *race* of criminals." This was translated into German, French and English (in 1918), and had a profound effect upon western legal attitudes. At the same time, a decree was issued in Bavaria which called for the strictest examination of documentation held by Rroma, both at the borders and inland, and the confiscation of their work-permits whenever the slightest reason warranted. Their horses were also to be examined and confiscated if they were deemed unhealthy. The movements of those who were allowed to remain were still to be carefully monitored (Strauß, 1989).

In 1883, Richard Pischel published his essay on the non-Aryan, and specifically Dravidian, origin of the Romani people, findings which are being substantiated by scholarship being undertaken in India today (Pischel, 1883; see also Hancock, 1995:17-28). This was also discussed in Martin Block's 1936 study, a profoundly racist document which had far-reaching influence upon Nazi policy regarding Rroma. Thus his chapter entitled "Gypsy race and racial preservation" begins (on page 58) "[t]heir ethnological type, like their language, indicates relationship with the original inhabitants of India, either Dravidians or even the still earlier Mon-Khmer peoples."

In 1886, Chancellor von Bismarck issued a directive to the governments of all the regions of Germany alerting them to "complaints about the mischief caused by families of Gypsies travelling in the Reich, and their increasing molestation of the population," and stated that foreign Rroma were to be dealt with particularly severely. This led to the creation of many regional policies designed to deport non-German-born Rroma (Hehemann 1987:246-50). In 1889 a survey was held by the Imperial Chancery which summarized the progress of the regional reports on Gypsy activity called for by Bismarck in 1886 (Hehemann, *loc. cit.*).

In the early 1890s, the Swabian parliament organized a conference on the "Gypsy Scum" (*Das Zigeunergeschmeiß*), and suggested means by which the presence of Rroma could be signalled from village to village by ringing church bells. The military was empowered to apprehend and move them on. In 1893 a dossier was published in Cologne demanding that Rroma and Jews be grouped together as criminals and charged equally for the same types of crime (Hehemann, 1987:114, 119-120, 126-127). An idea of the popular Gypsy stereotype held by the general public is found in Gustavus Miller's 1901 *Traumlexikon* ("Dictionary of Dreams"), where under "Gypsies" the following observations are found: "For a man to hold any conversation with a gypsy, he will be likely to lose valuable property; to dream of trading with a gypsy, you will lose money in speculation." Similarly under "Jew," the reader is told

> [t]o dream of being in company with a Jew, signifies untiring ambition and an irrepressible longing after wealth; for a young woman to dream of a Jew, omens that she will mistake flattery for truth.

An especially significant year in Romani Holocaust chronology was 1899, when Houston S. Chamberlain, whose father-in-law was the composer Richard Wagner, published his two-volume work *Die Grundlagen des neunzehnten Jahrhunderts* ("The foundations of the 19th Century") which credited the German people with the greatest scientific and cultural accomplishments, and which supported their philosophy of racial superiority. In it, he yearned for a "newly shaped" and "especially deserving Aryan race" (1899:I:266). This was regarded as complete academic justification for actions directed at the Romani minority and others throughout the German-speaking territories. On March 23rd, an information agency (*Nachrichtendienst in Bezug auf die Zigeuner*) was established in Munich under the direction of Alfred Dillmann to consolidate reports on the movement of Rroma throughout German lands, and a register of all Gypsies over the age of six began to be compiled. This included obtaining photographs, fingerprints and other genealogical data, and in particular all information relating to "criminality." None of these measures affected the Jews. This led in turn to two initiatives: Dillmann's *Zigeuner-Buch* (1905), and the policy conference of December 1911.

The Twentieth Century

In 1904, the Prussian Landtag unanimously adopted a proposition regulating the movement of Rroma and their means of livelihood. The following year, the groundwork was laid for what was to come a quarter of a century later, with the appearance of Alfred Dillmann's *Zigeuner-Buch* (the "Gypsy Book"). This consisted of three parts; an introduction which presented the arguments for controlling Rroma, a register, 310 pages long, of over 5,000 individuals, including name, date and place of birth, genealogy and kinship, criminal record and so on, and lastly a collection of photographs of Rroma from various police files. The introduction maintained that the German people were "suffering" from a "plague" of Gypsies, who were "a pest against which society must unflaggingly defend itself," and who were to be "controlled by the police most severely," being "ruthlessly punished" whenever necessary. The notion of the particular dangers of a mixed Romani and white gene pool, which Dillmann considered to characterize almost the entire Gypsy population, resurfaced in the Nuremburg Laws in 1935. Such racially motivated statements also supported the *Zigeuner-Buch*'s emphasis on the Gypsies' genetic tendency toward criminal behavior (Vaux de Foletier, 1978, and Cortiade, 1992). In 1943, the fear of race-mixing and a solution in sterilization was discussed in a book on the Danish Romani population, in which it was maintained that "mixed gipsies cause considerably greater difficulties [than "pure" Gypsies]; nothing good has come from a crossing between a gipsy and a white person" (Bartels & Brun, 1943:52). On February 17th 1906, the Prussian Minister of the Interior issued a directive entitled *Die Bekämpfung des Zigeunerunwesens* ("Combatting the Gypsy Nuisance") which listed bilateral agreements guaranteeing the expulsion of Rroma from those countries, with The Austro-Hungarian Empire, Belgium, Denmark, France, Italy, Luxembourg, The Netherlands, Russia and Switzerland (Hehemann, *loc. cit.*). Police were authorized to prosecute Rroma for breaking the law, which offenses included "lighting fires in the woods, illegal fishing, illegal camping" and so on. Temporary school attendance was forbidden for children whose families were travelling through an area. Prussia introduced "Gypsy licenses," required by all

Rroma wanting to stay in that region. These were issued only if the applicant had a fixed domicile, no serious criminal convictions, educational provision for their children, and proper tax accounts. Those qualifying were nevertheless still not allowed to settle locally (Günther, 1985:13-14).

In 1907 Hugo Herz wrote that Rroma, because of their "purely parasitical" existence, threatened normal society and the very State, concluding that "Gypsies represent an unhealthy social form within the organism of cultured people" (Hehemann, 1967: 114,119-20, 126-7). This was followed a year later a by sharp increase in anti-Gypsy terrorism throughout Germany, which led to an influx of Rroma into western Europe, including Britain. In 1909, Switzerland petitioned Germany, Italy, France and Austria to exchange information on the movements of Rroma across their shared borders, and while this attempt was unsuccessful, the Swiss Department of Justice began a national register of Gypsies, based upon the Munich model. Recommendations coming from a "Gypsy policy conference" in Hungary included the confiscation of their animals and wagons, and permanent branding for purposes of identification. In December 1911, a conference was organized at which the Munich Register was used as the basis for a larger file by incorporating data from the registers of six other German states. A year later, France introduced the *carnet anthropométrique*, a document containing personal data, including photograph and fingerprints, which all Rroma were required to carry. This requirement remained in effect until 1970. Despite the terms of Article 108 of the National Constitution of the Weimar Republic, reaffirmed in 1919, and again in 1921, which guaranteed Rroma full and equal citizenship rights, antigypsyism throughout the German-speaking lands was steadily escalating.

Another significant year in the pre-Holocaust chronology was 1920, which saw the publication of psychiatrist Karl Binding and magistrate Alfred Hoche's book, which argued for the killing of those who were "*Ballastexistenzen*," i.e. whose lives were seen merely as ballast, or dead weight, within humanity (discussed in detail in Burleigh, 1994:15*ff*.). The title of that study included the phrase "*lebensunwerten Lebens*," the concept of "lives unworthy (or undeserving) of life," which was first introduced by Liebich 57 years earlier and which became central to Nazi race policy in 1933, when a law incorporating this same phrase was issued by Hitler on July 14 that year. It singled out three groups which warranted this "euthanasia:" the terminally ill who specifically requested it, the incurably mentally ill, and people in comas grossly disfigured through accident or battle. The Romani population was seen as belonging to the second category, a belief which eventually crystallized in Hitler's 1933 law against them, and a later law issued on December 14, 1937 which allowed imprisonment for "genetically inherited criminality" as well as for actual criminal activity. On July 27, 1920, the Minister of Public Welfare in Düsseldorf forbade Gypsies from entering any public washing or recreational facilities, including swimming pools, public baths, spas and parks. In 1922 Viktor Lebzelter wrote about 41 Rroma from Serbia imprisoned in Kråkow, Poland, in language one would use "to describe a different species" (Hohmann, 1981:33). In Baden, requirements were introduced that all Gypsies be photographed and fingerprinted, and have documents completed on them.

In 1925, a conference was held on the Gypsy question, at which Bavaria proposed a law to settle Gypsies compulsorily, and to incarcerate those not regularly employed (referred to as *arbeitscheu* or "work shy") to work camps for up to two years, for reasons of "public security." This law applied equally to settled and non-settled Rroma. On July 16, 1926, the Bavarian "Law for Combatting Gypsies, Vagabonds and Idlers" proposed at the 1925 conference was passed. It was justified in the legislative assembly thus:

> [Gypsies] are by nature opposed to all work, and find it especially difficult to tolerate any restriction of their nomadic life; nothing, therefore, hits them harder than loss of liberty, combined with forced labor.

The law required the registration of all Gypsies, settled or not, with the police, registry office and unemployment agency in each district. Bavarian State Counselor Hermann Reich praised

> the enactment of the Gypsy law.... This law gives the police the legal hold it needs for thorough-going action against this constant danger to the security of the nation.

The Swiss Pro Juventute Foundation began, "in keeping with the theories of eugenics and progress" (Fraser, 1992:254), to take children away from Romani families without their consent, to change their names, and to put them into foster homes. Those pre-Nazi ideas of ethnic cleansing continued until 1973, and were not brought to public attention until the 1980s. Switzerland has apologized to the Rroma, but still adamantly refuses to allow access to the records which will help parents locate the children stolen from them. Again we must reexamine the accusation of the *Gypsy* as child-stealer.

On November 3, 1927, a Prussian ministerial decree was issued which required all Rroma to be registered by means of documentation "in the same manner as individuals being sought using wanted posters, witnesses, photographs and fingerprints." Even infants were fingerprinted, and those over the age of six required to carry identity cards bearing their photograph as well. Between November 23 and 26, armed raids were carried out by the police on Rroma communities throughout Prussia to enforce the decree of November 3. Eight thousand men, women and children were processed as a result. Bavaria instituted a law forbidding Rroma to travel in family groups, or to own firearms. Those over sixteen found themselves liable for imprisonment in work camps, while others without proof of local birth began to be expelled from Bavaria. A group of Rroma in Slovakia was tried for cannibalism, which Friedman (1950:3) interpreted as part of the growing campaign to increase negative public sentiment against the Romani population. After April 12, 1928, Rroma in Germany were placed under permanent police surveillance; the same directive was reissued and reaffirmed the following month, even though it was in direct violation of the provisions of the Weimar Constitution. Professor Hans F. Günther wrote in that year that "it was the Gypsies who introduced foreign blood into Europe." On April 3, 1929, resulting from the 1926 law, the jurisdiction of the Munich office was extended to include the whole of Germany; the German Criminal Police Commission renamed it The Central Office for the Fight Against the Gypsies in Germany. On April 16 and 17, police departments everywhere were ordered to send fingerprints and other data on Rroma both to that office and to the International Criminology Bureau headquarters in Vienna-Interpol. Working closely together, they enforced restrictions on travel for Rroma without documents, and imposed up to two years' detention in "rehabilitation camps" on those sixteen years and older.

In 1930, the Norwegian journalist Scharfenberg recommended that all Gypsies be sterilized, and on January 20, 1933, just ten days before Hitler came to power, officials in Burgenland called for the withdrawal of all civil rights for Rroma, and the introduction of clubbing as a punishment.

The Nazi Period, 1933-1945

It was stated earlier that a fuller chronology has been published elsewhere, and it does not need to be reproduced here; reference is made, however, to a number of the more significant events during this period, while the earlier chronology (and also Hancock 1989 and 1996) may be referred to for further details and references.

On January 30, Hitler was elected Chancellor of The Third Reich. March 18 saw the renewal of the cooperative agreement of German States for Combatting the Gypsy Menace, which was based on the Bavarian decree of 1926. It allowed any German state to issue additional regulations restricting licenses to Gypsies for itinerant work, the supervision of school-age Romani children by the welfare authorities, and it restricted travel. On May 26, the Law to Legalize Eugenic Sterilization was introduced. On July 14, Hitler's cabinet passed the law against "lives not deserving of life" (*Lebensunwertesleben*), called The Law for the Prevention of Hereditarily Diseased Offspring." It ordered sterilization for certain categories of people, "specifically Gypsies and most of the Germans of black color" (the so-called "Rhineland Bastards"). It also affected the Jews, as well as the disabled, and others seen as "asocial" (i.e. social misfits). The Law for the Revocation of German Citizenship was implemented against Rroma unable to show proof of German birth, as well as against the "Eastern Jews," who constituted nearly 20% of all Jews in Germany in 1933. During the week of September 18-25, the Reichsminister for the Interior and Propaganda called for the apprehension and arrest of Rroma, under the terms of the "Law Against Habitual Criminals." Many were sent to concentration camps and made to undertake penal labor. From January 1934 onwards, Rroma were being selected for transfer to camps for processing, which included sterilization by injection or castration. Over the next three years, such centers were established at Dachau, Dieselstrasse, Sachsenhausen, Marzahn and Vennhausen. On March 23 The Law for the Revocation of German Citizenship was reinstituted, and again directed at Rroma, Eastern Jews, stateless persons and other "undesirable foreigners;" on April 11th, the municipal housing policy in Düsseldorf withheld residence permits from Rroma wanting to live within city limits. In July, two laws issued in Nuremberg forbade Germans from marrying "Jews, Negroes and Gypsies."

In May, 1935, some five hundred Rroma were arrested simply because they were Rroma, and incarcerated in a camp on Venloerstraße in Cologne. The camp was surrounded by barbed wire and patrolled by armed police. On September 15, Rroma became subject to the restrictions of the National Citizenship Law (the *Reichsbürgergesetz*) and the Nuremberg Law for the Protection of German Blood and German Honor, which forbade intermarriage or sexual relationships between Aryan and non-Aryan peoples. It stated: "A marriage cannot be concluded when the expected result will put the purity of German blood of future generations in danger." A policy statement issued by the Nazi Party read "[i]n Europe generally, only Jews and Gypsies come under consideration as members of an alien people." Gypsies, Jews and Afro-Europeans were considered "racially distinctive" minorities with "alien blood."

On September 17, The National Citizenship Law relegated Jews and Rroma to the status of second class citizens, and deprived them of their civil rights. On November 26, the Central Reich Bureau and the Prussian Ministry of the Interior circulated an order to local vital statistics registration offices throughout Germany, prohibiting mixed marriages, specifically between Germans and "Gypsies, Black people, and their bastard offspring." In December, all Rroma in the town of Gelsenkirchen were incarcerated in camps on Crangerstraße and Reginenstraße, which were patrolled by the police, armed soldiers and dogs.

On March 4, 1936, a memorandum to the State Secretary of the Interior, Hans Pfundtner, addressed the creation of a national Gypsy law (*Reichzigeunergesetz*), the purpose of which was to deal with the complete registration of the Romani population, their sterilization, the restriction on their movement and means of livelihood, and the expulsion of all foreign-born and stateless Rroma. On March 20, "action against the Gypsies" was instituted in Frankfurt am Main, when the City Council voted to move the entire local population to an internment camp. The camp, on Dieselstrasse, was designated on September 22 that year, and the arrests and internment began a year later. In June, the main Nazi institution to deal with Rroma, the Racial Hygiene and Criminal Biology and Research Unit (which was Department 13 of the National Ministry of Health) was established under the directorship of Dr. Robert Ritter at Berlin-Dahlem. The National Interior Ministry supervised this entire project, partially funded by the *Deutsche Forschungsgemeinschaft* (the German Research Foundation). Its expressed purpose was to determine whether the Romani people and the Afro-Europeans were Aryans or sub-humans

(*Untermenschen*). By early 1942, Ritter had documented the genealogy of almost the entire Romani population of Germany. On June 5, a circular issued by the National and the Prussian Ministries of the Interior instructed the police to renew their efforts to "fight against the Gypsy plague." Information about Rroma was no longer to be sent to Vienna, but to the Munich Center for the Fight Against the Gypsy Nuisance. On June 6, 1936, the same ministries released a second circular, signed by Himmler which stated that "Gypsies live by theft, lying and begging, and are a plague.... It will be difficult for Gypsies to get used to an orderly, civilized way of life." Also on this day, a decree issued by the National and Prussian Ministry of the Interior brought into existence the Central Office to Combat the Gypsy Menace. This office in Munich became the headquarters of a national data bank on Rroma, and represented all German police agencies together with the Interpol International Center in Vienna, where it was located in the police headquarters on Roßauerlände. In June and July, several hundred Rroma were transported to Dachau by order of the Minister of the Interior as "dependents of the Munich Centre for the Fight Against the Gypsy Nuisance." Attempts to escape were punishable by death.

Also in 1936, Dr. Hans Globke, Head of Service for the Ministry of the Interior for the Third Reich, who served on the panel on racial legislation, declared that "in Europe, only Jews and Gypsies are of foreign blood," while race hygienist Dr. Robert Körber wrote in his paper *Volk und Staat* that "The Jews and the Gypsies are today wide apart from us because their Asiatic progenitors were totally different from our Nordic forebears" (quoted in Tenenbaum, 1956:400), a sentiment reiterated by Dr. E. Brandis, who wrote that "only the Gypsies are to be considered as an alien people in Europe (beside the Jews)." Dr. Claus Eichen published his book *Raßenwahn: Briefe über die Raßenfrage* ("Delusions of race: Notes on the race question") in which he justified sterilization of "asocial" and "criminal" elements in German society, *i.e.* Gypsies. German anti-Gypsyism became transnational in Europe when Interpol in Vienna established the Centre for Combatting the Gypsy Menace, which had grown out of the earlier Bureau of Gypsy Affairs. In Leipzig, Martin Block published his general study of Rroma, and justified Nazi racist attitudes, echoing Grellmann when he wrote of the "nauseating Gypsy smell," and the "involuntary feeling of mistrust or repulsion one feels in their presence." In Berlin, Rroma were cleared off the streets away from public view because of the upcoming Olympic games, so that visitors could be "spared the sight of the Gypsy disgrace" (Zimmermann, 1990:91). In 1937, an editorial in the Hamburger Tagblatt for August by Georg Nawrocki, took the Weimar Republic to task for its lenient attitude towards Gypsies:

> It was in keeping with the inner weakness and mendacity of the Weimar Republic that it showed no instinct for tackling the Gypsy question. For it, the Sinti were a criminal concern at best - we, on the other hand, see the Gypsy question above all as a *racial* problem, which must be solved, and which is being solved (Vossen, 1983:70).

On August 18, Rroma in Frankfurt were arrested and incarcerated in the Dieselstraße camp. In the same year, 1937, Heinrich Himmler issued a decree entitled *Bekämpfung der Zigeunerplage* ("The Struggle Against the Gypsy Plague") which stated, like Dillmann's *Zigeuner-Buch* 27 years before it, that Gypsies of mixed blood were the most predisposed to criminality, and that police departments should systematically send data on Rroma in their areas to the Reich Central Office (Döring, 1964:58-60).

Between June 12 and June 18, 1938, *Zigeuneraufräumungswoche*, "Gypsy clean-up week," took place, and hundreds of Rroma throughout Germany and Austria were rounded up, beaten and imprisoned (Novitch, 1968:7). This was the third such public action by the German state, earlier attacks having taken place on November 23-26, 1927 and September 18-25, 1933. Like *Kristallnacht*, it was a public sanctioning and approval of the official attitude towards members of an "inferior race." After March 16, Rroma were no longer allowed to vote, a directive shortly thereafter also applied to Jews. The first mention of the *Endlösung der Zigeunerfrage* ("Final Solution of the Gypsy Question") appeared in a document calling for its implementation signed by Himmler on December 8, 1938 (Ranz, 1995:11).

At the beginning of 1940, the first mass genocidal action of the Holocaust took place when 250 Romani children from Czechoslovakia were murdered during tests with the new Zyklon-B gas in the camp at Buchenwald (Proester, 1940; Novitch, 1968). Robert Ritter published a report in which he stated that

> we have been able to establish that more than 90% of the so-called "native" [i.e., German-born] Gypsies are of mixed blood.... Furthermore, the results of our investigations have allowed us to characterize the

Gypsies as being a people of entirely primitive ethnological origins, whose mental backwardness makes them incapable of real social adaptation.... The Gypsy question can only be solved when the main body of asocial and worthless Gypsy individuals of mixed blood is collected together in large labor camps and kept working there, and when the further breeding of this population of mixed blood is permanently stopped (Müller-Hill, 1989:57).

In August 1941, Himmler issued a decree listing the criteria for racial and biological evaluation. An individual's family background had to be investigated over three generations (compared to two generations for one's Jewish genealogy). He implemented a system of classification based on the degree of Romani ancestry in one's genetic descent: <Z> meant "pure Gypsy," <ZM+> meant more than half Gypsy, <ZM> meant half Gypsy, <ZM-> meant less than half Gypsy and <NZ> meant non-Gypsy. Having two great-grandparents who were even only part-Gypsy (*i.e.* if one were of 25% or less Gypsy ancestry) counted as <ZM->. On July 31, Heydrich, chief architect of the details of the Final Solution, issued his directive to the Einsatzkommandos to "kill all Jews, Gypsies and mental patients" (Müller-Hill, 1989:56; see also Friedlander, 1995). In September that year, Minister of Justice Dr. Otto Thierack wrote in a memo to Hermann Goebbels that

> With regard to the destruction of asocial life, Dr. Goebbels is of opinion that the following should be exterminated: (1) All Jews and Gypsies (2) Poles in prison for three or four year terms, and (3) Czechs and Germans who have been sentences either to death or to life imprisonment. The idea of exterminating them through work is best (*International Military Tribunal*, Vol. VI, *p.* 279).

On December 16, 1942, Himmler issued the order to have all Rroma remaining in Europe deported to Auschwitz-Birkenau for extermination, and so the end began for the second "major group which National Socialists proposed to exterminate in its entirety: the Gypsies" (Peukert, 1987:210).

The Post-War Period

The question is frequently asked regarding the number of Rroma murdered in the Holocaust. Estimates from as low as twenty thousand to as high as four million have appeared, with half a million having somehow become the default figure. This must be considered an underestimation for a number of reasons, expressed most clearly by König (1989:87-89):

> [T]he count of half a million Sinti and Roma murdered between 1939 and 1945 is too low to be tenable; for example in the Soviet Union many of the Romani dead were listed under non-specific labels such as "remainder to be liquidated," "hangers-on," "partisans," [&c...] The final number of the dead Sinti and Roma may never be determined. We do not know precisely how many were brought into the concentration camps; not every concentration camp produced statistical material ... Sinti and Roma often ... do not appear in the statistics.

Also, as the Auschwitz Memorial Book points out, Rroma were murdered unrecorded, sometimes by the hundreds, outside the camps, in the most numbers in the eastern territories, for which only scant records exist. As research continues, for example that being undertaken for Czechoslovakia by Polansky (Strandberg, 1994) or for Serbia by Acković (1995), the figures rise steadily higher. In order to estimate the percentage of total losses, we would have to know, in addition to the number of dead, the number of Rroma throughout Europe before 1933, and this we will never be able to determine accurately, although both *Colliers Encyclopedia* and the *Encyclopedia Americana* list the pre-war European Romani population as 700,000. A guess as good as any is that there were perhaps three million Rroma throughout the German-controlled territories at the period of their maximum extent, between one and one and a half a million of whom were murdered, i.e. between a third and a half of the population. The *world* population at the same time was probably *ca.* five million.

Only a few thousand survived in the Nazi-controlled territories, and none was asked to testify in behalf of the Romani victims at the war crimes trials. Reparations to Rroma as a people have yet to be made by the German government, which has only in recent years even admitted the racial motivation of the Nazi genocidal campaign against the Romani people.

The massive increase in neo-Nazi activity since the reunification of Germany and the collapse of Communism has been documented in a series of book-length treatments published by Helsinki Watch, and in a 50-page report by the Geneva-based U.N. Human Rights Commission. And in poll after poll, the Romani population in Europe stands as the prime target of both sanctioned and unsanctioned discrimination. In 1995 alone, in the Czech Republic alone, there were over 450 documented attacks against Rroma, several resulting in death; those were only the reported incidents. There have been rapes and house-burnings in Romania and Bulgaria; letter bombs and booby-trap explosives have killed four Rroma and blinded and maimed many more. At the October 1995 OSCE meeting in Warsaw, one of our delegates was hit and robbed by four youths on the street shouting racial epithets; another was turned back at the Polish border simply because he was a Rrom, and as a result was not able to attend the meeting. The previous year, in the same city, a group of nine of us, all Rroma, were refused service in a restaurant.

One of the issues at the 1995 conference in Warsaw was the official protest of Romania's resolution to replace the words *Rom* and *Romani* with *Ţigan* in all official documents. The word, which was a synonym for "slave" during the five and a half centuries of Gypsy slavery in that country, is as offensive for Rroma as the word "nigger" is for African Americans. The Romanian government's reason for this is that *Romani* sounds too much like *Romanian*, and outsiders might think that Romanians were Gypsies. In November, 1995, Amnesty International released a 62-page document on human rights abuses in Romania which referred in part to

> "reports about torture and ill-treatment by police officials [and their] violent abuse of power.... Massive arbitrary measures against the Romani minority and the lack of protection of this group against racist attacks have continuously posed a problem since March, 1990.

The Romanian government has responded by declaring that "hereafter, slandering of the state and the nation will be prosecuted by imprisonment of up to five years" (*Romnews*, No. 46, November 19, 1995, p. 1.).

Echoes of the Holocaust

Attention is drawn to Romania deliberately here, because a frightening link with the Third Reich is having repercussions in the present day, though it has so far gone unheeded. In the pages of the newsletter of the Virginia-based Romanian Children's Connection, attention has been brought to the appalling conditions of the orphans in Romania's state institutions. In some places Rroma constitute as many as 80% of the children, although Rroma make up only between 10% and 20% of the national population. The Romanian government is struggling to address this situation, which is a legacy left it by Nicolae Ceauşescu. Like Hitler before him, Ceauşescu was intent on creating a superior "Dacian" race by genetic manipulation. His fascination with Hitler's race policies was no secret; Pacepa (1988:281) describes this as follows:

> In the early 1970s, when Ceauşescu learned that Romania had over 600,000 emigrés abroad, he became very interested in Hitler's Fifth Column. This was not too surprising, as Ceauşescu had always studied Hitler's "charisma," and had repeatedly analyzed the original Nazi films of Hitler's speeches.... In almost every speech, he recalls the Romanian people's origins in proud Roman and Dacian warriors, just as Hitler harped on the Aryans.

Because he took pains to conceal his actions, however, and because little documentation has yet come to light, much of it having been destroyed, the means by which Ceauşescu tried to accomplish his aims are only now being pieced together.

The establishment of his "death camp" orphanages apparently predated his fascination with Hitler by some years. On July 28th, 1991, using footage secretly filmed by Hans Hunink, who was working with the human rights organization Terre des Hommes which is based in Den Haag, Mark Jones presented a documentary on NBC's Cable News Network in which he reported that

> Ceauşescu started the camps as early as 1965; there had been years of planning. When Auschwitz, the Nazi concentration camp, was discovered in January, 1945, Nicolae Ceauşescu was 27 years old. Like the Nazis, Ceauşescu advocated racial purity. Years later, he would express his concern for, quote, "the new human type we intend to mold in our society." Ceauşescu had Romania's history books rewritten. He argued that the true Romanians were Dacians, far more advanced than what he called "the other aboriginal races ... superior even to ancient Rome." Ceauşescu wanted a huge robot work force.

His intention was to breed on the one hand large numbers of "pure" Romanians and on the other, those who were to make up his "robot work force," the status the Romani slaves had already endured for over five hundred years in his country. In both cases, the weak were allowed to die, since they were of no use to either population. Terre des Hommes reported that the annual death rate in some of the homes was between 50% and 65%. Such children were classified as "irrecuperable" or "irrecoverable" by the government, and no attempt was made to sustain them. Hans Hunink's film showed the mass graves where their bodies had been dumped, sometimes not even in boxes, after they had been allowed to die. According to that report, irrecuperables were sent to Riu Sadului, near Sibiu,

> ... one of 170 isolated "forbidden zones." No visitors were allowed inside; one mile up the road is a mass grave, four football fields long. Dutch humanitarian Hans Hunink discovered the mass grave last winter; Hunink believes that most of the dead are children.

Women, married or not, were encouraged to have many children; they were rewarded publicly for giving birth to five or more, and birth control was made illegal. Romanian officials have since maintained that Rroma were not therefore discriminated against, since the policy affected both populations equally, but the awful difference lay in what was destined for each group. Because of the state of the Romanian economy, and because Ceaușescu was executed in December 1989, this bizarre plan never materialized, but it has left a legacy in the surplus children who languish in Romania's orphanages, and whose bodies fill the graves reported by Terre des Hommes.

A report dated August 28, 1991, indicated that the coercive sterilization of Romani women in Czechoslovakia and the permanent removal of their children was still going on, despite assurances from the Czech government that it had been stopped (Pellar, 1991; see also Offner & de Rooj, 1990).

The age-old charge of spying re-emerged a few years ago in 1989, when the British government used it as a reason for their not allowing the construction of a site for Rroma near a Ministry of Defence research facility. It was said that the presence of Gypsies near the establishment would "pose a risk to security ... and allow terrorists near the top-secret site for reconnaissance work" (*The Surrey Advertiser*, May 25th, 1990).

Lombroso's and Dillmann's and the Nazis' insistence that criminality is a genetic characteristic of the Romani people was the focus of a 1981 article in a police journal by American criminologist Terry Getsay, who wrote about the "criminal propensity" of the Gypsies as a people; two entire books on the topic appeared in 1994, published by police specialty presses: Jack Morris' *The Master Criminals Among the Gypsies* and Marlock & Dowling's *Licensed to Steal*; the latter talks about "dishonest Romani, the *true* Gypsies" (*p.* 17), and cautions that "no one is invulnerable to Gypsy crime" on the dust-jacket. Such crime, it says, "has a feel, a smell and an aura that screams 'Gypsy'" (p. 5). An article on Gypsies published in the *FBI Law Enforcement Bulletin* in 1994, in wording reminiscent of the 1899 police conference in Germany, stressed that "interagency cooperation represents the greatest asset law can employ [against Gypsies]" (Mazzone, 1994:5).

An unsettling echo of the 1920 decree which forbade Rroma to use public facilities came on October 18, 1995, when the mayor of Vsetin in the Czech Republic issued a similar order banning Rroma from using public bathing and swimming facilities in that city (Open Media Research Institute, *Daily Digest*, 20 October 1995).

History also repeated itself in Munich in October 1988, when the City Council announced its intention forcibly to relocate Rroma refugees to a containment center on the site of an earlier Nazi deportation and slave-labor camp in that city; it was a toxic waste dump, and was to have guards and guard dogs patrolling it (*Die Tageszeichnung* for October 26, 1988). The same action was taken in the same city in May 1935.

In 1936, Rroma had been cleared from the streets of Berlin in anticipation of the Olympic Games; fifty-six years later, the police in Spain did exactly the same thing in preparation for the 1992 Olympic Games in Barcelona, when Spanish Rroma were moved to the Campo de la Bota outside the city for the same reason - to hide the Gypsy "eyesore" from the public.

When attempts to create a robot work force for a master race were being made forty years after the fall of Nazi Germany, when the coercive sterilization of Romani women is being reported in the 1990s, when Germany can deport its unwanted Rroma to neighboring countries and pay those countries to take them, we must ask ourselves how far we have come since the days of Hitler. When we watch the present-day rise of neo-Nazi activity, not only overseas but here in our own country, and stand impotently by as Rroma are beaten and murdered in Europe, sometimes by the very police meant to protect them, we must face the fact that the writing is clearly on the wall. If the situation is not regarded seriously and steps are not taken to prevent it, then the world will have another *porrajmos*, another massive devouring of Romani lives, to account for.

Notes

1. This is a modified version of a paper originally presented at the Conference entitled *Gypsies in the Holocaust: The Nazi Assault on Roma and Sinti,* co-sponsored by the Drew University Center for Holocaust Study and The United States Holocaust Research Institute, Drew University, Madison, New Jersey, Thursday, November 9th 1995.

2. Though not entirely: Kimmerling (1995:63, *fn.* 26) notes that

Most mainstream Israeli historians and social scientists agree upon the incomparability of the Holocaust with other organized genocides and invest much energy in "proving" this argument. Any counter-argument is seen as "revisionism" and virtually seen as equivalent to the denial of the Holocaust itself. When in 1995 the Ministry of Education tried to introduce an optional curricular program for high schools about the Armenian and Gypsy genocides, the plan was vetoed by several respectable history professors, who argued that the subject was better presented as part of the more general program dealing with World War II.

3. Friedlander deals in particular with the targeting of the handicapped in his new book, the one other population selected for extermination according to Nazi genocidal policy, and the one on which race-engineering techniques for dealing with Rroma and Jews were later based.

4. There is considerable confusion about the terminology used when discussing the Romani people, and some clarification is in order. All Romani populations throughout the world share a single common origin in India, having left there as a single group about a thousand years ago as a result of the spread of Islam (Hancock, 1995); at the time of arrival in Europe between 1250 and 1300 AD, the Rroma were one people speaking one language. The fragmenting into the various sub-groups occurred after this time, as a result of different sociohistorical factors. These divisions were accompanied by the acquisition and use of different names; *Sinti* refers to the Romani population in northern Europe, a population which suffered especially severely at the hands of the Nazis. The Sinti refer to their language and culture as *Romani,* and use the word *Rom* only to mean (Romani) husband. Other groups use the word *Rom* in the same way as *Sinti,* i.e. as the larger group designation; the Sinti do not refer to themselves as a group as *R(r)oma.* When referring to the Sinti specifically, the word Sinti should be employed. The International Romani Union recognizes the historical unity of all Romani populations, and that all populations furthermore have the word *Rom* in their respective dialects of Romani, either to mean "(Romani) husband" (as opposed to "non-Romani

husband"), or to refer to the group as a whole, or else to mean both. Thus, the word *Rrom* (plural *Rroma*) is now used in all IRU documents as the general ethnonym for all peoples who descend from Romani-speaking populations, including the Sinti, Vlax, Manuš, Romničel, Kale, &c. The spelling with double-/rr/ is in accordance with standardized orthography, there being two /r/ phonemes in the language (Cortiade *et al.*, 1996).

5. Romani cultural restrictions on contact with outsiders, while probably having their origins in Hinduism and the caste system, are not maintained for religious reasons today. They are based in the concept of ritual pollution, which must be guarded against by the proper preparation of food, handling of animals, washing and placement of clothes and bedlinen, and by proper male-female relationships. Since non-Rroma do not observe these behaviors, they are in a state of defilement, and thereby able to defile others (specifically Rroma themselves) by association. Not all Romani groups maintain all of these restrictions to the same extent.

Works Mentioned in the Text

Acković, Dragoljub, *Roma Suffering in the Jasenovic Camp.* (Belgrade: Struča Knjiga, 1995).

Bartels, Erik, & Gudrun Brun, *The Gipsies in Denmark.* (Copenhagen: Munksgaard, 1943).

Bauer, Yehuda, "Whose Holocaust?," *Midstream,* (November, 1980), pp. 42-46.

Bauer, Yehuda, "Gypsies," in Gutman & Berenbaum, eds., (1994), pp. 441-455.

Beck, Sam, "The Romanian Gypsy Problem," in Grumet, ed., (1985), pp. 100-109.

Biester, Johann Erich, "Ueber die Zigeuner," *Berlinische Monatsschrift,* (1793), p. 21, pp. 108-165, 360-393.

Binding, Karl, & Alfred Hoche, *Die Freigabe der Vernichtung Lebensunwerten Lebens.* (Leipzig: Felix Meiner, 1920).

Bischoff, Ferdinand, *Deutsch-Zigeunerisches Woerterbuch.* (Ilmenau: Voigt Verlag, 1827). Block, Martin, *Die Zigeuner: Ihre Leben und Ihre Seele.* (Leipzig: Bibliographisches Institut, 1936).

Block, Martin, *Zigeuner: Ihre Leben und ihre Seele.* (Leipzig: Bibliographisches Institut A.G, 1936).

Burleigh, Michael, *Death and Deliverance.* (Cambridge: The University Press, 1994).

Chamberlain, Houston S., *Die Grundlagen des Neunzehnten Jahrhunderts.* (Leipzig, 1899).

Cortiade, Marcel, *The "Zigeuner-Buch" or, When the KL Were Still Paper and Ink.* (Fondàcija Rromani Baxt Occasional Paper, 1992).

Cortiade, Marcel, Nicolae Gheorghe & Ian Hancock, *Romani Ethnic Terminology.* (Toulouse: Collection Interface, Centre de Recherches Tsiganes, 1996).

Crowe, David, & John Kolsti, (eds.), *The Gypsies of Eastern Europe.* (Armonk: E.C. Sharpe, 1989).

Dillmann, Alfred, *Zigeuner-Buch.* (Munich: Wildsche, 1905).

Döring, Hans-Joachim, *Die Zigeuner im NS-Staat.* (Hamburg: Kriminalistik Verlag, 1964).

Dunstan, G.R., "A Note on an Early Ingredient of Racial Prejudice in Western Europe," *Race*, 6(4), (1965), pp. 334-339.

Eccard, J.G., *Corpus Historicum Medii ævi.* (Leipzig, 1723).

Eichen, Claus, *Raßenwahn: Briefe über die Raßenfrage.* (Paris: Carrefour, 1936).

Fings, Karola, & Frank Sparing, *Nur Wenige Kamen zurück: Sinti und Roma im Nationalsozialismus.* (Cologne: Stadt-Revue Verlag, 1990).

Fox, John P, "The Nazi Extermination of the Gypsies: Genocide, Holocaust, or a 'Minor Irritant?,'" paper presented at the conference of the Association of Genocide Scholars, Williamsburg, Virginia, June 14-16, 1995.

Friedlander, Henry, *The Origins of Nazi Genocide from Euthanasia to the Final Solution.* (Chapel Hill: North Carolina University Press, 1995).

Friedman, Philip, "How the Gypsies Were Persecuted," *Wiener Library Bulletin*, (1950), pp. 3-4.

Getsay, Terry, "GYP-sies and Their Criminal Propensity," *Spotlight*, (1981/2). 1(1) pp. 12-17, 1(2) pp. 14-19, 2(1) pp. 10-20.

Gilbert, Martin, *The Holocaust: A History of the Jews of Europe During the Second World War*, (New York: Henry Holt & Co., 1985).

Gobineau, Joseph Arthur, *Essai sur l'inégalité des races Humaines*. Paris, 1855.

Gobineau, Joseph Arthur, "Die Wanderstämme Persiens," (*Zeitschrift der Deutscher Morganländische Gesellschaft*, 1857), 11, pp. 689-699 [on Gypsies in Iran].

Grautoff, H., *Die lübeckischen Chroniken*, (Lübeck, 1972), 2 vols.

Grumet, Joanne, *Papers From the Fourth and Fifth Annual Meetings of the Gypsy Lore Society, North American Chapter*, (New York: GLS (NAC), 1985), Monograph 2.

Günther, W., *Zur Preußischen Zigeunerpolitik Seit 1871*, (Hannover: ANS Verlag, 1985).

Gutman, Israel, & Michael Berenbaum, eds., *Anatomy of the Auschwitz Death Camp*, (Bloomington & Indianapolis: Indiana University Press, 1994, in association with the U.S. Holocaust Memorial Council).

Hancock, Ian, *The Pariah Syndrome: An Account of Gypsy Persecution and Slavery*. (Ann Arbor: Karoma Publishers, 1987).

Hancock, Ian, "'Uniqueness' of the Victims: Gypsies, Jews and the Holocaust," *Without Prejudice: International Review of Racial Discrimination*, 1(2), (1988), pp. 45-67.

Hancock, Ian, "Gypsy History in Germany and Neighboring Lands: A Chronology Leading to the Holocaust and Beyond," *in* Crowe & Kolsti, eds., 1989, pp. 11-30.

Hancock, Ian, *A Handbook of Vlax Romani*. (Columbus: Slavica Publishers, 1995).

Hancock, Ian, "Jewish Responses to the Porrajmos," in Rosenbaum, 1996.

Hobson, R.F., [Commentary on Racism] in Dunstan, 1965, p. 338.

Hohmann, Joachim S., *Geschichte der Zigeunerverfolgung* in *Deutschland,* (Frankfurt & New York: Campus Verlag, 1981).

Hehemann, Rainer, *Die "Bekämpfung des Zigeunerunwesens"* im *Wilhelminischen Deutschland und in der Weimarer Republik, 1871-1933.* (Frankfurt am Main: Haag & Herschen Verlag, 1987).

International Military Tribunal, 1948. Nuremberg.

Kenedi, János, "Why is the Gypsy the Scapegoat and Not the Jew?," *East European Reporter*, 2(1), (1986), pp. 11-14.

Kenrick, Donald, & Grattan Puxon, *The Destiny of Europe's Gypsies,* (London: Sussex University Press, 1972).

Kimmerling, Baruch, *History and Memory,* (Tel Aviv: Spring-Samlea, 1995).

Knox, Robert, *The Races of Men.* London, 1850.

König, Ulrich, *Sinti und Roma unter dem Nationalsozialismus.* (Bochum: Brockmeyer, 1989).

Körber, Robert, [Jüdische u. Zigeunerische Artfremdesblut], *Volk und Staat,* 1936, (cited in Tenenbaum, 1956 p. 400).

Kulemann, Rudolph, "Die Zigeuner," *Unsere Zeit,* (1869) 5(1), pp. 843-871.

Liebich, Richard, *Die Zigeuner in ihrem Wesen und ihere Sprache*, (Leipzig: Brockhaus, 1863).

Lombroso, Cesare, *Crime: Its Causes and Remedies,* (Boston: Little, Brown & Co., 1918).

Marlock, Dennis, & John Dowling, *License to Steal.* (Boulder: Paladin Press, 1994).

Mason, Philip, "But O! My Soul is White," *Encounter*, April, 1968, pp. 57-61.

Mayall, David, *Gypsy-Travellers in Nineteenth Century Society*, (Cambridge; The University Press, 1988).

Mazzone, Gary L., "Traveling Criminals," *FBI Law Enforcement Bulletin*, 63, (1994) pp. 1-5.

Mihalik, Eva von, & Doris Kreutzkamp, *Du kriegst auch einen schönen Wohnwagen: Zwangslager für Sinti und Roma während des Nationalsozialismus in Frankfurt am Main,* (Frankfurt: Brandes & Apsel, 1990).

Miller, Gustavus Hindman, *Das Traumlexikon* (1901), (published as *The Dictionary of Dreams: 10,000 Dreams Interpreted,* (New York: Simon & Schuster, 1992).

Morris, Jack, *The Master Criminals Among the Gypsies.* (Loomis: The Palmer Press, 1994).

Müller-Hill, Benno, *Murderous Science: Elimination by Scientific Selection of Jews, Gypsies and Others, Germany 1933-1945,* (Oxford: The University Press, 1988).

Nicoll, Ruaridh, "Bimbo Tribe Lures Men into Foxglove Trap," The (London) *Observer,* November 29, 1995, *p.* 25.

Novitch, Miriam, *Le génocide des Tziganes sous le Régime Nazi,* (Paris: AMIF, 1968).

Ofner, Paul, & Bert de Rooj, "Survey on the Sterilization of Roma Women in Czechoslovakia," (Amsterdam: Report of the Lau Mazirel Foundation, 1990).

Okely, Judith, *The Traveller Gypsies,* (Cambridge: The University Press, 1983).

Pacepa, Ion Mihai, *Red Horizons,* (Washington: Regnery-Gateway, 1988).

Pellar, Ruben, "Sterilisierung von Roma-Frauen in der ESSR," *Pogrom,* 159 (May-June, 1991) p. 49.

Peukert, Detlev, *Inside Nazi Germany: Conformity, Opposition and Racism in Everyday Life,* (London: R.T. Batsford, 1987).

Pischel, Richard, "Der Heimath der Zigeuner," *Deutsche Rundschau,* 36, (1883), pp. 353-375.

Proester, Emil, *Vraždní čs. Cikánů v Buchenwaldu.* Document No. ÚV ČSPB-K-135 of the Archives of the Fighters Against Fascism. (Prague, 1940).

Ranz, S., "Buchenwald: 50 Years Later," *Jewish Currents*, October, 1995, pp. 10-13.

Rosenbaum, Alan, ed., *Perspectives on the Uniqueness of the Holocaust*, (Boulder: Westview Press, 1996).

Scharfenberg, J., "Omstreiferondet," *Arbeiderbladet*, Oct. 31 & Nov. 25, 1930.

Scheier, Alfred (ed.), *Arnim's Werke*, (Leipzig: Bibliographisches Institut, 1925).

Sibley, David, *Outsiders in Urban Societies*, (Oxford: Basil Blackwell, 1981).

Smith, Julia, "People Seem to Imagine that Martin is Such a Sap," The (London) *Times*, Friday, October 27, 1995, p. 18.

State Museum of Auschwitz-Birkenau, *Memorial Book: The Gypsies at Auschwitz-Birkenau*. Documentary and Cultural Centre of German Sintis and Roma, (Munich: K.G. Saur, 1993).

Strandberg, Susan, "Researcher Claims Thousands of Gypsies Exterminated by Czechs," *The Decorah Journal*, May 5, 1994, pp. 1-2.

Strauss, Eva, "Gipsy Policy and Persecution in Bavaria from 1885 to 1945." Leiden Fonds paper, translated from the Dutch by Margit von Stetten and Christopher Martin, 1989.

Tenenbaum, Joseph, *Race and Reich: The Story of an Epoch*, (New York: Twayne Publishers, 1956).

Vaux de Foletier, François, "Un Recensement des Tsiganes de Bavière en 1905," *Etudes Tsiganes*, 24 (3), (1978), pp. 8-14.

Vossen, Rüdiger, *Zigeuner*, (Frankfurt & Berlin: Ullstein Sachbuch, 1983).

Walters, E. Garrison, *The Other Europe: Eastern Europe to 1945*, (Syracuse: The University Press, 1988).

Wippermann, Wolfgang, *Das Leben in Frankfurt zur NS-Zeit: Die nationalsozialistische Zigeunerverfolgung*, (Frankfurt am Main: W. Kramer & Co., 1986).

Chapter 3

UNIQUENESS AND UNIVERSALITY IN THE HOLOCAUST: THE NEED FOR A NEW LANGUAGE

John T. Pawlikowski

Introduction

Was the Holocaust primarily the result of classical antisemitism in modern guise, or was it essentially the result of new realities made possible by advances in technology, science and bureaucratic development with traditional antisemistism serving to generate popular support? If the latter, then were the non-Jewish victims merely adjuncts to the annihilation of the Jews? Or is their victimization to be understood as intimately related to the basic processes that unleashed the Holocaust?

My principal argument is that there is need for a basic paradigm shift in Holocaust interpretation, which moves our understanding of the event from a mere repetition of classical antisemitism to a distinctly modern phenomenon whose central intent went beyond making Europe (or even the world) *Judenrein*. In that context, while the annihilation of the Jews became all-consuming as an initial Nazi goal (and classical antisemitism undoubtedly influenced the designation of the Jews as the primary victims), there is now sufficient evidence to suggest that the Nazis intended to do much more.

Victimization During the Holocaust

Since the development of scholarship on the Holocaust in the 1970s, an intense discussion has ensued regarding its uniqueness. This debate has focused to some extent on the relationship between Jews and other

Nazi victims, but even more on the comparability of the Holocaust to other examples of mass death and genocide, such as the slaughter of the Armenians in the early years of this century, the mass exterminations that took place in Cambodia under the Khmer Rouge, and the elimination of indigenous peoples and their cultural traditions in the Americas. Jewish scholars and activists in the main have argued for some measure of uniqueness for the Jewish experience, with some going so far as to maintain that any comparisons between the fate of the Jews under the Nazis and other instances of massive human brutality inevitably distort the magnitude of the crime against the Jews. Others, while recognizing the special character of the Nazi attack on the Jewish people, have searched for an authentic way to include the other Nazi victims within the general umbrella of human suffering during the period and have acknowledged the need for carefully stated comparisons between the Jewish experience and other genocides.

The various scholars addressing the issue of universality have lent their own particular interpretation. Michael Berenbaum, Director of the U.S. Holocaust Memorial Museum's Research Institute, has attempted to group the differing perspectives within two general categories. The first of these Berenbaum terms uniqueness by reason of *intention*. The second he calls uniqueness by reason of *results*.[1]

Those scholars locating the uniqueness of the Holocaust primarily in the intentionality of the perpetrators emphasize the central role of ideology and directed decision-making in the carrying out of the Nazi plan. On the other hand, those who favor the "results" perspective concentrate far more on the processes of human destruction designed by Hitler and his collaborators. For these scholars, how the annihilation took place assumes far greater importance than its philosophical or theological roots, which may always remain somewhat ambiguous.

One of the principal proponents of the *intentionality* viewpoint is Yehuda Bauer. In several of his published works,[2] Bauer situates the uniqueness in the deliberate and conscious decision by the Nazi leadership to move towards the total extermination of the Jewish people. No calculated plan of that kind had ever been put forward previously, with respect to Jews or any other people. The Nazi ideologues had become convinced that it was impossible for humankind to advance to a "higher" human plateau without the complete disappearance of Jews from the face of the earth. They were "vermin" whose continued presence within the human family threatened it with biological stagnation if not actual retardation. The Jews were regarded as the central barrier to the Aryanization of Europe, which would in turn bestow upon the Nazis absolute control over the world.

Bauer also adds a religious component to his understanding of the Holocaust's uniqueness. While this "sacral" element has definite ties to the long history of Christian antisemitism, it takes on for the Nazis a "demonic" quality that gives the antisemitic tradition new force. As Bauer sees it, there existed a "quasiapocalyptic" dimension to the Nazi embrace of the classical antisemitic legacy found in the Christian tradition.[3] This dimension had never occurred prior to the emergence of the Nazis, nor has it happened since.

Bauer's stress on *intentionality* as the root of the Holocaust's uniqueness is shared in some measure by several other scholars, including Uriel Tal, Steven Katz, George Mosse and Lucy Dawidowicz. Tal, for example, argued for an understanding of the Holocaust as the end result of distinctly modern philosophical and scientific theories emerging in western Europe throughout the century or so preceding the emergence of the Nazi movement. Central to this modern consciousness was strong belief in the possibility of genuine human progress and in the importance of biological "cleansing" in promoting such progress.

The most thorough articulation of the *intentionality* perspective to appear of late is the first of a projected three-volume work by Steven Katz.[4] As Katz interprets the Nazi phenomenon, Hitler suffered from an obsession with racial views that pitted the Aryan race against the Jews, whom he regarded as a parasitic people that fed on the lifeblood of Germany. Katz clearly differentiates Hitler's belief in the Aryan myth and the struggle for world domination between Aryans and Jews from the classical Christian myth that portrayed the Jews among the minions of the devil and Antichrist. For him Nazi racial ideology represented a step beyond the traditional Christian approach to the Jewish people. The Church, he argues, was content to persecute and proselytize. It left Jews the option of conversion. The Nazis eliminated any and all options for Jews to survive. That was the fundamental difference. Katz defines the Holocaust as

phenomenologically unique by virtue of the fact that never before has a state set out, as a matter of intentional principle and actualized policy, to annihilate physically every man, woman, and child belonging to a specific people.[5]

In discussing the uniqueness of the Holocaust, Katz deliberately refrains from any theological conclusions. In his judgement both the theological "radicals" (e.g., Rubenstein, Cohen, Fackenheim, Greenberg, the Eckardts, and to a degree Moltmann, Littell, Sherman, van Buren, Cargas, Tracy, Thoma and Pawlikowski) and the theological "conservatives" (e.g., Berkovits, Neusner, Barth, Schneerson, and Journet) have all exceeded the available evidence in arriving at their conclusions.[6]   In his view their conclusions are extrinsic to the experience of the death camps and depend largely on prior theological positions. It is interesting in this context that he ignores the writings of Elie Wiesel who, while not a theologian in a formal sense, has deeply influenced the formulation of both Jewish and Christian post-Holocaust theologies.

On the question of the non-Jewish victims of the Nazis and the implications of their deaths for Katz's theory of the Holocaust's uniqueness, he offers only a skeletal outline in volume one. The issue, he says, will be discussed at length in the final volume of his projected trilogy.   He argues that though the slaughter of these peoples was "abhorrent," and while it forms an integral part of the overall plan of Nazism, it was a distinctive part of that plan which in the final analysis is different from the plan directed against the Jews who alone were singled out for total extermination.

In his bibliographic citations in volume one Katz displays considerable familiarity with the growing body of literature on the non-Jewish victims; however his overall provisional conclusion does not answer all questions in my judgment, at least not with respect to the Gypsies, the disabled, and the Poles. Some distinctions still need to be drawn among the victim groups because the Nazis drew them.

The *results* perspective on the Holocaust's uniqueness is advanced by several important scholars, in particular Raul Hilberg, whose work, *The Destruction of the European Jews,* still remains the most comprehensive study on the Nazis' systematic extermination of European Jewry. In a special way Hilberg has highlighted the central importance of the German railroad system which transported Jews to the death camps on a daily basis in a highly efficient manner.   Other prominent names associated with this viewpoint are Lawrence Langer, Hannah Arendt, Joseph Borkin and Emil Fackenheim.

For Fackenheim, who in some ways could also be included with the *intentionality* advocates, the uniqueness of the Holocaust is multi-faceted. For one, its scope was unprecedented when compared to other instances of the mass slaughter of human beings. The Nazis aimed at eliminating every Jew then alive simply because of Jewish parentage. Faith and ideology played no role in determining the fate of a Jewish person. Ultraorthodox Jews died alongside atheistic Jews and Jews who had converted to Christianity. Liberal and socialist Jews were killed together with socially conservative Jews. For the Nazis, says Fackenheim, the destruction of the Jews was an end in itself. The death camps were not accidental by products of the Nazi plan but part of its very essence.

Joseph Borkin and Lawrence Langer are both struck by the way in which the Holocaust totally deprived its victims of any meaningful choices. Langer describes the world of the death camps as a universe of "choiceless choices." It is nearly impossible for us to imagine how this world was experienced in terms of inner consciousness by those who found themselves confined within its perimeters. Borkin, focusing much more on the objective level, sees the death camps as the perverse perfection of slavery where the human being was reduced to raw material. The only value attached to the camp inmates by the Nazis related to their hair, gold teeth, ashes, etc., which could be converted into profit upon their death.

Michael Berenbaum and Richard Rubenstein, in different ways, each advocate a position that affirms the uniqueness of the Jewish experience under the Nazis but insists on relating that experience to a larger context. For Berenbaum that context is primarily the victimization of the Poles, the Gypsies, the disabled and the other groups. He is convinced that Jewish uniqueness (which results from the Nazi view of Jews as not merely symbols of evil but as evil's actual embodiment coupled with the universal death sentence pronounced upon them as a consequence of this perspective) can be preserved while fully acknowledging the victimization of the other groups under the Nazis. Berenbaum uses imagery (drawn from Dante's Inferno) suggested by philosopher Bohdan Wytwycky depicting the Nazi victims in terms of concentric rings extending out from the center of hell, which is occupied by the Jews.[7]

Rubenstein shares Berenbaum's conviction that the Holocaust is a distinctly modern phenomenon that cannot be seen as merely the continuation of historic anti-Judaism/antisemitism. He too is unwavering in seeing the Jewish situation under the Nazis as unique because of the Jews' status as permanent Nazi targets who lacked any options whatsoever for ameliorating their situation and whom the Nazis envisioned as "disgusting parasitic vermin and at the same time the embodiment of absolute evil that must be eliminated to complete the Nazi dream of salvation."[8] But he joins Berenbaum in stressing the broader implications of the Holocaust, in his case the insights it can provide in modern socio-political life. He especially focuses on how those who control the use of violence in a given society can go far in acting with impunity against others under their control. The Holocaust enables us to understand better the world in which we live, "a world more complex, more obsessed with power, more difficult to humanize than one might have guessed before."[9] Unlike Berenbaum, Rubenstein does not address the issue of the other Nazi victims in any depth, though he does acknowledge their presence at certain points of his analysis.

The "Other" Victims

Writers on the Holocaust who have addressed the specific situations of the non-Jewish victims such as Richard Lukas for the Poles and Ian Hancock for the Gypsies have tended to underline the links between Jewish victimhood and the Nazi attack against other "social undesirables."

I cannot in this limited space detail my argument for a close affinity (at least in principle) between the Nazi attack on the Jews and at least some of the other victim groups, particularly the Poles, the Gypsies, the disabled and to some extent the homosexuals, but I can provide a short synopsis of the attack on the Poles and present a few examples of the victimization of the other groups in order to make clear the basic thrust of my argument.

The Attack on the Polish Nation

On September 1, 1939, Poland was invaded by one of the world's strongest and most modern armies. Over 1,800,000 soldiers, representing the elite of the German army, took part in the campaign against it. The German army was vastly superior to any counterforce Poland could mount because of its tremendous fire-power and mobility enhanced by its motorization. On September 3, 1939, in fulfillment of their treaty obligations to Poland, Great Britain and France declared war on Nazi Germany.

From the very outset of the German invasion of Poland, it was apparent that the Nazis were not engaged in a conventional war to defeat the Polish military, nor even to subdue the state politically.

Instead, as the contemporary Polish-American historian Richard Lukas puts it, "... the Germans waged war against the Polish people, intent on destroying the Polish nation."[10] This point is very crucial and is often overlooked in writings on Polish victimization under the Nazis. Poles were not killed first and foremost as individual dissenters, whether religious or political. Nor did the Nazi leadership wish only to conquer Poland in a military or political sense. Rather, Poland fell victim as a nation to the same basic ideology which eventually turned its attention with even greater fury to the annihilation of the entire Jewish population of Europe.

The Nazi theory of racial superiority totally dehumanized the Polish people. In the Nazi perspective, Poles were considered *Untermenschen* (subhumans) who lived on land coveted by the superior German race. Poland was not simply to be defeated and occupied, the primary goal of the subsequent Nazi invasions of other western European countries. "The aim is not the arrival at a certain line," declared Hitler, "but the annihilation of living forces."[11]

Even prior to the actual invasion of Poland, Hitler had authorized on August 22, 1939, killing "without pity or mercy all men, women, and children of Polish descent or language. Only in this way," he insisted, "can we obtain the living space we need."[12] The person placed in charge of implementing Hitler's Polish "plan," Heinrich Himmler, said outright that "all Poles will disappear from the world. It is essential that the great German people should consider it as its major task to destroy all Poles."[13]

From the above quotations it becomes evident that key Nazi operatives, including Hitler himself, seriously contemplated the total extermination of the Polish population in due time. Whether the Nazis would have carried out this plan fully if they had been given the opportunity is a matter of conjecture at best. However, the annihilation of Jews is a fact, not merely a possibility. But on the level of theory, in trying to understand where the Poles fit into the Nazi victimization scheme, no other conclusion can be drawn except that they belonged with the Jews, Gypsies, the disabled and, to a degree, the homosexuals in the category of candidates for eventual total extinction in the gradual emergence of the new Aryan humanity.

As the Nazis set out to "purify" German society of Jewish blood and influence, they also included Gypsies or Rroma in their "purification" net. At least 250,000 Gypsies died in the process, perhaps more. They were regarded as *artfremd* ("alien to the German species"), a term also applied to the Jews. Additionally, they were termed "parasites," "congenital criminals," "asocial," and a "threat to the purity of German blood." Beginning in 1933 they were increasingly subject to harassment, arrest, and involuntary sterilization. By 1936 local and national laws for "eliminating the gypsy plague" became commonplace. In concentration camps neither Gypsies nor Jews had any legal rights; they could be killed at will.[14]

The attack on the disabled began slowly in 1939 with the killing of a few individuals. Hitler issued an order which he dated September 1, 1939 (the day World War II commenced) which authorized the process of executing anyone deemed unfit to live by reason of physical or mental condition. The effort escalated rather rapidly into a fullscale euthanasia program directed against those defined as unfit to live by psychiatrists or physicians. Gas chambers first appeared in the process of exterminating the disabled, so too the use of burning to dispose of bodies. And during the thirties a series of laws were enacted against the disabled which Sybil Milton again maintains closely resemble the anti-Jewish legislation.[15] I sense a rapidly emerging consensus among Holocaust scholars that at least for the Gypsies, if not for the other groups I have mentioned, there is no option but to speak of their planned extermination *in toto* by the Nazis.

Finally, when we come to the homosexual victims, we are on much more uncertain ground. This is especially true for the lesbian community, though some new research is beginning to develop. Not much solid inquiry has been done on homosexuals until fairly recently, in part because survivors from this community were extremely hesitant to identify themselves. There is also some initial evidence that the Nazis confined their attacks primarily to German homosexuals and that they did believe that at least in some cases "rehabilitation" might be a possibility. The question, let me emphasize, is not whether gay people suffered brutal treatment under the Nazis inside and outside the concentration camps. A play such as *Bent* has captured well the depth of their pain. The only question is whether they were intentionally included in the Nazi plan for human purification. It is hard to say with certainty at this point whether the attack on the gay community was seen primarily as one effort to rid German society of the liberal culture associated with the Weimar Republic and to overcome the lack of "manliness" which led to the devastating German surrender at Versailles, or whether the Nazis regarded it as integral to the plan for biological cleansing. In my judgement this question remains open though the *existing* evidence would push us towards a "social parasite" interpretation of the Nazi attack on gay people rather than a "biological" interpretation.[16]

The Uniqueness of Jewish Victimization

My basic assertion that the Jewish victims can no longer be regarded as totally unique in their victimization does not mean I eschew all important differences between them and the others discussed in this study. There are indeed differences, and these should not be lost in the process of reworking our more fundamental descriptive categories. First of all, to repeat what has been emphasized earlier, European Jewry nearly disappeared as a result of the Nazi attack. While this may have been the ultimate goal of the Nazis for some or all of the other groups, it was never realized to the same degree. This is a difference we can never forget.

Secondly, there was both a "sacral" and a historical dimension to the Nazi hatred of Jews. Antisemitism had not only been around for centuries, it had also become an integral part of religious tradition. This clearly added a distinctive dimension to the victimization of the Jews, as Richard Rubenstein has emphasized. Ian Hancock and others have shown the existence of a continuing pattern of discrimination against Gypsies for most of the second millennium of European society. While this discriminatory pattern somewhat parallels that developed in relation to the Jews, it lacks any corresponding "sacral" dimension. This "sacral" dimension clearly rendered Jewish victimization distinctive. It accounts for the selection of the Jews as the primary victims who always received the harshest treatment in the camps. It likewise accounts for the considerable popular support, or at least indifference, that the Nazi attack on the Jews generated among the masses, even among other victim groups. This religious antisemitism combined with political nationalism during the period between the two world wars to produce an intense religio-political nationalism which came to regard Jews as the pre-eminent "outsiders" who constituted a grave threat to authentic political and cultural sovereignty. Some feelings along these lines were sometimes directed against Gypsies, but without the same intensity because the religious compulsion was missing.

In short, then, the need obviously remains to maintain a clear measure of distinctiveness relative to the attack on the Jewish people. However, no longer can we regard Jewish victimization as wholly unique. We must begin to acknowledge, far more than we have thus far, that the Jews, Gypsies, Poles and the disabled (and perhaps the homosexuals) fell under the same umbrella effort to purify humanity and raise human consciousness to a new, supposedly higher level of maturity. The best paradigm for such an acknowledgment remains, in my judgment, the proposal of Berenbaum/Wytycky referred to earlier which is highly dependent on theological understandings (contrary to Katz). In a word, the non-Jewish victims must now be seen as integral, not peripheral, to our basic understanding of the Holocaust.

Notes

1. Michael Berenbaum, "The Uniqueness and Universality of the Holocaust," in Michael Berenbaum, (ed.), *A Mosaic of Victims: Non-Jews Persecuted and Murdered by the Nazis* (New York and London: New York University Press, 1990). 26.

2. See Yehuda Bauer, "Whose Holocaust?," *Midstream* XXVI:9 (1980), 34-43; *A History of the Holocaust* (New York/London/Toronto/Sydney: Franklin Watts, 1982); and "Is the Holocaust Explicable," in *Remembering for the Future: The Impact of the Holocaust on the Contemporary World.* Papers from the International Scholars' Conference, Oxford, 10-13 July, 1988, Theme II. 1967-1975.

3. As quoted in Michael Berenbaum, "The Uniqueness and Universality of the Holocaust," in John K. Roth and Michael Berenbaum (eds.), *Holocaust: Religious & Philosophical Implications* (New York: Paragon House, 1989), 88.

4. Steven T. Katz, *The Holocaust in Historical Context.* Vol. 1. The Holocaust and Mass Death before the Modern Age. (New York/Oxford: Oxford University Press, 1994).

5. Katz, *The Holocaust*, 28.

6. I do not agree with Katz's assessment. It is somewhat difficult to argue the issue with him, however, since he has failed to offer any of his criteria for "authentic" theologizing. The Eckhardts have written a strong response ("Steven T. Katz and Eckardts: Response to a Misrepresentation"), originally presented to the Christian Study Group of Scholars, which will appear in a forthcoming issue of *Shofar*.

7. See Berenbaum, "The Uniqueness," in Roth and Berenbaum, (eds.), *Holocaust*, 95-96. Also see Bohdan Wytycky, *The Other Holocaust: Many Circles of Hell.* (Washington: The Novak Report on the New Ethnicity, 1980).

8. Richard L. Rubenstein and John K. Roth, *Approaches to Auschwitz: The Holocaust and Its Legacy* (Atlanta: John Knox Press, 1987), 17.

9. Rubenstein and Roth, *Approaches*, 20.

10. Richard C. Lukas, *Forgotten Holocaust: The Poles Under German Occupation 1939-1944* (Lexington, KY: The University Press of Kentucky, 1986), 1.

11. See Eugeniusz Duraczyński, *Wojna i Okupacja: Wrzesień 1939-Kwiecień 1943* (Warsaw: Wiedza Powszechna, 1974), 17. Also see Nora Levin, *The Holocaust: The Destruction of European Jewry 1933-1945*. (New York: Schocken, 1973), 163; 193; and *Destruction of the Jews of Europe* (New York: Holocaust Library, 1979), 263.

12. Janusz Gumkowski and Kazimierz Leszcyński, *Poland Under Nazi Occupation* (Warsaw: Polonia Publishing House, 1961), 59.

13. See Karol Popieszalski, *Polska pod Niemieckim Prawem* (Posnań: Wydawnictwo Instytutu Zachodniego, 1946), 189.

14. Sybil Milton, "The Context of the Holocaust," *German Studies Review* 13 (May 1990), 270-271. Also see Gabrielle Tyrnauer, "Holocaust History and the Gypsies," *The Ecumenist* 12 (September-October, 1988), 90-94; Ian Hancock, "Uniqueness, Gypsies and Jews," in Yehuda Bauer et al., *Remembering for the Future*, Vol. 2 (Oxford: Pergamon Press, 1988), 2017-2025; and Henry Friedlander, *The Origins of Nazi Genocide: From Euthanasia to the Final Solution* (Chapel Hill: University of North Carolina Press, 1995).

15. Milton, "The Context of the Holocaust," 270-271. Also see Robert Proctor, *Racial Hygiene: Medicine Under the Nazis* (Cambridge: Harvard University Press, 1988); Robert J. Lifton, *The Nazi Doctors: Medical Killing and the Psychology of Genocide* (New York: Basic Books, 1986); and John J. Michalczyk (ed.), *Medicine, Ethics and the Third Reich* (Kansas City, MO: Sheed and Ward, 1994).

16. See Richard Plant, *The Pink Triangle* (New York: Holt, 1986); Ruediger Lautmann, "The Pink Triangle: The Homosexual Male in Concentration Camps," *The Journal of Homosexuality* 6 (1981), 35-51; and Günter Grau, (ed.). *Hidden Holocaust? Gay and Lesbian Persecution in Germany, 1933-45*. With a contribution by Claudia Schoppmann (London and New York: Cassell, 1995).

Chapter 4

"THESE PEOPLE ARE UNDESIRABLE...:" AUSTRALIAN RESPONSES TO REFUGEES FROM NAZISM BEFORE WORLD WAR II

Paul R. Bartrop

> *I desire to emphatically protest at the continued landing in Aust. of Alien Jews. I have observed their conduct & demeanour & I consider that these people are undesirable. ... All my acquaintances are of the same opinion. I suggest an immediate embargo be placed on Jews before the people realise fully what is happening.*

D.G. Simpson, Sydney, to the Secretary, Department of the Interior, 15 January 1939.[1]

Up to now, scholarship on Australia and the Holocaust has typically fallen into one of two categories: examinations and evaluations of government policy towards Jewish refugees fleeing Nazi persecution;[2] or the role and response of the Australian Jewish community in trying to facilitate their rescue.[3] There has not, on the whole, been much coverage concerning the attitudes of non-Jewish Australians to the refugee crisis, the Jewish plight in Europe, or the relationship between the government and the people over these issues.[4] In view of the relative dearth of coverage of a great many areas of the Australian response, this is not surprising,[5] but it does point to the fact that Australian scholars have, in the main, identified that the government and the Jewish community were the only major players in the fashioning of a response. Other social forces have not generally been considered in discussions of Australia and the refugee crisis of the 1930s.

The time has come, therefore, to reflect upon the attitude of the Australian public toward the refugees, particularly those refugees who had already arrived in the country. It was from this attitude that the Federal government could gauge how its policies were being received, and whether these should be modified. In this regard the reaction of the Australian public served an important function for both the government and the refugees themselves, for here were real cases of social interaction which had to be acknowledged and which required a response. Taking stock of public opinion meant that the refugee issue was not just an abstract problem to which the government formed policies in isolation; for many, the situation facing Australia by the refugee ingress had a real potential to create a cleavage within the community, thereby rendering the nation vulnerable to harm.

At the beginning of the Nazi period, Australia did not have a refugee policy, but soon after the Nazi seizure of power, when it seemed likely that Germany's Jews might wish to escape antisemitic persecution, a rapidly improvised position was developed by the conservative United Australia Party government and the officials of the Department of the Interior who administered immigration. This position held that care would have to be taken to see to it that no undue influx of Jews came to Australia, a stance that was rigidly adhered to from mid-1933 until the destruction of the Third Reich twelve years later.

The response of the Australian public to this position was on the whole one of agreement and endorsement, creating a situation in which both government policies and the popular will coalesced to form an unsympathetic and anti-refugee Australia. The government, as I have shown elsewhere,[6] consistently searched for ways in which to keep out refugees; the argument here is that most Australians, whenever they thought about the problem, came down on the side of an abstract sympathy for Europe's Jews, though not sufficiently to accept them into the country as immigrants. This was especially the case from late 1938, after which the refugee issue assumed hitherto unparalleled dimensions.[7] In short, there was a very strong undercurrent of opposition to Jewish refugee immigration, and it was this opposition which carried the day in the twelve months leading up to the outbreak of war in September 1939.

Public opinion was, however, difficult to gauge. Opinion polls did not yet exist, and the only measures available for government analysts were newspaper editorials, letters to the editor, correspondence forwarded directly to politicians, and public statements from leading citizens. Where competing positions were put forward, it was usually up to the bureaucrats in the Commonwealth public service to interpret them and provide an approximation of which way the wind was blowing.

On one point, however, all seemed agreed: despite debates concerning numbers of refugees to be allowed into Australia, something had to be done with those already in the country; the refugees had to be absorbed and assimilated as quickly as possible. An argument can be made to show that by the outbreak of war public opinion felt this process was not happening fast enough. Consequently, a general hostility came to typify the broad Australian public response to the refugee presence.

This hostility did not, it must be said, emerge overnight. Since 1933 Australians had continually been refining their position *vis-à-vis* Jewish refugees, until the point was reached whereby both their potential ingress and their presence once in the country were opposed. The reasons for this opposition are complex, but may be summarized along the following lines: 1) Australia at the outset of the period carried a number of prejudices toward foreigners from its previous history that had been formed according to racial criteria; 2) the Australian economy had been cruelly tormented by the effects of the Depression on unemployment, which on a global scale had seen only Germany hit more severely; 3) there was a powerful intolerance and xenophobia towards "alien" (that is, non-British) immigrants, which saw every new foreign arrival as an object of suspicion and uncertainty; and 4) there was also the existence of antisemitism in some sectors, which provided an additional justification for refugee rejection.

On July 14, 1939 the pro-refugee *Sydney Morning Herald* published a story which set out to relieve concerns that Jewish refugees were arriving in Australia at too fast a rate. Total arrivals of all central Europeans for 1938, the report stated, were 3,585; for the first four months of 1939 the figure was 2,983. Despite this growth, argued the *Herald*, the overall position "is now well in hand."[8] The main problem -- though it was not stated at this time -- concerned the degree to which refugees could be successfully absorbed into a British, monolingual, homogeneous and xenophobic Australia. The process would not be easy, and the opposition would often be both loud and cruel. Yet absorption did take place, and the refugees were ultimately accepted as authentic Australians. On the way, as we shall see, the pressures from much of Australian society were substantial.

In early 1940 a memorandum was forwarded to the minister responsible for immigration, Interior Minister Senator Hattil Foll. This document outlined the position of refugees in Australia as it stood in 1939, and showed that the refugee influx was a cause of concern for many Australians:

> ... newspapers recorded, almost every week, that several hundred refugees had arrived; publicity was given to many of the newcomers who usually were described as prominent men in their trades, professions or business and thus easily evoked fear of competition. The appearance of a growing number of foreign-looking and differently-dressed ... men in the principal city streets quickly tended to reverse the initial feeling of pity and interest into one of concern.[9]

Yet despite these misgivings, and the threat that Australia's "ratio of Jewish population would ... have increased to an extent unparalleled in history and might conceivably have entailed serious racial dangers," the report stated that a measure of assimilation was taking place relatively quickly after the refugees' arrival. It was observed that most refugee families mixed among themselves, but this social isolation was expected to change with time. It was observed that refugees had an overwhelming desire to fit into Australian society, and that many went to great lengths in order to achieve acceptance.

Most Australians would agree that this assimilation should take place as quickly as possible. One correspondent to the *Sydney Morning Herald* noted that the "desire of the Government and of the refugees themselves is that they should mingle in the community and be absorbed,"[10] but experience showed that not all Australians felt the same way. Indeed, it was observed by one *Herald* reader that

> Many of the new foreign immigrants have had a wretched time since arrival in Sydney -- rebuffed and insulted when they seek employment, treated with suspicion and resentment, and often not a single friendly door has been held open to them.[11]

This acute problem was not confined only to gentile Australians. True to the general approach of the 1930s, the Australian Jewish community adopted a position every bit as circumspect as the majority population. Suzanne D. Rutland has concluded that the refugees "were considered inferior by the [Jewish] establishment, even though they came from the centres of European culture and were generally well educated."[12] In fact, many Australian Jews assumed a patronizing attitude, instructing refugees on such matters as polite behavior and etiquette.[13]   In a much-quoted statement issued by the Australian Jewish Welfare Society, newly arrived refugees were warned about their behavior in the following way:

> Above all, do not speak German in the streets and in the trams. Modulate your voices. Do not make yourself conspicuous anywhere by walking with a group of persons all of whom are loudly speaking in a foreign language.... Remember that the welfare of the old-established Jewish community in Australia as well as of every migrant depends on your personal behaviour. Jews collectively are judged as individuals. You personally have a grave responsibility.[14]

Refugees were admonished at every turn to learn Australian ways and to act as exemplary citizens following the middle-class Anglo-Australian manner.

This question of assimilation was almost always invoked for the same reason: a fear of the emergence of an otherwise absent antisemitism if rapid absorption did not take place. As examples, in early 1939 paper swastikas were scattered around the Sydney Conservatorium during a recital at which Jews were expected to be present,[15] and a spate of stone-throwing and window-smashing incidents had been directed at Melbourne's Kadimah Yiddish library.[16]   The refugees were themselves only too aware of the strictures Australians placed over their acceptability, and wherever possible they sought ways to demonstrate their loyalty and desire to do well in the new country.   This was expressed no more clearly than at a mass meeting of Jewish migrants called by their representative organization in Sydney, the Migrants' Consultative Council, on 16 April 1939.   In his opening address the Chairman, Walter Hirst, stated that "we feel at home in Australia."   It was this feeling of being at home

> that determines our attitude towards our new country. We do not only feel mere gratitude for having found a "haven." We take sincere interest in all vital problems of Australia, we wish to take part in its life, to share citizenship and responsibilities.[17]

The international situation was, however, catching up with the refugees:

> We do not know what the future may hold for the world and for Australia in particular.   But we do know, that whatever will come, we

shall stand to Australia and shall do all in our power to strengthen her cause, as loyal and active members of her community.[18]

On 28 August 1939, with the international situation growing bleaker by the day and war less than a week away, the Migrants' Consultative Council reaffirmed its declaration of loyalty to Senator Foll, and expressed the desire

> to be given the opportunity by the Commonwealth Authorities to show [the refugees'] allegiance to the British Empire in a practical manner by being permitted to participate in any emergency duties and share responsibilities in the same manner as their fellow Australian citizens.[19]

Neither the government nor the Anglo-Jewish establishment were completely convinced, welcome though such expressions of loyalty might be. The loyalty question would be revisited often after the outbreak of war in September 1939, when all refugees were assumed to be potential enemies prior to an investigation of their cases.

As it turned out, not all responses toward Jewish refugees were negative, though as we shall see, it appeared as though few Australians had positive comments to make. When there were expressions of support, they often came from unlikely sources. Within some of the professions, for instance, not all was totally gloomy. In February 1939, the president of the New South Wales Chapter of the Royal Institute of Architects issued an appeal to all Australian architects to welcome refugees who were members of the profession, as he saw their appearance as "nothing but an acquisition to the cultural side of Australian life."[20] Then, in August, the New South Wales Institute of Accountants suggested that refugees from Germany holding accounting qualifications be exempted from most of the local examinations and thus be eligible to practice.[21] From the blue collar workers a further breakthrough had taken place in May: the New South Wales Trades and Labour Council recommended the admission of European refugees in Australia to membership of its constituent unions.[22] It is not clear whether this gesture was because unemployment had by now declined or because the Trades and Labour Council feared an influx of non-unionized cheap labor, but motives aside, it was a significant recommendation.

Others were less broadminded. In January the patriotic Australian Natives' Association passed a resolution at its annual meeting calling for immediate steps to be taken in order to ensure that "only the best type of migrant" be encouraged into Australia.[23] An issue which became increasingly topical throughout 1939 concerned the supposed inassimilability of the refugees, and in its April 6 edition the Australian Labor Party newspaper *Labor Call* foresaw that

> Continuation of the present suspicion, dangers and fears must result in the development of an anti-foreign, and particularly anti-refugee, psychology among the people.[24]

By April 27, *Labor Call's* scenario had crystallized into something far worse, with reference being made to the possibility of "riots taking place when least expected."[25] Such thoughts could, of course, only serve to panic the Australian people, resulting in further negative publicity for the refugees. Clearly, there was an increasing disquiet running through some sectors of Australian society that the presence of Jewish refugees in large numbers could lead to racial friction and communal strife, developments for which the Commonwealth was neither in need nor prepared.

The "front-line" areas in which all the dramas of assimilation were played out were in Sydney and Melbourne, where there was a great fear of foreign colonies forming. The Australian Jewish Welfare Society gave every encouragement to attempts by the new arrivals to settle in country towns and districts, and the idea of "congregating" was just as anathema to the Jewish community as it was to wider society. Unfortunate, therefore, was the consideration that refugees in certain localities were opening businesses which were squeezing out Australians. According to the *Sydney Morning Herald*, local non-Jewish shopkeepers did not object to newcomers engaging in business, "but they allege that Australian conditions and local awards are not being observed."[26] Members of the Australian Jewish community saw this problem no less clearly than the majority population, as an editorial in the *Westralian Judean* of May 1 showed:

> The bone of contention is that refugees are displacing Australian workers.... We emphatically agree that not one of our employed Australian workers should be permitted to stand aside while preference is given to a refugee migrant. The cry from suffering humanity overseas must not deafen us to the cry from distressed workers in this country, and it is the solemn duty of the Jewish communities everywhere in Australia to co-ordinate their work on behalf of the refugees with an attempt to solve local unemployment problems.[27]

For some Australians this matter had been at the core of opposition of refugee migration since 1933; for others the gravity of the situation took a little longer to penetrate. The position was clearly summed up by a Melbourne resident who wrote to Senator Foll in July 1939:

> there are hundreds of men with the qualifications claimed by these people who are at the present time walking the streets of the capital cities of Australia seeking employment ... [and it is] definitely unfair to bring to Australia foreigners who are taking positions our own Australians could well fill.[28]

Other citizens certainly felt the same way, and a major concern -- perhaps *the* major concern -- was that the refugees were allowing themselves to be economically exploited in such a way as to threaten living standards and industrial conditions for all Australians. The Shop Assistants' Union in Melbourne expressed the fear that

> foreign refugees who have come to Australia were being employed in Melbourne at rates far below those stipulated by the award

and that

> foreign workers coming here have earned a reputation for accepting low wages and working long hours, which is economically unsound, and a serious threat to our living standards.[29]

A company manufacturing artificial flowers in Sydney protested against the sweating of refugees in factories which were providing unfair competition in a very restricted marketplace, expressing the hope that strict supervision would be imposed on the refugees in the future in order "to prevent our Standard of living from being endangered."[30]

Examples such as these could be dismissed as anecdotal were it not for the fact that their growing prevalence throughout 1939 came to be viewed seriously by some politicians at both the State and Federal level. In May and June of 1939 opposition to the refugee presence found expression in a number of particularly vicious statements made by Australian politicians both inside and outside of parliament, and it can be concluded that these statements, made across the political spectrum, were representative of a wide body of opinion within Australia.

Amongst these attacks, the greatest stir came from the president of the Victorian Legislative Council, Sir Frank Clarke, on 8 May. Speaking to a branch meeting of the Australian Women's National

League in the respectable Melbourne middle-class suburb of Malvern, Clarke shocked the ladies by referring to the:

> slinking, rat-faced men under 5 ft. in height, and with a chest development of about 20 inches, who worked in backyard factories in Carlton and other localities in the north of Melbourne for 2/- or 3/- a week pocket money and their keep.[31]

Prior to this time Clarke had not shown any tendencies towards antisemitism, or even political extremism. That he should be making statements of this kind was significant for another reason, however; as a very senior member of Victoria's Upper House, and a member of the party which ruled Australia federally, Clarke was in effect declaring to his parliamentary colleagues that the Federal party's policy of allowing in any Jews at all was wrong and having a deleterious effect on the fabric of Australian society. It was an important statement, taken up by opponents of Jewish migration throughout the country. Here, for the first time, was a major pronouncement by a member of Australia's conservative ruling elite -- a stark contrast to the frequently expressed labor antagonism which had been opposed to refugee migration almost from the start.

Yet this was not all. Clarke continued his speech by contemplating with horror that "such people would want to marry Australian girls, or even to bring here their own undernourished and underdeveloped women, and breed a race within a race;" he also expressed with consternation that on the wharves of the port of Melbourne "the tongues of Babel could be heard, and in the third-class accommodation of ships there were hundreds of weedy East Europeans." Medical certificates which had been produced upon landing in Australia "were apparently dictated more by friendship than the truth;" otherwise many of these refugees would not have obtained entry. Clarke continued by lambasting the sweating of refugee labor and the flouting of factory regulations by unscrupulous employers. Upon concluding his speech, a vote of thanks was expressed by the Leader of the Opposition in Victoria, Sir Stanley Argyle, and Sir Frank was cheered enthusiastically. Argyle himself referred to the refugees as "the refuse of European countries, where bad living and bad government had developed them into what they were." He declared that Australia should not be allowed to become "a receptacle for them," and noted with concern that the

Australian people "should firmly resist an evil such as ... [that] described by Sir F. Clarke being built up in our midst."[32]

Response to Clarke's outburst was swift. Melbourne's *Age* newspaper immediately invited Prime Minister Menzies to comment, and his reply appeared on the same page as Clarke's speech. Menzies considered that the allegations made were "very serious," and announced that he would personally have them investigated. Without direct reference to Sir Frank's stereotyping of the refugees, he declared that

> the policy of the Government is to protect Australian standards, and if we find that they are in effect being broken down we will certainly take every step in our power to prevent such a course.[33]

The refugee organizations, horrified at the allegations, hastened to refute publicly Clarke's claims. In a joint statement prepared by the Australian Jewish Welfare Society and the Victorian International Refugee Emergency Committee, attention was drawn to the fact that "a large majority of Jewish migrants reaching Australia are not eastern Europeans, but German and Austrian," and that they were "of excellent physique, many of the males having served in the armies of their respective countries."[34] The Honorary Secretary of the Victorian Branch of the Australian Jewish Welfare Society offered similar comments, stressing that those coming into the country "were skilled men with occupations, had undoubted testimonials and were carefully hand-picked."[35] The conservative *Argus*, on the other hand, took such protestations with a grain of salt, and basically accepted Clarke's allegations. In an editorial the day after the story broke, the paper stated, "Most Australians will agree with the strictures uttered by Sir Frank Clarke," but recognized that "the Jewish refugees must be taken as they come, mixed lot though they may be."[36]

Clarke's accusations were soon taken up in the Federal parliament in Canberra. On May 17, Senator Donald Cameron (Labor, Victoria) asked Senator Foll whether inquiries were being made as to the veracity of Clarke's statements. Foll's response was that an investigation had been ordered as soon as Clarke's speech was reported, and that information had already been received to the effect that his evidence was only hearsay. On further questioning, Foll said that Clarke could not verify any of his allegations.[37] He went on to reassure the Senate that "every effort is being made by the Government to ensure that the state of affairs suggested in the statement attributed to Sir Frank Clarke shall not be allowed to occur."[38] Foll, it will be recalled, was the

Federal Minister responsible for Jewish refugee migration, and it was in his direct interest to demonstrate that Clarke's comments were neither accurate nor representative of conservative opinion. He was only partly successful. Clarke had articulated an issue which had until now been spoken of only informally or by those with polarized views, but henceforth outbursts such as his became both acceptable and persistent.

Another such comment, more extreme than Clarke's, and uttered in a forum of the Federal parliament, came from the Labor Member for Kalgoorlie in the House of Representatives on June 15. Tom Green, from Western Australia, rose to speak during the debate on the Supply Bill, but clearly what he had to say bore no relevance to the matter at hand. Addressing Jewish refugee immigration, he announced that his opposition was "far stronger than if the immigrants were of the Nordic race, and came from northern European countries, from the north of Italy or from Jugo-Slavia." Were immigrants to come from these countries, the development of Australia would be enhanced. Jews, on the other hand, would not develop Australia, as they "are essentially a trading people..., and the Jews who are coming here will be of no help to a producing country like Australia."[39] Where Jews were not merchants, they were professionals; this, too, was not suitable for Australia's needs, because "for every Jew who is given a professional job ... an Australian will be shut out." Green asked why it should be necessary for Jews to wish to leave Europe at all; it was "only fair," he felt, "to point out that there may have been some reason for [Hitler's] wishing them to go elsewhere."[40] For Green, that reason centered around Jewish internationalism, economic domination and exploitation. Now, the Jewish presence was increasing; they were "trying to dominate Australia" in the following ways:

> Most of the cut-price tobacco shops in the suburbs of Melbourne and elsewhere are run by Jews, most of them recent arrivals.... The fur shops are completely in the control of Jews. Even little shops for the mending of stockings, some of them a mere hole in the wall where a little Australian girl can be seen working, have behind them a Jew who controls the business. The mantle shops, where mantles priced at ten and twenty guineas, allegedly exclusive models from Paris, are for sale, are also Jewish-owned, though the Jew's name does not appear, of course.... There is a well-known mammoth emporium in Melbourne which is controlled by Jews. When trade is slack, the workers are told to take a couple of weeks off, and they are not paid for that period. In Western Australia, there is another great emporium under the control of Jews. In

that business Australian workers are being dismissed, and their place taken by Jews. The very press of this country, including the Melbourne evening papers, is controlled by these people who are now stretching out their tentacles to South Australia.[41]

Green concluded his speech by stating that Jews "are not wanted here; we have enough exploiters among our own people, but these other people are the kings of exploiters." He then declared his intention to continue his remarks at some future date, and resumed his seat.

Green's comments came at a time of concern over the alien presence in Australia. By mid 1939, security fears were beginning to be expressed, and on May 3 the Member for the Northern Territory, A.M. Blain, asked the Prime Minister whether immigration administration could be transferred forthwith "to the direct control of the Department of Defence, where it rightly belongs."[42] At this time a bill for the compulsory registration of all aliens in Australia was receiving its Second Reading in the Lower House, and numerous members were expressing their thoughts concerning aliens' control.

The bill, moreover, had general agreement from all sides of the House. During the Second Reading debate, speaker after speaker rose commending it and stressing the need for some form of control over the activities of aliens once they were in the country.[43] Some did not want aliens in Australia at all. From antisemites such as Tom Green, who did not want refugees because they were Jews, the focus shifted to those who advocated restriction on the grounds of economic necessity. Much of this agitation came from the Labor Party, which sought to protect the interests of Australian workers from any potential ingress into the very tight labor market. On May 16, Senator J.S. Collings made the clearest possible statement of Labor's attitude:

We hear a great deal these days about refugees. Although I have the greatest sympathy with men and women who have been persecuted through detestable forms of government in other countries, my parliamentary salary is paid by Australians to enable me to do a job in this chamber for Australia. Therefore, I must not allow my sympathy with foreign refugees to make me overlook the fact that my first duty is to Australians. I hope that I shall not be accused of cruelty, but, if I had my way, not one foreign refugee, man or woman, would be admitted until every good Australian had been taken off the dole or relief work, and given a job under award conditions....[44]

Although this statement was made by a Labor politician (and hence a member of the opposition), it should be recalled that both sides of the House were aware that the government was pursuing an immigration policy rather than a "rescue-from-the-Holocaust" policy. To issues of ethnic assimilation and economic integration could be added that of national security, clearly an important matter as Australia (and the world) moved closer and closer toward war. Yet even without this, it must be stressed that Australians had had a long tradition of suspicion towards strangers, and certainly would not have tolerated a government policy which opened the gates to a large number of Jewish refugees. The challenge before the policy-makers was a steep one. If Australia accepted refugees, the country's racial homogeneity -- 97 per cent British, so the racial purists alleged -- would be diluted. Worse, in some quarters, was the fear that Australia would fall under Jewish "domination," and that the Australian standard of living would consequently drop.

On the other hand, if the Australian government deliberately excluded refugees, the Commonwealth would surely miss the opportunity of acquiring some useful skills and capital brought to the country by potentially "good" Jews who did not fit the stereotype. Australia would then also miss the opportunity of adding to the country's white population at a time of considerable apprehension about Australia's relative underpopulation and increased fear of Asia, particularly Japan.

After weighing the pros and cons, the Australian government took a compromise position. *Some* Jewish refugees would be accepted: Australia would not be seen as renouncing its humanitarian obligations, and the nation's racial composition would remain essentially intact. The solution was to carry out a covert policy of discrimination against Jewish admissions, with the bureaucracy playing a major role in shaping and executing policy decisions.

Jewish immigration to Australia increased after December 1, 1938, but it is highly questionable whether the increase was matched in tolerance, understanding or humanitarian feelings. On the surface, there was no reason it should have. The refugees were still foreign, still Jewish, and still applying to come in what were seen as alarming numbers. No government could hope to legislate tolerance or approval; that could only come through wholehearted commitment and an intensive education program, but there was nobody within the Australian power elite with that sort of commitment. The policy of the Australian government began as a niggardly one; it remained so, and the actual number of refugees admitted to the country bore no relationship to the thoughts or motivations underscoring their arrival. For most Australians, there was a world of difference between admittance and acceptance, and no government in the interwar years could tell the Australian people which attitude they should adopt over *any* issue -- least of all one concerning foreigners, the outside world, or the future ethnic composition of the Commonwealth.

The majority of the refugees came in 1939 close to the outbreak of war and hence were more alien and less assimilated than the significantly fewer numbers who had arrived in the preceding five years. The issue had always been construed as a Jewish problem; now, with the outbreak of war, it became an "enemy alien" problem. Given this change, there would be new grounds for opposition, particularly as the refugees would be seen to remain at large as free persons. There remained an enormous residue of prejudice towards them: as Jews; as foreigners; as economic competitors; and now, as enemy Germans or Austrians. There was, moreover, absolutely no guarantee that the Australian people would willingly depart from their cherished standard of a 97% British Australia. Yet the presence of even a few refugees did play an important part in the future approach of Australians toward the wider world. It was that presence which signaled to British Australians that other groups of people existed who were just as eager to help build the country as they were.

The overall response offered by Australians towards Jewish refugees by 1939 was far from welcoming, even though there were of course always exceptions (sometimes in important areas). The main argument of this paper, that the Australian public and government on the whole conspired with each other in order to uphold a policy of restriction, does not allow for the possibility of large-scale philosemitic tendencies within Australian society, though it must be admitted that these were expressed in innumerable individual instances between 1933 and 1945. Once war broke out, however, the Australian public had the opportunity to stand back and take stock of those who had already been admitted. On balance, they were not comfortable with what they saw, and the subsequent security measures (including internment) placed over the refugees during the early days of the war confirmed for many that they had been right to oppose refugee entry and a Jewish presence in Australia.[45]

Public opinion was an important determinant in helping the government to chart its course over the refugee issue. Just how far positive forces may have come into their own had the government pursued a policy of openness and welcome can, of course, never be ascertained; in view of the eagerness with which much Australian opinion embraced an anti-Jewish line when the government offered one, however, the potential for positive action on behalf of the refugees could not be deemed as promising. Whether this attitude was likely to change would to a large degree depend upon the outcome of the war; under peacetime conditions, however, it must be concluded that the Australian government assessed the mood of public opinion correctly, and set its policy direction accordingly.

Notes

Abbreviations used in these notes are as follows:

AA A   Australian Archives, Canberra
CPD   Commonwealth Parliamentary Debates (Hansard)
H. of R.   House of Representatives

1. AA A445, file 235/5/6, "Protests re. Jewish Immigration (1938-1946)," D.G. Simpson, Sydney, to the Secretary, Department of the Interior, 15 January 1939.

2. See, for example, Paul R. Bartrop, *Australia and the Holocaust, 1933-45*, Melbourne: Australian Scholarly Publishing, 1994; Michael Blakeney, *Australia and the Jewish Refugees, 1933-1948*, Sydney: Croom Helm Australia, 1985; and, for a contrary position, W.D. Rubinstein, "Australia and the Refugee Jews of Europe: A Dissenting View," *Journal of the Australian Jewish Historical Society*, vol. X, part 6 (May 1989), pp. 500-23.

3. See, for example, Suzanne D. Rutland, *Edge of the Diaspora: Two Centuries of Jewish Settlement in Australia*, Sydney: Collins Australia, 1988; Hilary L. Rubinstein, *The Jews in Australia: A Thematic History*, vol. 1, *1788-1945*, Melbourne: William Heinemann Australia, 1991; P.Y. Medding, *From Assimilation to Group Survival: A Political and Sociological Study of an Australian Jewish Community*, Melbourne: Cheshire, 1968; and Konrad Kwiet, "Responses of Australian Jewry's Leadership to the Holocaust," in W.D. Rubinstein (ed.), *Jews in the Sixth Continent*, Sydney: Allen and Unwin, 1987, pp. 201-15.

4. In *Australia and the Holocaust*, however, I make an attempt at doing so: see especially chapter 9, "Responses to Jewish Refugees in Australia 1939," and chapter 10, "News About the Holocaust: The Press Reports, 1939-45."

5. As I have written elsewhere, the historiography contains some glaring omissions:

> The degree to which non-Jewish refugee relief took place has been covered in only a few short studies: there is nothing on organisations such as the Society of St Vincent de Paul, the Salvation Army or the Red Cross. The attitude of the general Australian community to the refugee question has been completely passed over by researchers. The labour movement, political parties, pressure groups, state governments, educational and professional bodies, newly-arrived non-refugee immigrants - the entire range of Australian society has barely been considered.

See Bartrop, *Australia and the Holocaust*, p. xiv.

6. *Ibid.*

7. On this, see Paul R. Bartrop, "'Not a Problem for Australia:' The *Kristallnacht* Viewed from the Commonwealth, November 1938", *Journal of the Australian Jewish Historical Society*, vol. X, part 6 (May 1989), pp. 489-99.

8. *Sydney Morning Herald*, 14 July 1939, p. 10.

9. AA A433, file 40/2/520, "Absorption in Australia of Refugees from Central Europe," unsigned memorandum (*The Absorption, in Australia, of Refugees from Central Europe*) written by "an alien resident qualified to express a reliable opinion," forwarded to Senator Foll by Colonel Harold Jones (Director, Commonwealth Investigation Branch), 2 February 1940.

10. *Sydney Morning Herald*, 13 July 1939, p. 4.

11. *Ibid.*

12. Rutland, *Edge of the Diaspora*, p. 187.

13. *Hebrew Standard*, 22 December 1938, p. 3.

14. *Sydney Morning Herald*, 13 May 1939, quoted in Suzanne D. Rutland, "Australian Responses to Jewish Refugee Migration Before and After World War II," *Australian Journal of Politics and History*, vol. 31, no 1 (1985) p. 38.

15. *Sydney Morning Herald*, 3 July 1939, p. 11.

16. *Argus*, 6 April 1939, p. 3.

17. AA A433, file 39/2/402, "AJWS Sydney. Large Numbers of Jewish Migrants Desire to Enlist in Militia," Address of Mr W. Hirst, 16 April 1939.

18. *Ibid.*

19. *Ibid.*, Migrants' Consultative Council to Senator H.S. Foll, Minister for the Interior, 28 August 1939.

20. *Sydney Morning Herald*, 16 February 1939, p. 9.

21. *Ibid.*, 1 August 1939, p. 10.

22. *Ibid.*, 6 May 1939, p. 16.

23. AA A433, file 44/2/1566, "A.N.A. Annual Conference Sydney. Resolutions Concerning Immigration," H.R. Redding (General Secretary, ANA) to the Secretary, Prime Minister's Department, 16 January 1939).

24. *Labor Call*, 6 April 1939, p. 14.

25. *Ibid.*, 27 April 1939, p. 2.

26. *Sydney Morning Herald*, 13 June 1939, p. 13.

27. *Westralian Judean*, 1 May 1939, p. 2.

28. AA A659, file 39/1/1551, "Austro-Australian Jewish Relief Committee. Purpose of," Reginald L. St John (South Melbourne, Victoria) to Senator Foll, 4 July 1939.

29. *Argus*, 16 February 1939, p. 1.

30. AA A433, file 43/2/4588, "European Refugees. Views of Public Re. Admittance of," Madame Gennie Pty Ltd (Sydney) to the Secretary, Department of the Interior, 21 February 1939.

31. *Age*, 9 May 1939, p. 11.

32. *Ibid.*

33. *Ibid.*

34. *Argus*, 10 May 1939, p. 2.

35. *Age*, 11 May 1939, p. 12.

36. *Argus*, 10 May 1939, p. 8.

37. CPD, Senate, vol. 159, 17 May 1939, p. 358.

38. *Ibid.*, p. 359.

39. CPD, H. of R., vol. 160, 15 June 1939, p. 1965.

40. *Ibid.*, p. 1966.

41. *Ibid.*, pp. 1966-67.

42. *Ibid.*, vol. 159, 3 May 1939, p. 37.

43. See *ibid.*, vol. 159, 3 May 1939, pp. 55-57; and ibid., vol. 160, 15 and 16 June 1939, pp. 2014-24.

44. CPD, Senate, vol 159, 16 May 1939, p. 349.

45. The absurdities of Australian legislation governing the classification of so-called "enemy aliens" are described in Paul R. Bartrop, "Enemy Aliens or Stateless Persons? The Legal Status of Refugees from Germany in Wartime Australia," *Journal of the Australian Jewish Historical Society*, vol. X, part 4 (November 1988), pp. 270-80.

Chapter 5

"LIBERAL DEMOCRACY - THE END OF HISTORY" OR CARL SCHMITT REDIVIVUS? THE NEED FOR AN ANAMNESTIC CULTURE FOR GERMANY AFTER AUSCHWITZ

Jürgen Manemann

The year 1989 seemed to be a promising one for Germany concerning its longing for identity -- not just for nationalists but for liberals, too. The liberals view the events of 1989 as a definitive confirmation of their conviction that liberal democracy is the best way of living together and, as Francis Fukuyama said, the "end of history."[1] First of all 1989 was not the victory of a new nationalistic Germany, but a victory of liberalism and capitalism over communism, a victory of the West over the East.

But this triumphal procession of liberal democracy did not last long. Far from having now secured for itself a position as "the endpoint of mankind's ideological evolution" (Fukuyama), liberal democracy has, by virtue of the victory it has won, actually entered a period in its development in which it is likely to be tested as severely as it has ever been before.[2] And yet, our democracy is in trouble, caused by the absence of the so-called negative guarantor and the necessity to define itself without opposing "real existing socialism."[3] Ernst Wolfgang Böckenförde, justice at the German Constitutional Court, characterizes the situation as follows: "Our democratic state cannot guarantee its own foundations."[4] The secular state doesn't give definitive justification of the freedom it guarantees. Thus, this justification is transferred to the responsibility of the individual. But the freedom in our society depends on resources regulating it in order to make interpersonal life possible, and these resources are not naturally given. Therefore, they need protection because they are in danger from modernization, with its destruction of traditions and increasing atomization.

Briefly, by the way of summary: Living in a liberal democracy requires us to live with uncertainty.[5] But what happens if this uncertainty gets into our "habits of heart?"[6] Where will be the source of meaning, of a new appropriate meaning?

Some discourse theorists in our country suggest a horizontal model of society with a communicative understanding of political power. This model notes that the perpetuation of political institutions does not depend on transcendental guarantees but on the communicative energy included in the founding of the institution. In this model the memory of the founding of the institution becomes essential.[7] So we could say democracy needs a culture of remembrance, or like Johann Baptist Metz says, an anamnestic culture.[8]

But where could we find such a culture in our accelerating society and what would be its signs?

Instead of asking for an anamnestic culture in a so-called post-traditional society, most of the liberals in Germany spoke just of the end of history without recognizing the above-mentioned problems. Thus, they created a vacuum of meaning bearing a need for another mental orientation. Therefore, the ground was already prepared: The so-called German *Historikerstreit*[9] in 1986 (the quarrel about the uniqueness of Auschwitz) could be characterized as the overture of a new consciousness.

Junge Freiheit (Young Liberty), the periodical of this new mental orientation, does not talk of the end of history but of the end of politics. For this reason the so-called Neue Rechte (the "new right" is a complex of different movements and journals grounded in ideas of the "Konservative Revolution," the intellectual right wing who fought the Weimar Republic, with connections to neo-nazism), which has become more and more influential since the unification, makes Carl Schmitt (1888-1985) its spokesperson. Described both as "the Hobbes of our age" and "the philosophical and juristical godfather of Nazism," Schmitt defined policy as the ability to distinguish between friend and enemy.[10] For him social life was grounded in civil war. His political theory, which he called a political theology (inheriting special Catholic counter-Enlightenment traditions of the 19th century) demands a democracy grounded in homogeneity, a homogeneity excluding the nonhomogeneous other.

As early as 1923 Schmitt wrote:

Every actual democracy rests on the principle that not only equals are
equal but unequals will not be treated equally. Democracy requires
therefore, first homogeneity and second -- if the need arises -- elimination
or eradication of heterogeneity. ...A democracy demonstrates its political
power by knowing how to refuse or keep at bay something foreign and
unequal that threatens its homogeneity. The question of equality is
precisely not one of abstract, logical-arithmetical games. It is about the
substance of equality.[11]

The danger of Schmitt's ideas for the present Germany becomes
obvious by realizing that not just the *Neue Rechte* accepts his theories.
Ernst Nolte's arguments during the *Historikerstreit* are a complex
mixture of thoughts of two nazis, Martin Heidegger and Schmitt.[12]
Currently, we can see a renaissance of the civil war theory by left
intellectuals. On the ground of such an anthropological foundation we
find a frontal attack against all universal ethics such as human rights,
which are being criticized for having an inherent theological core,
making man responsible for everything.[13]   But this negative approach
of universal ethics itself is rooted in a specific theological tradition, too.
Its negative, pessimistic anthropology is based on a specific
interpretation of original sin propagated by traditional Catholics (Joseph
de Maistre, Donoso Cortes etc.).

But how could the government find a point of view if human rights
are abolished. Schmitt wrote: "Who says humanity will betray."[14]   For
him a sovereign government gives meaning to its sovereignty by making
decisions on its own by and by being able to abolish law because of its
right for self-preservation.[15]

Toward an Anamnestic Culture

The described renaissance is an expression of the current amnesia in
our public and private life concerning the period of Nazism. Since
1945 this amnesia caused a German identity mainly based on two
perennial lies: the first lie arises in the time when Konrad Adenauer was
chancellor, by contending we are all democrats. And the second has
evolved since 1989, talking ourselves into believing that we are now
normal. But the proponents of these lies never directly confronted the
problem of National Socialism.[16]   In the face of these repressions we
see that the present decline of morality in our society is connected with

forgetting Auschwitz. The lack of sensitivity for the past reflects itself in the absent sensitivity for the present injustice. Here we return to the question at the beginning: If democracy depends on an anamnestic culture, how could such a culture become a reality in our society?

As long as the catastrophe of Auschwitz is forgotten in order to bear a meaning just for ourselves, we live on the so-called "bright side of life." As long as the discussion about how to remember Auschwitz articulates itself in the language of interest and in behalf of self-interest, the negativity will be minimized because Auschwitz is purposeless and meaningless. You cannot extrapolate a doctrine from Auschwitz. It is required that one remember Auschwitz without giving sense to it. To remember Auschwitz for the sake of the victims means to remember without purpose.[17]   This is not denying the "dialectics of the enlightenment" (M. Horkheimer/Th.W. Adorno). It brings about the danger of forcing the victims into being objects again: this time objects of our research and our point of view of meaning. Such a memory would be an expression of calling into responsibility without functionalization because this memory is grounded in an asymmetrical relationship challenged by the other, by the victim whose otherness is rooted in his experience, in his suffering. The other demands me to remember his suffering. Such a remembrance stands in continuity with the *memoria passionis*, the memory of suffering in biblical tradition.

As such, biblical memory is an expression of conscience which consisted in the ability to take into account the true interests of others. Thus, it is a responsibility with the emphasis on response, a response of Cain's question: "Am I my brother's keeper?" The brother in the bible is not my neighbor in a simple sense. He is the other, the victim, the poor. Helping him would not be a positive reward for me. Judaism and Christianity remember this call for a universal responsibility. This responsibility is an expression of a world conscience. It demands what Elie Wiesel has stated:

> If human life is threatened, if human dignity is in danger then national borders and national considerations will become irrelevant. Wherever men or women are persecuted, by virtue of their race, their religion, or their political views -- this place must be -- in the same moment -- the center of the universe.[18]

Judaism is the representative of this culture of remembrance, unable to distance itself successfully from the suffering which leads into a responsibility for the other. But Judaism is not just the culture of remembrance. It is its inventor and therefore the target of antisemitic hate risen from a triumphalist Christianity which has often forgotten this remembrance and become more a cult of anamnesis than an anamnestic culture. In most part Christianity has preserved memory liturgically. But it has not cultivated it publicly.[19]

But, what does this anamnestic culture mean for the liberal democracy in our country?

An anamnestic culture rooted in the *memoria passionis* is aware that the need to lend a voice to suffering is the precondition to all justice. It shows two kinds of responsibility: justice and care.[20] Both are different because justice, located on the cognitive level, is the symmetrical principle of responsibility with rights and duties toward everyone. At this level the other has the role of the generalized other.[21] At the other level, the affective level, responsibility is the result of compassion and not of a procedural process and thus it comes from an asymmetrical responsibility. This responsibility is basic because it refers to a non-representative individual for whom I am responsible. It is the basis for the existence of moral sensitivity. According to the discourse ethics, I think it is indeed the appropriate form of ethics in liberal democracies; everything has to be subjected under the practical discourse and its formal principles. In this way, the values of our social environment must campaign - Habermas uses the verb *Kandidieren* - in the discourse to become norms. In comparison, Emmanuel Lévinas emphasizes the need for the other level when he says:

> Morality arises not from equality, it arises through the infinite demands which converge in the universe in one point, that you serve the poor, the stranger, the widow, and the orphan.[22]

The way present discourse ethics appear is centered in the value of reciprocity influenced by Greek thought. Memory of suffering is the fracture of this immanent concord, it breaks the reciprocity, interrupts the danger of a totalitarian equality, and urges a society build upon justice to transform to a progressively more just community. This memory interrupts the liberal discourse and total policy. It doesn't allow a restriction of our responsibility like some authors are preaching today. My church became late, maybe too late, aware of the danger of immunizing ourselves against the harm of others. The document *Unsere*

Hoffnung (Our Hope) published in 1975 by the West German bishopric says:

> Our country's recent political history is darkened by the systematic attempt to wipe out the Jewish people. Apart from the admirable efforts by individuals and groups, most of us during the time of National Socialism formed a church community preoccupied with the threat to our own institutions. We turned our backs to the persecuted Jewish people and were silent about the crimes perpetrated on Jews and Judaism. Some have been guilty out of pure anxiety for their lives.

Liberal democracy has long lived parasitically on the fruits of ideas to which liberal theory itself has not been particularly congenial.[23] In this situation liberal democracy could not fight against a violent homogeneity à la Schmitt if it is not rooted in an asymmetry implying the knowledge that morality and meaning of life never arises from equality but from the claims of the other as the victim. If liberal democracy in our country does not perceive the necessity of dangerous memory, and even destroys the memory of the victims by defining itself in a functional anti-utopian and anti-historical way which only values the ability to adapt to technological and economical developments, then this kind of liberal democracy will be the foundation of fascism: First, because it produces an emptiness of life and second, because it leads to total indifference, an indifference which, as Wiesel and Adorno have already said, made Auschwitz possible. The memory of Auschwitz reminds us that politics must be rooted in an anamnestic culture, keeping track of the forgotten and being grounded in the priority of the other.

But Will There Still be a Chance for Such a Culture?

Maybe religions could play an important role in this situation as resources of memory. For my church the task would be to become an institution of memory, but of dangerous memory calling the church into question because this memory demands a remembrance of the most radical protest against Christianity -- Auschwitz. The church is obligated not to leave the memory of the God of Abraham, Isaac, and Jacob for the sake of the hopeless because this God reminds the church that the hope He is promising is one for the others. Thus, the church would not have its interest in self-preservation but in the victims of the world. It would remember a messianic future which does not extend our future but interrupts it.[24]   It would not confirm our "habits of heart" as the theorists of democracy intend; it would demand the changing of our heart. Encountering the problems of responsibility in the liberal democracy in Germany we emphasize the difference between civil religion and a religion rooted in biblical traditions. We indeed see, as Habermas has pointed out, that

> today what is at stake is adapting Germany's political role to new realities, without letting the process of civilizing politics that was underway until 1989 be broken off under the pressure of the economic and social problems of unification, and without sacrificing the normative achievements of a national self-understanding that is no longer based on ethnicity but founded on citizenship.[25]

However, we also know that this is theoretically and practically not enough. What is at stake is solidarity based in an anamnestic culture.

But will there be a chance for remembering this God in our present situation in Europe which could be described as a crisis of God?[26]

To Nietzsche's proclamation of God's death the jurist and Catholic Schmitt reacted with his concept of policy and his kind of political theology. But instead of the belief in God he installed a belief in the Catholic Church as a form of power or as he calls it a "katholische Verschärfung"[27] (Catholic aggravation).

To resist this aggravation which reflects itself in the present discussion about the right for asylum, we need a passion for God which means a passion for God and a passion unto God so that Europe will never be again the graveyard of those who invented this God -- the Jews. Finally, there are a few reasons to assume that the fascists did not murder Jews because they had murdered God, as the Christians maintained, but because the Jews have invented Him.[28]

Notes

1. Francis Fukuyama, *The End of History and the Last Man* (New York: Free Press, 1992). For a critical view of Fukuyama's theory: Jürgen Manemann, "Geschichte und Gedächtnis - Plädoyer für eine anamnetische Kultur nach Auschwitz," in Erich Geldbach (ed.), *Vom Vorurteil zur Vernichtung? "Erinnern" für morgen* (Hamburg/Münster: Lit-Verlag, 1995), pp. 264-280.

2. R. Bruce Douglas, "Liberalism After Good Times: The 'End of History' in Historical Perspective," in R. Bruce Douglas/David Hollenbach (eds.), *Catholicism and Liberalism. Contributions to American Public Philosophy* (Cambridge: Cambridge University Press, 1994), p. 101.

3. Helmut Dubiel, *Ungewißheit und Politik* (Frankfurt: Suhrkamp Verlag, 1994), p. 93.

4. Ernst-Wolfgang Böckenförde, "Erfolge und Grenzen der Aufklärung," in Universitas. Zeitschrift für interdisziplinäre Wissenschaft 8 (1995), p. 720.

5. Jürgen Manemann, "An den Grenzen der Moderne. Zu Kulturkampf und Demokratiefeindlichkeit in der gegenwärtigen Gessellschaft," in: Jürgen Manemann, (ed.) Jahrbuch Politische Theologie. Bd. 1: Demokratiefähigkeit (Hamburg/Münster: Lit-Verlag, 1995), pp. 137-154.

6. Robert Bellah et al., *Habits of Heart. Individualism and Commitment in American Life* (Berkeley: Harper & Row Publishers, 1985).

7. Helmut Dubiel, p. 54.

8. Johann Baptist Metz, "Plädoyer für eine anamnetische Kultur," in: Franz-Michael Konrad, Reinhold Boschki, Franz Josef Klehr (eds.), *Erziehung aus Erinnerung. Pädagogische Perspektiven nach* (Auschwitz: Akademie der Diözese Rottenburg-Stuttgart, 1995), pp. 11-18.

9. Jürgen Manemann, *Weil es nicht nur Geschichte ist.* Die Begründung der Notwendigkeit einer fragmentarischen Historiographie des Nationalsozialismus aus politisch-theologischer Sicht (Hamburg/Münster: Lit-Verlag, 1995).

10. Carl Schmitt, *Der Begriff des Politischen.* Text von 1932 mit einem Vorwort und drei Corollarien (Berlin: Duncker und Humblot, 1963), p. 32.

11. Carl Schmitt, *The Crisis of Parliamentary Democracy* (Cambridge, MA: Mit Press, 1994), p. 9.

12. Ernst Nolte, *Der europäische Bürgerkrieg 1917-1945. Nationalsozialismus und Bolschewismus* (Frankfurt/Berlin: Propyläen, 1987).

13. For example: Hans Magnus Enzensberger, *Aussichten auf den Bürgerkrieg* (Frankfurt: Suhrkamp, 1994).

14. Carl Schmitt, *Der Begriff des Politischen,* p. 55.

15. Carl Schmitt, *Politischen Theologie.* Vier Kapitel zur Lehre von der Souveränität (Berlin: Duncker und Humblot, 1993), pp. 18-19.

16. Jürgen Habermas, *Normalität einer Berliner Republik.* Kleine Politische Schriften VIII (Frankfurt: Suhrkamp, 1995), p. 161.

17. Jürgen Manemann, *Weil es nicht nur Geschichte ist,* pp. 146-292.

18. Elie Wiesel, *Rede anläßlich der Verleihung des Friedensnobelpreises,* Oslo, December 10, 1986.

19. Johann Baptist Metz, *Plädoyer für eine anamnetische Kultur,* pp. 14-15.

20. Jacques Derrida, *Politics of Friendship,* in: Journal of Philosophy (1988), pp. 632-644. Azel Honneth, *Das Andere der Gerechtigkeit,* in Peter Fischer (ed.), Freiheit oder Gerechtigkeit. Perspektiven Politischer Philosophie (Leipzig: Reclam-Verlag, 1995), pp. 194-240.

21. Jacques Derrida, *Gesetzeskraft. Der "Mystische" Grund der Alterität* (Frankfurt, 1991), p. 44.

22. Emmanuel Lévinas, *Totalität und Unendlichkeit. Versuch über die Exteriorität* (Freiburg/Munich: Alber-Verlag, 1987), p. 361.

23. R. Bruce Douglas; *Helmut Dubiel.*

24. Johann Baptist Metz, *Jenseits bürgerlicher Religion. Reden über die Zukunft des Christentums* (Mainz: Grünewald-Verlag, 1984), p. 10.

25. Jürgen Habermas, *Struggles for Recognition in the Democratic Constitutional State,* in *Multiculturalism. Examining the Politics of Recognition. Charles Taylor et al., ed. by Amy Gutmann* (Princeton/New Jersey: Princeton Paperbacks, 1994), p. 148.

26. Johann Baptist Metz, *Gotteskrise. Versuch zur geistigen Situation der Zeit,* in *Diagnosen zur Zeit. Mit Beiträgen von Johann Baptist Metz. Günther Bernd Ginzel, Peter Glotz, Jürgen Habermas, Dorothee Sölle* (Düsseldorf: Patmos-Verlag, 1994), pp. 76-78.

27. Carl Schmitt, *Glossarium. Aufzeichnungen der Jahre 1947-1951* (Berlin: Duncker und Humblot, 1991), p. 165.

28. Jürgen Manemann, *Weil es nicht nur Geschichte ist,* pp. 202-205.

Chapter 6

AUSCHWITZ OR HOW GOOD PEOPLE CAN DO EVIL: AN ETHICAL INTERPRETATION OF THE PERPETRATORS AND THE VICTIMS OF THE HOLOCAUST IN LIGHT OF THE FRENCH THINKER TZVETAN TODOROV

Didier Pollefeyt

Introduction

The commemoration of the fiftieth anniversary of the liberation of the Nazi concentration and extermination camps brought us once more strongly face to face with the horrible and striking pictures of genocide by the Nazis. Once again we were confronted with perplexity and dismay by the shocking archive films, the moving testimonies and the nearly unbelievable "statistics of death" of the Holocaust. Now that the official addresses are over and the world media refocus their attention on the pressing moral issues of our time, the question presents itself whether and in which respect this commemoration has also urged us to draw vital ethical conclusions as to how to organize our individual and social life in a more thought-out manner. There is indeed a danger that we might tremble in a very sincere way in the face of the evil of Auschwitz, but that after our initial moral indignation, we shake our heads powerlessly and continue our lives just as before, as if such a moral catastrophe could never (again) happen to us. In so doing, and in spite of all our good intentions, we risk forgetting that the Nazi genocide was a product precisely of *our* Christian and modern civilization.[1]   If we are not searching for the roots of this moral catastrophe in our individual and political way of life today, then we do not have reason to be confident about the impossibility of such evil in the future. Reflection upon the violent and even genocidal mechanisms of evil is not a luxury in the contemporary socio-political context; new forms of extreme intolerance, antisemitism, nationalism and racism are rearing their ugly heads again.   Indeed, democracy is undergoing a profound crisis. The regeneration of right-wing political parties is a widespread phenomenon in Europe. At some universities revisionism is even being defended in the name of so-called "academic freedom." The tragedies in Rwanda and former Yugoslavia teach us that the danger of genocidal violence never definitively belongs to the past.

In this contribution we explore the question of what Auschwitz can teach us about the origins of human evil.[2] The answer to this question will be of importance for the way in which we will socially organize the prevention of evil in the future. Through this quest it will become clear how we always implicitly use a particular anthropology, a specific portrayal of humanity. Are we human beings fundamentally unethical beings whose egocentric dynamic should be under the strict supervision of a rigorous ethics? Is not every one of us being directed towards evil, and is not each of us potentially capable of inhumanity and racism? Or are we humans essentially orientated towards the good, and is it this human goodness that can disappear under the fragments of our own fears and brokenness, our socio-historical conditions and the finitude of our own lives? Furthermore, is it possible to reconstruct an ethics for a humanity that has been so deeply undermined by its own destructive potential? Should such ethics be built on a moralizing struggle against evil?   Or should it first of all be orientated towards an honest application of human creativity in the good?

These reflections will critically examine the answers to these questions as found in the French anthropologist and ethicist Todorov,[3] especially as he has developed them in his recent and insightful ethical study on Nazi genocide, *Face à l'extrême* (Paris, 1991, 2° revised ed., 1994), and secondarily in his *Au nom du peuple: témoignages sur les camps communistes* (Paris, 1992), *Une tragédie française: été 44: scènes de guerre civiles. Suivi de souvenirs d'un maire* (Paris, 1994) and *Les abus de la mémoire* (Paris, 1995). In answering these questions we will distinguish two different perspectives: that of the perpetrators and that of the victims. In the first part of this article we ask ourselves the question of whether the perpetrators of such evil should be seen as moral monsters or as human beings. We argue with Todorov in favor of the humanity of the perpetrator and ask how human beings like you and I can become such terrible criminals?

In the second part we pose the even more difficult question of whether human beings who have lost, or been stripped of, the thin cloak of civilization display their "real" identity by becoming "wolves" (Hobbes) to each other? With Todorov we demonstrate that the victims of the camps were not only ruled by the "law of the jungle," but that even "*face à l'extrême*" the human concern for what is good, true and beautiful could never be completely destroyed. Finally, based on this double perspective, we attempt to summarize our answers to the anthropological and ethical questions of this introduction in our conclusion.[4]

I. Human or Inhuman Character of the Perpetrators?
The Perpetrator as Moral Monster

When people describe the Nazi perpetrator, we mostly get an extremely moralizing and diabolical representation. Morally considered, Nazis were completely perverted beings; they were moral monsters, sadists or barbarians.[5] Yet according to Todorov, this interpretation is founded on a pessimistic anthropology (37-39 & 133): in each of us sleeps a dangerous, unethical beast that awakes when the cloak of civilization becomes threadbare. The Nazi is paradigmatic of this ethically derailed human. In this popular point of view, the Holocaust is not a result of our modern culture, but a regressive moment or an *accident de route* in the line of our civilization and is apart from the ascending of humanity. Herein Nazis appear as moral savages, beasts who strive after evil for evil's sake.[6] In this commonly held point of view, the Nazi is sometimes called the incarnation of evil or the modern embodiment of the devil. An argument for this interpretation is sometimes based on the *Kristallnacht* (1938) when the whole German population seems to have been in the spell of a "spontaneous" surge of antisemitic hatred, and the beast rose to the surface.

There are, however, some very convincing arguments against this dehumanizing interpretation of the perpetrators (149-170). The testimonies of most of the survivors indicate that only a minority of the perpetrators can be considered as sadistic or monstrous.[7] Instead of diabolic personalities, most of the perpetrators appears in this literature as very average and even petty officials. Furthermore, the proposition of the monstrousness of the perpetrators is incapable of explaining how thousands of simple and even well-educated people (such as doctors, industrials, educators, lawyers, philosophers, etc.) could collaborate in the destruction of the Jewish people for more than a decennium without stopping to see themselves as ethical human beings. Nor can it explain how the executioners once again became "decent" and well-functioning citizens after the war. There were undoubtedly monsters among the Nazis, but they were not enough in number to be really dangerous by themselves.

One of the basic points of our exposition will be that in circumstances such as the Holocaust, the greatest danger actually arises from normal people like you and me.[8] *Kristallnacht* can not be used as an argument to prove the monstrosity of the Nazis. If the murder of the Jewish people were carried out at the rate of the *Kristallnacht* (i.e. 100 murders per day), then the Nazis would have needed 140 years, instead of five years, to kill as many Jews as they did. Hate per se is a very inefficient means for the successful completion of such large-scale enterprise.[9] Nor should we forget that the Nazis did not violate the ruling social contract of their time by killing the Jews; by their participation in this genocide, Germans did not break the law of their country, but on the contrary were obedient to it. From this, we can see that people who apply the law can be more dangerous than people who disobey it. Perhaps the perpetrators had better followed more their human intuitions and less the prevailing decrees (133). Finally, we can learn from psychology that there is a physical boundary to the amount of people one can kill out of hate, fanaticism or sadism.[10] These critics on the monstrousness of the perpetrators form an invitation to search for other explanations of human evil, especially in its genocidal form.

The Perpetrator as Victim of the Political System

In the beginning of the 1960s the Jewish philosopher Hannah Arendt wrote a book on the trial against Adolf Eichmann under the subtitle *The banality of evil.*[11] Through her analysis it became clear that although the evil he did was undoubtedly horrible, the Nazi Eichmann was not a sadistic monster, but an ordinary bureaucrat. In this Jerusalem trial, the opposition between the banality of the criminal and the evil for which he was responsible became clear. In Arendt's view, Eichmann was not a perverted being,[12] but "terribly normal." Speaking about the "banality of evil," however, was not accurate since she actually thought that the criminal was banal, not evil itself. She never did, nor would, call the evil of Auschwitz itself banal. On the contrary, she meant that precisely because evil is such an ordinary human ability, we can never banalize it, but should always take it seriously as a universal human possibility.

In Arendt's view, moreover, the evil of Auschwitz was not a consequence of the violation of the law, but rather a result of the total obedience to it. The Holocaust, then, was possible because people complied with bureaucratic prescriptions and rules without thinking any further. According to Todorov, this interpretation is founded on a more optimistic anthropology:[13] the evil of Auschwitz is not the result of giving free rein to a monstrous desire for evil, but stems from a restriction of human commitment towards the good (135). Auschwitz is neither a tragic *accident de route* nor an unexpected moment of regression, but a logical consequence of our modern civilization with its anonymous, bureaucratic structures.[14] To understand this restriction of human involvement towards the good, in the view of Todorov (134-142), we should not look at the (monstrous) character of individuals, but at the political and social influences that made the transformation of human beings into criminals possible,[15] especially the totalitarian system that ruled in Germany and influenced the moral behavior of its citizens in three very typical ways.[16]

First of all, totalitarian systems are always manicheistic:[17] they split human beings in two radically different categories (based, for example, on race or class). In such dualistic interpretations, the world is unambiguously divided into (wholly) good people and (wholly) evil people. Herein, every action undertaken against evil people is morally acceptable and even praiseworthy.[18] Moreover, a totalitarian state always tries to replace human conscience by appointing itself as the ultimate source and measure of good and evil. Consequently, in such regimes an individual can concentrate on the means and no longer need ask difficult questions about the (un)ethical goals or consequences of social life. A totalitarian system can ask its citizens even to realize unethical, instrumental tasks without affecting the private moral infrastructure of the individual. Even in the camps the perpetrators were able to distinguish good from evil. The Nazis, however, believed that the cruelties against the Jews were necessary because the State was commanding these things of them. The perpetrators, then were not stripped of every ethical concern, but had a new kind of (professional) ethics. Finally, a totalitarian system controls the totality of society; the entire social midfield (trade unions, youth movements, etc.) is destroyed. Because every individual is isolated, effective ethical protest becomes impossible or involves great risk of life (165).

These characteristics show how an important cause of the evil of Auschwitz cannot be found primarily in individuals, but in the reigning political system. An important part of the population risks becoming an accessory to such crimes once such a system becomes almighty. For Todorov, Auschwitz reveals that involvement in crimes is very easy and that even ordinary persons can become perpetrators.

It is of course much more comfortable to think that the evil of Auschwitz is something outside ourselves, that we have nothing in common with these inhuman "monsters of Auschwitz." If we choose to forget Auschwitz, it is usually out of fear of the fact that Auschwitz is not something strange to humanity. For the most part, choice for the thesis of the monstrosity of the perpetrators is inspired by the fear of a confrontation with ourselves.[19] The dividing line between good and evil, however, is not running between non-Nazis and Nazis, between "we" and "they," but through the heart of every human being. People very easily choose for the monstrous interpretation of evil because this is very comforting, especially in the context of the Nazi genocide. The idea that human beings who murder every day are not fundamentally different from us, is very threatening for our own identity. It is very comforting if we can say that such criminals are sick, extremely racist, sadistic or possessed by the devil. In this way, we very carefully locate evil outside ourselves, thereby enabling us to condemn it in a moralistic manner in the other. If we have no resemblance to the monstrous image of evil, then we need not ask ourselves difficult questions about our own ethical functioning and we can confront ourselves with the Nazi genocide, full of indignation, but with a quiet conscience.[20] Therefore, we often find the belief that such Nazi genocide is a "typically German" phenomenon. Evil then becomes the guilt of the Other, the immoral individual, the extreme antisemite, the supreme antagonist. The Other is doing evil for evil's sake, whereas we know ourselves by experience: we long for goodness, integrity and authenticity. We can thus so aesthetitize perpetrators in their inhumanity that we create a safe manicheistic distance between ourselves and them. In this way we can strategically absolve ourselves of every possible evil and reorganize our own identity without blemish in confrontation with Auschwitz.

A final argument against the monstrousness of the perpetrators is that this presentation bears a remarkable resemblance with the demonization that the Nazis themselves used; with the diabolicalization of the perpetrators, we risk reproducing the Nazi *Weltanschauung* itself. The Nazis attributed precisely those characteristics to the Jews that they feared most in themselves: the Jews were the incarnation of the devil, sexually perverse, avaricious, bloodsuckers, unreliable, murderers of God, etc.[21] Every form of racism is in fact a cowardly way to deal with one's own fears. When we externalize evil in the demonically dangerous Nazi, we risk falling into the same dualistic scheme. By combatting evil only in the other, we risk rendering evil permanent in ourselves. Instead of fighting evil, we unconsciously imitate it. If we do not want to give the perpetrators a "posthumous victory" (Fackenheim) by becoming like them, we must be careful not to internalize evil. One of the problems of humanity has always been that it only tries to eliminate evil in the other. Using the manicheistic categories of good and evil, Germans and Jews, *Übermenschen* and *Untermenschen*, the Nazis did likewise; the Jew was the incarnation of absolute evil and as such was *unpardonable*.[22] And the only solution for radical evil, is a final solution, an *Endlösung*.

Evil as a Universal "Daily Vice"

A honest confrontation with the evil of Auschwitz demands that we unmask the manicheistic, "nazistic" mechanisms of defense that we spontaneously develop in confrontation with evil and which consists in our seeing evil only in the other. Perhaps we should be most careful when indignant about the moral offense of others. The acceptance of evil as a possibility in each one of us would seem to be the first, very difficult but crucial step in the development of an authentic understanding of evil. Without being beasts or monsters, we all possess some universal characteristics to do evil. It is only when we recognize this potential for evil in ourselves, that we can also effectively understand and combat evil. The Dutch Jewess Etty Hillesum has shown us from her experience in the camp of Westerbork that one of the biggest problems of humanity consists in that people always want to destroy in the other, precisely what they dare not recognize first of all in themselves.[23]

Like Todorov, we introduce here the idea of evil as "daily vice" (*vice quotidien*), as the human capacity that is not born out of an unambiguous choice of evil for evil's sake, but that arises in a silent and subtle way, step by step, in the "little wickedness" of the every day (165-170). We will examine three "daily vices:" fragmentation, depersonalization and enjoyment of power. We do so because they were basic conditions that undergird the realization of Auschwitz, but yet are general human attributes that can be found on a smaller scale in

our own social life as well.[24]   Our plea to understand evil as a
universal human possibility does not, of course, mean that we no longer
distinguish wrongdoers from the wronged, perpetrators from innocent
victims. One must, however, distinguish between the capacity to act
and the act itself, lest we mistake anthropology (human nature) for
jurisprudence (human acts).

Fragmentation

The behavior of most of the Nazi perpetrators looks very incoherent;
both humane feelings and cruelty can easily be found in one and the
same person (170-189). The commandant Kramer of Bergen-Belsen,
for example, wept with emotion listening to his favorite music, but
could mercilessly kill a Jew who did not obey his orders. Kramer
declared in his trial that "he did not feel emotions during these
crimes."[25]   This disunity or "doubling" (Lifton)[26] in the lives of most
of the perpetrators points to a radical discontinuity in their inner lives
between the public and the private. During the day in the camps they
did the cruelest of things, but in the evening in their rooms they wrote
very romantic letters to their spouses. Their minds seem to have been
compartmentalized like the waterproof bulkheads of a submarine. On
Christmas night 1943 the *Einsatzkommando IIb* received an order to kill
3000 Jews and Gypsies in Russia. The order was executed doubly
quick in order to enable the soldiers to go to Midnight Mass (180).
During the Nuremberg trials, the Nazi criminal Speer declared that "on
the affective level he only had sentimental reactions, but on the level of
decisions only rational principles count for much."[27]   Such
fragmentation is the creation of a difference in the inner life between
various spheres of life, so that human compassion can no longer
interfere with public work (genocide), while the private life remains
intact. On the basis of fragmentation it becomes clear how normal
human beings can become mass-murderers and how a member of a
totalitarian system can (try to) reconcile his submission to immoral
orders with the preservation of his private moral self-respect.

This fragmentation is not "typically German," as is sometimes argued
referring to the specifically Lutheran distinction between the rational,
public life on the one hand, and the private, religious life on the other.
This manicheistic and defensive reasoning tries to escape from the idea
that fragmentation is in fact a common and widespread modern
phenomenon.[28]   Due to the growing complexity of professional tasks,
modern society is characterized by an increasing specialization. In

modern society people are forced to restrict themselves to very specific and highly technical duties, while losing sight of the totality of the process of production. Eichmann himself had a purely technical view of his job. Wiesenthal once stated that if Eichmann would have been ordered to kill all people whose name began with a "P," he would have performed this task just as zealously and accurately.[29]   In the Jerusalem trial, Eichmann declared that he had nothing to do with the executions of the Jews: "I did not kill one Jew."[30]   He merely saw himself as one link in a complex process and tried to avoid conflicts with other departments.   The result of such fragmentation was that ultimately no one feels responsible for the whole.   In short, fragmentation leads to the shutdown of conscience. Since in Auschwitz only the *Sonderkommando* and some Nazis effectively *saw* the extermination, responsibility could always be attributed to an other (unseen) link in the process of destruction, while in the meantime the crimes could occur more readily.

Fragmentation, then, is the preservation of an inner disunity to maintain essential moral principles in some spheres of life, while at the same time one does evil in other spheres. In this fragmentation one becomes a "double" with a "double-conscience." This phenomenon is not restricted to Germans; indeed, we all need a certain degree of fragmentation in order to survive psychologically in the modern world. Everyone has his or her limits. Fragmentation makes the emergence of evil easier, but is not evil in itself. Sometimes fragmentation is the only possibility to maintain oneself (e.g., soldiers, priests, policemen, doctors, etc.). In a similar sense where a fever is not only a part of the illness, but already a defense against the illness, fragmentation is not only part of evil, but in fact also already a defense against evil. Fragmentation becomes a part of evil, however, just as the fever becomes a part of the illness (187). The question then arises at what point does fragmentation become criminal (*see also below*).

Depersonalization

For totalitarian ideologies human beings are never considered as goals in themselves (philosophically) nor as images of God (theologically). Individuals are always thought in terms of a bigger cosmic project (such as Hitler's thousand-year Reich) in which they themselves are of no importance. For Todorov, one of the goals of totalitarianism is depersonalization (190-211): the reduction of individuals to merely ingredients of an enormous project that completely transcends them (191). The camps were the first and foremost place to experiment with this process of depersonalization.[31]

Yet the transformation of human beings to non-humans is not immediately evident, requiring the overcoming of a great deal of inner moral resistances. Therefore the Nazis used (modern) technics to neutralize the "appeal of the face of the other" (Levinas)[32] thereby wiping out the humanity of the other.[33] These techniques might be illustrated with some examples that make clear how the evil of Auschwitz was more the result of depersonalization than of sadistic monstrosity (190-201). "The road to Auschwitz was built by hate, but paved with indifference" (Littell).[34] A first technique was the deprivation of victims of their clothing just prior to killing them. Normally we do not see naked people in groups. Since clothing is an expression of humanity, by stripping victims of their clothes, it became much easier to consider them non-human. This technique made it more difficult for the perpetrators to identify with the victims and easier for them to kill with a clear conscience. Another technique was to make people live in their own waste without food or sanitation, so that they became completely unrecognizable and, like animals, preoccupied only with food. After the war, the journalist Sereny asked commandant Stangl why it was necessary to humiliate people so much when they would only be killed afterwards. Stangl answered her: "to make the work of the executers easier."[35] A third technique consisted in the reduction of persons to numbers tattooed on their arms.[36] In this way, a person loses his or her name, the first indication of his or her being human. One could give many other similar examples of this depersonalizing use of language by the Nazis.[37] A fourth technique was the continuous use of large quantities. It is more difficult to kill two persons than to kill two thousand. A last technique was the avoidance of direct confrontation with the victims. It is well-known that Himmler became sick during his two visits to Auschwitz. Precisely to avoid this kind of "moral nausea," the gas chambers were created so that the machine could take over the human work and that every personal contact with victims could become superfluous. Once again, this depersonalization is not "typically German," but a feature of modernity and modern war. It has become psychologically much easier to drop a bomb on a city that kills 20,000 people than to shoot one child who stands before you.

Totalitarian systems are reducing every human being to an element of a larger cosmic project. Because the perpetrators renounced their free will, they might also in some way be seen as victims of this system

(197-201). They, for the most part, were not aware that their obedience to the immoral rules of the regime also meant their own depersonalization.[38] In fact they accepted becoming means and no longer ends in themselves. It is not surprising that after the war for a lot of them obedience (*Befehl ist Befehl*) was a real excuse. "We only obeyed" as if this would dismiss people from their responsibility. In Jerusalem Eichmann declared: "my guilt was my obedience."[39] Eichmann referred to the categoric imperative of Kant that requires one to do one's duty. Perhaps it was not very efficient of the prosecuting attorneys to try to prove that the SS were working on their own initiative. Blind obedience is clearly an important feature of totalitarian regimes. As we have already pointed out, depersonalization is not "typically German," but a characteristic of modern life. The extreme circumstances of the camps only brings to light the worst consequences of this general human phenomenon. Today, our way of life is full of moments of depersonalization; people sometimes obey certain systems, regimes or ideologies without thinking.

Enjoyment of Power

A third characteristic of the anthropology of the perpetrator is the enjoyment of the exercise of power (*Schadenfreude*).[40] This is a kind of depersonalization in which the other is reduced to only a means, while the power-holder remains an end (212-227). This enjoyment of power was already known by Freud as *Bemachtigungstrieb* or *libido dominandi*:[41] to enjoy the submission of the other to one's own arbitrariness. Of course, one can also enjoy making someone else happy. There is, however, an asymmetry between the effects of making someone else happy and unhappy. By making someone else unhappy, one receives a much stronger proof of one's power over that person. But when one makes someone else happy, one can never be sure that this person's happiness is not also thanks to his or her own will. When one makes someone else unhappy, one can be more certain about the effectiveness of one's power, because normally no one wants to be unhappy (213). Killing the other is the absolute proof of my power over that person (but at the same time the absolute limit of my power!). Yet it is not the suffering of the other itself that causes my enjoyment, as in sadism, but the consciousness of having had power over the other.[42] Instead of sadism, then, it was the enjoyment of power that was the central passion behind the evil of Auschwitz. There are not many proofs for this claim in the biographies of perpetrators because most of these were written with apologetic purposes. We can nonetheless see that perpetrators in camps became angry when, for example, an order was not executed quickly or the victim risked to look into the eyes of the executioner.[43] What was new for the camps was that this enjoyment of power was no longer limited by any legal or moral boundary. The only boundary left was the death of the other person.[44] The desire to exercise such power over the victim was for the most part the consequence of the perpetrator's own restriction of freedom within the system. Many perpetrators within the totalitarian system were tyrants to those below because they were slaves to those above (215).

Enjoyment of power is not a phenomenon restricted to Nazis. Torodov refers to the story of the president of the Jewish Council in Lotz, Chaïm Rumkowski, who behaved as master and king of the ghetto during the war.[45] Due to his tyrannical attitude he implicitly created within the ghetto a mini-totalitarian state on the Nazi model. But then neither is the enjoyment of power "typically Jewish." In all social relations, people like to enjoy of the power they possess over others (policemen, teachers, parents, children, etc.).

Fragmentation as Self-Deception

The most significant daily vice is fragmentation. This fragmentation could be used to exonerate the perpetrators of every guilt. In some cases, deculpabilization on psychological and social grounds might be appropriate, but not always. We have indicated that fragmentation always happens as a kind of protection against evil. Yet there are always gaps in the bulkheads of fragmentation so that there always remains a certain level of consciousness of one's own fragmentation.[46] Fragmentation is always characterized by self-deception.[47] This idea, however, is missing in the thought of Todorov.[48]

Generally, people do not explicitly choose evil for evil's sake, but do evil while deceiving themselves. In self-deception the evildoer is simultaneously deceiver (active) and deceived (passive), perpetrator and victim.[49] The self-deceiver knows that he or she does wrong, but tries to convince him or herself with (pseudo-)ethical arguments that this is not the case. For the most part, perpetrators are not "adherents of evil"; they are not conducting a crusade against the good. Each human being - including the perpetrator - tries to remain an ethical being, even when doing evil. Even in the most extreme forms of evil, a person does not abandon his or her engagement towards the good. On the contrary, in such situations the attempts to avoid guilt and shame become even greater. A normally socialized moral person feels very uncomfortable when continuously violating his or her own moral principles.[50] The human desire to be good and consistent is very strong. Self-contradiction, inner conflict and ambivalence are sources of pain and fear. It is the anxiety of disintegration in the light of the immoral character of one's existence that makes one cling to self-deceptive strategies. In other words, every human being has an "inhuman" desire for self-justification. One will think oneself good, even if one does evil. One can reach this state by psychologically manipulating one's inner and outer reality. Is it remarkable, then, that human beings can (mis)use ethics? Ethics can become a means by which human beings try to justify themselves.

The Nazi "ethic"[51] (Haas) was such a closed "ethical" system with very clear descriptions of good and evil. The Nazi very rigorously and anxiously obeyed these rules out of fear that his protest might cause total rejection by others and by him or herself. Anxiety was thus the foundation of this Nazi "ethic." Everything that called into question the safe and closed system, especially the stranger, could only be seen as a threat. Out of fear of real ethical provocation, people closed themselves off from everything that might call into question their secure and unquestionable "ethical" existence.[52] It is anxiety that causes self-deception, and through self-deception perpetrators create a *Weltanschauung* (Fackenheim)[53] that closes them off from the ethical appeal of the vulnerable and suffering victims of evil.

II. Are We Wolves to Each Other (Hobbes) or Are We Each Other's Keepers (Genesis)? About the Victims of the Holocaust

Now we concentrate on the victims of the Nazi genocide. The camps reveal a very hard reality, namely that in extreme circumstances every trace of ethical life disappears, and human beings become beasts in a merciless struggle for life (37-50). In a certain ideological literature, the camps are sometimes used to demonstrate that in humanity "the law of the jungle" ultimately reigns, that every ethical law crumbles and brute power rules. To substantiate this, we can find illustrations in some testimonies of survivors about the terrible indifference that victims had for the suffering of their co-prisoners.

Todorov demonstrates that in the camps there were many matters of conscience among the victims, indicating the elementary possibility of free choice and therefore of moral life (37-50). For example, Ella

Lingens-Reiner, a physician in Auschwitz, had the choice of using a single medicine for one very ill person or for several less ill persons. Should the newborn babies in the camps be killed in order to increase the chance of survival of their mothers or not? There are many similar examples that demonstrate how camp life was not only ruled by "the law of the jungle."

The notion of "war of all against all" is not specific to camp life, but can also be found in a certain philosophical literature of the two latest centuries, for example, in the work of Schopenhauer and Nietzsche. While the camps may have been created in a Nietzschean spirit, this does not mean that they demonstrate the perfection of this ideology. One should distinguish the philosophy that was the basis of the camps and the philosophy that one can deduce from a study of their victims. It is evident that with very extreme means one can destroy the ethical attitudes that exist between people and reduce human beings to a bundle of animal instincts. But this does not mean that morality is only a superficial convention that loses its truth very quickly under unfavorable circumstances. For Todorov, Auschwitz teaches us that morality is always present and can only be destroyed by very extreme and violent means. Auschwitz is not simply a proof for animality as the ultimate truth of human nature. The so-called natural inclination of human beings for immorality is not so natural. The "war of all against all" has to be imposed through very violent means. When social Darwinists use Auschwitz to prove the correctness of their pessimistic ideology, are they not raising the factuality of Nazi ideology to a moral truth?

For Todorov, the difference between camp life and normal life is not the respective absence and presence of moral life. In daily life we do not notice the contrasts between morality and immorality so easily since egocentrism is usually better camouflaged. In the camps one sometimes had to choose between losing one's bread or losing one's human dignity. For victims, then, the camps sometimes became a purification of their conscience (e.g., Hillesum), sometimes a total destruction of it, but for the most part were something in between. The direction of this ethical evolution was mostly dependent upon the moral starting point victims had before the war. The camps project on large scale what is mostly hidden from view in daily life. Precisely because of this, one thinks one can draw general lessons of immorality from the camps, while egoism reigns unnoticed in daily life.

Goodness as a Universal "Daily Virtue"

It would seem that the most important lesson to be learned from the study of the victims of the Holocaust is that although evil was inevitable in these circumstances, goodness was not completely absent. And even if there are only a few testimonies illustrating this insight, they still show how human beings *can* be stronger than the tragic destiny imposed upon them. Sometimes evil among the victims is seen as the most relevant and sensational aspect of the life in the camps. Yet it was the moments where victims developed "daily virtues" (*virtus quotidiennes*) in these extreme situations that were in fact much more spectacular. Like Todorov, we base this claim on the analysis of three important ethical attitudes, attitudes which could be seen at work in the life of the victims in the camps and which each of us -- without being superhumans -- can develop in our lives today: dignity, care and creativity.

Dignity

Dignity is understood by Todorov as the capacity to act through one's own will (66-77). In difficult situations one is dignified insofar as one tries to influence one's environment through one's own initiative. In extreme situations this can be by transforming a deterministic situation into a reality of freedom. In the camps one sees that this final freedom could never be completely suppressed. At times, however, dignity was only possible at great risk of life. In Ravensbrück, for example, Milena Jesenska systematically refused to line up correctly in rows of four. She never hurried carrying out an order. She sometimes sang a melody, which not only roused the anger of her supervisors, but also of the co-prisoners who had completely internalized the ruling order.[54] Dignity depends on such little actions with no apparent effect, but that nonetheless keep the human spirit alive.

At times, in the extreme circumstances of the camps, this affirmation of human dignity could only exist in the following of an order "as if" with one's own free will. Gradowski, a member of a *Sonderkommando* in Auschwitz-Birkenau, tells in a manuscript, buried next to the crematoria, how victims walked with pride (and dignity) to the gaschambers "as if" they walked to life.[55] In such situations, even suicide can be a final expression of one's dignity. Olga Lengyel always carried poison with her and declared after the war that being the ultimate master of her own life represented her last freedom.[56] The perpetrators knew that for the victims the choice of the moment and manner of their own death was a final affirmation of their own freedom, while the camps aimed at the destruction of this freedom. In the camps suicide was therefore "forbidden." When Mala Zimetbaum tried to commit suicide just before her execution in Auschwitz, the SS who discovered her, was furious; killing was *their* job. Todorov gives the example of a hunger strike that broke out among the prisoners of a Russian concentration camp where the guards forced the victims to eat, even though their death was otherwise of no importance. Within the limits of their situation, these people tried to use their freedom as optimally as possible. They chose to have hunger, rather than undergo hunger passively. They knew that even worse than death was a total alienation from their own will.[57] With this dignity they implicitly reacted against the process of fragmentation they saw at work in the perpetrators, as they became unfree by following the inhuman ideology of their superiors.

Another attempt at saving one's dignity was trying to keep oneself clean, even in miserable circumstances of the camps. By so keeping their self-respect, victims would sometimes even raise their chances for survival.[58] Other victims systematically refused to follow a logic of pure self-interest and immediate self-profit. Some of them tried to be interested in others, not humiliating them in confrontation with their superiors. They sometimes refused a favor they did not deserve. Dignity does not always serve the struggle for survival! Others enjoyed the work they did, not because it was ordered, but out of professional love. It was precisely because of this that the Nazis imposed so many meaningless tasks, work one could never do without losing one's self-respect.

Acts of dignity, however, can never be automatically called moral acts (75-77). We also need to consider the function and the ethical or unethical consequences of these actions for others. Even for the professional builder, constructing a good wall around a concentration camp cannot be considered a moral good.[59] Indeed, were there not also Nazis who knew love for their work? Hoess called himself obsessed by his work. The subordination of other human beings to the perfection of one's own work is immoral. Neither is cleanliness always moral. Were not Nazis also obsessed by neatness? We can, indeed should, distinguish moral from immoral self-respect. Dignity alone does not suffice. We must always consider whether the well-being of our fellow human being is not violated through the manifestation of our dignity. This brings us to a second daily virtue: care.

Care

Every survivor of the Holocaust will remember how he or she was once helped, saved or encouraged by a co-prisoner (78-98).[60] So also mothers soothed their children by singing songs or caressing them, to the very doors of the gas chambers. Mala Zimetbaum became a very strong symbol of this helping human hand in Auschwitz. She used her privileged position as interpreter to establish contact between families, to smuggle medicine, to change working lists, etc.[61]

Todorov, however, distinguishes care from certain forms of solidarity that exist among people of the same group (89-92). In such kinds of solidarity one always automatically helps those who are in one's own group, but does not feel responsible in the same way for those who are outsiders. This kind of solidarity is for Todorov merely a quantitative extension of the principle of self-interest. Egoism is replaced by "nosism" (egoism of the *nous*). This form of solidarity excludes the outsider; the stranger cannot but be the victim of such "nosism." In the camps, for example, newcomers were frequently the victims of the solidarity of the group that was already formed and that feared losing its privileges. Solidarity with one group in this case sometimes means the death of the others. In caring one is not acting automatically on the basis of the other's nationality, language, job, etc., but only on the basis of the other's humanity. Solidarity can nevertheless function as a kind of school for learning more universal care. Yet care also differs from a charity that excludes no one (92-93). A typical example of charity is the giving of alms to an anonymous beggar. Such charity always happens within an asymmetric relation and can thus be very humiliating for the person who undergoes it. Care, for its part, engenders care again (i.e., children-parents, parents-children). Care is likewise different from self-sacrifice (93-94). In care one is not losing time and money, but one is devoting oneself to the other and draws intrinsic happiness out of that. In care one is never poorer but ultimately richer. In the offer of charity and self-sacrifice one is sometimes frustrated because one is not rewarded for the effort; care, however, bears its reward in itself.[62]

The famous Jewish psychiatrist and camp survivor Viktor Frankl claimed that caring for the well-being of others was an important factor for survival in the camps.[63] Through experience in the camps he learned that prisoners who had a purpose beyond their own self-preservation had a greater chance to withstand the very hard circumstances of camp life. Victims found more vitality when they could orient themselves towards a goal, a life value outside themselves, than when they were only occupied with their own survival. Of course, care for the other also carries risks: one becomes more vulnerable because in addition to one's own suffering, one is also bearing the suffering of the other. In this sense one is better protected when fighting for an idea because the suffering and death of an individual can be relativized in the light of one's ideal.

Care stands opposed to the daily vice of depersonalization, just as dignity stands opposed to fragmentation. In care the other person is an end in him or herself, while in depersonalization the other is reduced to a means. Care likewise stands opposed to the daily vice of enjoyment of power. In the care I am a means and the other is the end; in the enjoyment of power the other is a means and I am the end.

Creativity

A further possibility for retaining their integrity in the camps was the human capacity to be creative (99-126). Creativity is related to experiences of truth and beauty. In one of his works Viktor Frankl tells how a sunset in the camp brought him an extraordinary aesthetic experience (99). In such experiences one leaves one's direct preoccupation with survival and contemplates what is true and beautiful. The experience of creativity can also take the form of reading books, reciting poems, exchanging ideas, writing stories, drawing, making music, dancing, praying, etc.[64] And in this search for meaning barbarity is combatted.[65]

Creativity, however, does not automatically generate goodness. Sometimes aesthetics and crimes coincide. Some Nazis, for example, read poetry after their duty. We should always ask ourselves what are the consequences of our creative activities. Creativity can be perverted! The famous violist Alma Rose, who was the *Kapellmeister* of the women's orchestra of Auschwitz, was prepared to "offer up" some of her musicians to improve the quality of her orchestra's music.[66] When creativity and care are in conflict, care should always take precedence. No matter how impressive human creativity might be, it should never foster the depersonalization of the persons who surround the artist or scholar.

Conclusion

Our analysis has shown how, for self-protective reasons, people in confrontation with extreme forms of evil very easily choose strategies of diabolication. They look to Auschwitz as into an aquarium, i.e. as into a very well-delineated and fascinating world populated with beings who are completely different from themselves. In the approach we developed here, Auschwitz is not presented in a comforting way as an extra-human reality. With the notion of daily vices, we have tried to hold Auschwitz up as a mirror in which we can see the features of our own faces. The daily vices of fragmentation, depersonalization and enjoyment of power demonstrate how the evil of Auschwitz was not a demonic reality, but an extremely enlarged version of an universal human possibility which finds a very receptive ground in modernity. The daily vices combined with the notion of self-deception reveal how "good" people can do evil without stopping to see themselves as ethical beings.

The study of the daily vices can save us from a contra-productive discourse about evil and destructiveness. These vices teach us that we should not fixate ourselves only on (or better: not let ourselves be dazzled by) the excessive apex of human destructiveness, as the camps were, but that we should also and especially concentrate on the first steps, the little, daily processes that lead us to that point. Such an approach is no longer comforting because it confronts us with our modern way of life and our subtle and daily manipulations of good and evil.

In the second part of our reflections we showed how even in extremely violent circumstances human commitment to the good can never be completely destroyed. This is indeed a very hopeful perspective: in every system there always remains *espaces de liberté* (Falise) which can be sought and broadened by ethically sensitive human beings. The choice for the good in the camps mostly happened in neither a very noisy nor heroic embrace of "the Good,"[67] but rather in thousands of little and unseen daily virtues. We have analyzed three of these daily virtues based on the so-called "structure of intersubjectivity" (110-111). Human dignity is based on the relation of the subject with itself (the first person: I to I); interpersonal care is orientated by the relation of the subject with the other (the second person: I to You); creativity is always developed in relation with more people, here and elsewhere, today and tomorrow (the third person: I to They). With the development of the daily virtues in the midst of the

Holocaust, the victims already formulated an implicit answer to the daily vices they saw at work among the perpetrators. With human dignity they criticized the processes of fragmentation; with human care they condemned the depersonalization of victims; with their constructive creativity they resisted the misuse of art by the perpetrators. In short, their choice for the good *in* Auschwitz is the foundation for our possibility of the good *after* Auschwitz.

In spite of and in the vulnerability of their existence in the camps they carried this very rich treasure through this dark period in history, a treasure they offer us as a valuable legacy and of which we unfortunately do not always realize the worth and the fragility. In this sense we cannot only speak about the "banality of evil" (Arendt), but also about the "banality of good,"[68] that is, about goodness as a universal and daily human possibility, also today. This conclusion is not simply optimistic. We need only recall that in Auschwitz many very ethical victims did *not* survive.[69]

Moreover, today we see how some victims of crimes against humanity, based on their very deep injuries, react to their suffering by diabolicalizing the perpetrators. This reaction is very understandable from their (defensive) point of view. In the coming years the question will become of major importance how people who are divided by very serious evil (on micro-, meso- and macro-levels) can live together in the future, without forgetting evil, but with and in memory of the victims of this evil. The theme of authentic reconciliation cannot but be a question of crucial significance in the beginning of the next millennium.

Notes

1. See F.H. Littell, *Ethics after Auschwitz. A Covenant Between Christians and Jews*, in H.J. Cargas (ed.), *When God and Men Failed. Non-jewish Views of the Holocaust* (New York: Macmillan, 1981), pp. 38-50, pp. 43-44: "Six million Jews were murdered efficiently and scientifically by baptized Christians in the heart of Christendom."

2. For a more extensive investigation of this topic, see our doctoral dissertation D. Pollefeyt, *Voorbij afschuw en verschoning. Een antropologisch, wijsgerig en ethisch onderzoek naar verschillende paradigmatische benaderingen van het kwaad van Auschwitz als aanzet tot een "be-vreemdende" theologie van het heilige.* Unpublished doctoral dissertation in Moral Theology, Louvain, 1995, vol. I: lxxxix+170 p.; Vol. II: pp. 171-412; Vol. III: pp. 413-629.

3. Tzvetan Todorov was born in Sofia (Bulgaria) in March 1939. He studied at the universities of Sofia and Paris. He is Doctor in Language and Literature. At the moment he is a Director of Research of the *Centre National de la Recherche Scientifique* of France (Paris). He is married and father of three children. Some of his most important works are *Introduction à la littérature fantastique* (Paris: Seuil, 1970); *Littérature et signification* (Paris: Larousse, 1977); *Théories du symbole* (Paris: Seuil, 1977); *Les morales de l'histoire* (Paris: Seuil, 1991); *La conquête de l'Amérique: la question de l'autre* (Paris, Seuil, 1991); *Nous et les autres: la réflexion française sur la diversité humaine* (Paris: Seuil, 1992); *Au nom du peuple: témoignages sur les camps communistes* (Paris: Editions de l'Aube, 1992); *Une tragédie française: été 44: scènes de guerre civiles. Suivi de souvenirs d'un maire* (Paris: Seuil, 1994); T. Todorov, *La vie commune. Essai d'anthropologie générale* (La couleur des idées) (Paris: Seuil, 1995). First published in 1991 (Seuil: Collection La couleur des idées), his work on the nazi genocide *Face à l'extrême* was revised in 1994 (Seuil: Collection Points 295). In this text the numbers between brackets refer to this new edition. There is also a German translation of this work *Angesichts des Äussersten* (Munich: Fink, 1993, 348 p.) and in 1996 will appear also the First American Edition *Facing the Extreme: Moral Life in the Concentration Camps* (New York: Henry Holt, 1996).

4. I wish to thank Dr. John Ries for proofreading this text.

5. For a more philophic foundation of this view, see, for example, G. Steiner, *In Bluebeard's Castle: Some Notes towards the Re-definition of Culture,* (London: Faber & Faber, 1971) p. 111.

6. See the view of B. Lang, *Act and idea in the Nazi Genocide* (Chicago: University of Chicago Press, 1990), p. 32: "(...) the Nazis implemented the policy of genocide at least in part *because* it was wrong: wrongdoing has assumed for them the status of a principle."

7. Ella Lingens-Reiner cited by G.M. Kren and L. Rappoport, *The Holocaust and the Crisis of Human Behavior,* New York, Holmes & Meier, 1980, p. 100 (footnote 33) from B. Naumann, *Auschwitz: A Report on the Proceedings Against Robert Karl Ludwig Mulka and Others before the Court of Frankfurt* (London, Pall Mall Press, 1966), p. 91.:

I know of almost no SS man who could not claim to have saved someone's life. There were few sadists. Not more than 5 or 10 percent were pathological criminals in the clinical sense. The others were all perfectly normal men who knew the difference between right and wrong.

8. W.K. Thompson, *Ethics, Evil and the Final Solution,* in A. Rosenberg and G.E. Myers (eds), *Echoes from the Holocaust, Philosophical Reflections on a Dark Time* (Philadelphia: Temple University, 1988) pp. 181-197, p. 184: "ordinary people can commit demonic acts."

9. S. Sabini and M. Silver, *Destroying the Innocent with a Clear Conscience: a Sociopsychology of the Holocaust,* in J.E. Dimsdale (ed.), *Survivors, Victims and Perpetrators. Essays on the Nazi Holocaust* (New York: Hemisphere, 1980), pp. 329-358, pp. 329-330.

10. H. Askenasy, *Sind wir alle Nazis? Zum Potential der Unmenschlichkeit* (Frankfurt & New York: Campus Verlag, 1979) pp. 35-36.

11. H. Arendt, *Eichmann in Jerusalem: A Report on the Banality of Evil* (New York: Viking Press 1st ed., 1963; new edition: Harmondsworth: Penguin Books, 1984).

12. See the view of G. Hausner, *Eichmann and His Trial. The Full Story of the Nazi Who Murdered Six Million Jews. How the Gruesome Evidence Was Collected Against Him and How He Was Convinced,* in *Saturday Evening Post* November 3, 11, and 17, 1962 and more extensive in G. Hausner, *Justice in Jerusalem. The Trial of Adolf Eichman,* (London & Beccles: William Clowes & Sons, 1966).

13. For a discussion between optimistic and pessimistic anthropologies, see T. Todorov, *La vie commune. Essai d'anthropologie générale* (La couleur des idées) (Paris: Seuil, 1995).

14. The same idea can be found in Z. Bauman, *Modernity and the Holocaust* (Cambridge: Polity Press, 1989).

15. See also the thesis of F.E. Katz, *Ordinary People* and *Extraordinary Evil: A Report on the Beguilings of Evil* (New York: State University of New York Press, 1993).

16. See also H. Arendt, *The Origins of Totalitarianism. New Edition with Added Prefaces* (Harvest book 224) (New York: Harcourt, Brace & Jovanovich, 5th ed., 1993).

17. For a description of "manicheism:" R.M. Wilson, *Mani and Manichaeism,* in P. Edwards (ed.), *The Encyclopedia of Philosophy* (New York: Macmillan, 1967) 8 volumes, volume 5, pp. 149-150, p. 149:

Evil stands as a completely independent principle against Good, and redemption from the power of Evil is to be achieved by recognizing this dualism and following the appropriate rules of life.

18. H. Kaplan, *Conscience and Memory: Meditations in a Museum of the Holocaust,* (Chicago & London: University of Chicago Press, 1994), p. 49:

Declare that you have an enemy and he will become the enemy. Declare a people to be of inferior race and you will soon write the scenarios that will fulfill your theory. This was Hitler's effort and his success. He defined Jews and made them become, through methodic abuse and torment, the proof of his definition.

19. H. Ofstad, *Our Contempt for Weakness: Nazi Norms and Values - and Our Own.* A translation from the Norwegian original by C. Von Sydow (Gothenburg: Almquist & Wiksell, 1991), p. 75.

20. A.J. Herzberg, *Eichmann in Jeruzalem* (Den Haag: Bert Bakker, 1962), pp. 14-15.

21. Hitler in *Mein Kampf* in L. Dawidowicz, *The War Against the Jews 1933-1945* (London: Weidenfeld & Nicolson, 1975), p. 21: "Two worlds face one another," said Hitler, "the men of god and men of Satan! The Jew is the anti-man, the creature of another god. He must have come from another root of the human race. I set the Aryan and the Jew over and against each other."

22. See, for example, these two citations of Hitler in E. Jäckel, *Hitler idéologue.* A translation from the German original *[Hitlers Weltanschauung: Entwurf einer Herrschaft]* by J. Chavy (Paris: Calmann-Lévy, 1973), p. 71: "Il n'y a aucun pacte possible avec les Juifs, mais seulement l'implacable eux ou nous," and p. 72: "Je crois donc aujourd'hui agir selon l'esprit du Créateur tout-puissant: en me défendant des Juifs, je combats pour l'oeuvre du Seigneur."

23. E. Hillesum, *Etty. De nagelaten geschriften van Etty Hillesum* (1941-1943). Edited by K.A.D. Smelik (Amsterdam: Balans, 3rd revised ed., 1986), p. 254.

24. The difference between "*une usage littérale*" et "*une usage exemplaire*" of the *Shoah* is carefully analyzed in T. Todorov, *Les abus de la mémoire* (Collection Violet) (Paris: Arléa, 1995), pp. 28-33, p. 31.

25. Cited in G. Tillion, *Ravensbrück* (Paris: Editions du Seuil, 1988), 3rd ed., Part II, p. 209: "Je n'ai ressenti aucune émotion en accomplissant ces actes."

26. R.J. Lifton, *The Nazi Doctors: Medical Killing and the Psychology of Genocide* (New York: Basic Books, 1986), p. 418: "the psychological principle I call 'doubling:' the division of the self into two functioning wholes, so that a part-self acts as an entire self."

27. M.K. Billson, *Inside Albert Speer: Secrets of Moral Evasion,* in *The Antioch Review* 37 (1979), pp. 460-474, p. 473.

28. *Ibid.,* p. 427.

29. A citation from H. Askenasy, op. cit., p. 24.

30. In an interview with Captain Avner Less in 1961: P. Joffroy and A. Less (eds), *Eichmann par Eichmann,* (Paris: Grasset, 1970), pp. 339-340.

31. H. Fein, *Accounting for Genocide: National Responses and the Jewish Victimization during the Holocaust,* (New York: Free Press, 1979), p. 8:

But leaders could not have chosen annihilation (rejecting assimilation) had not the victims been previously defined as basically of a different species, outside of the common conscience, and beyond the universe of obligation, this was the precondition.

32. D. Pollefeyt, *The Trauma of the Holocaust as a Central Challenge of Levinas' Ethical and Theological Thought,* on Marcia S. Littell, et al., [CD-Rom] The Holocaust, Remembering for the Future II (Stamford: Vista InterMedia Corporation, 1996), and D. Patterson, *Subjectivity and Responsibility: Wiesel per Levinas,* in *Cahiers Roumains d'études littéraires* 4 (1987) 130-144.

33. H.C. Kelman, *Violence without Moral Restraint: Reflections on the Dehumanization of Victims and Victimizers,* in Journal of Social Issues 29(4) (1973), pp. 25-61.

34. F.H. Littell, *The Credibility Crisis of Modern University,* in H. Friedlander and L. Milton, *The Holocaust: Ideology, Bureaucracy and Genocide* (The San Jose Papers) (New York: Kraus International Publications, 1980), p. 274.

35. See G. Sereny, *Into That Darkness: From Mercy Killing to Mass Murder* (London: Deutsch, 1974) and (New York: Random House, 1983), p. 101.

36. P. Levi, *Is dit een mens?* A translation from the Italian original by F. De Matteis-Vogels (Amsterdam: Meulenhoff, 1987), pp. 31-32.

37. D. Le Breton, *L'homme défiguré. Essai sur la sacralité du visage,* in *Les temps modernes* 44 (510) (1989) pp. 99-112, p. 100: "Si le visage est le signe de l'être de l'homme, la négation de l'homme passe par celle de son visage."

38. E. Fackenheim, *To Mend the World. Foundations of Future Jewish Thought* (New York: Schocken Books, 1982), p. 237:

As for the Third Reich, its heart and soul was the aim to destroy just this principle - by no means only in the case of Jews ... but also, and perhaps above all, in the case of the "master race" itself.

39. H. Arendt, op. cit., p. 179.

40. P. Levi, *De verdronkenen en de geredden. Essays.* A translation from the Italian original by F. De Matteis-Vogels (Amsterdam: Meulenhoff, 1991), p. 104.

41. S. Freud, *Gesammelte Werke: Chronologisch Geordnet* (Frankfurt: Fischer, 5th ed., 1972) part V (*Werke aus den Jahren 1904-1905*), pp. 93-94 (of *Drie Abhandlungen zur Sexualtheorie,* pp. 29-145):

Die gründliche psychologische Analyse dieses Triebes ist bekanntlich noch nicht geglückt; wir dürfen annehmen, daß die grausame Regung vom Bemächtigungstrieb herstammt und zu einer Zeit im Sexualleben auftritt, da die Genitalien noch nicht ihre spätere Rolle aufgenommen haben.

42. See J. Laplanche and J.B. Pontalis, *Vocabulaire de la Psychanalyse* (Paris, P.U.F., 11th ed., 1992), pp. 364-367 (*"Pulsion d'emprise"*) p. 364:

une pulsion d'emprise qui n'aurait pas originellement pour but la souffrance d'autrui, mais simplement n'en tiendrait pas compte (phase antérieure aussi bien à la pitié qu'au sadisme); elle serait indépendante de la sexualite.

43. See, for example, E.E. Cohen, *Human Behavior in the Concentration Camp.* With a New Preface by the Author and a Foreword of Dinora Pines. A translation from the Dutch original by H.M. Braaksma (New York, 1st ed., 1954; London: Free Association Books, 1988), pp. 246-253 and A.J. Herzberg, *Amor fati. De aanhandelijkheid aan het lot. Zeven opstellen over Bergen-Belsen,* (Amsterdam: Querido, 1977), pp. 11-12.

44. A. Pawelczynska, *Values and Violence in Auschwitz: A Sociological Analysis*. A translation from the Polish original by C.S. Leach (Berkeley: University of California Press, 1979), p. 19.

45. See the story in P. Levi, *De verdronkenen en de geredden*, pp. 62-65.

46. A good illustration is this citation from A. Speer, *Inside the Third Reich. Memoirs*. A translation from the German original by Weidenfeld & Nicolson (London: R. & C. Winston, 1970), pp. 112-113:

> Hitler's hatred for the Jews seemed to me so much a matter of course that I gave it no serious thought. I felt myself to be Hitler's architect. Political events did not concern me.... Today it seems to me that I was trying to compartimentalize my mind.... It is ... true that the habit of thinking within the limits of my own field provided me, both as architect and as Armaments Minister, with many opportunities for evasion.... But in the final analysis I myself determined the degree of my isolation, the extremity of my evasions, and the extent of my ignorance.

47. S. Hauerwas and D.B. Burrell, *Self-Deception and Autobiography: Reflections on Speer's Inside the Third Reich*, in S. Hauerwas, R. Bondi, and D.B. Burrell, *Truthfulness and Tragedy: Further Investigations in Christian Ethics* (Notre Dame: University of Notre Dame Press, 1977), pp. 82-98.

48. An extraordinary elaborated alternative is D.J. Fasching, *Narrative Theology after Auschwitz. From Alienation to Ethics* (Philadelphia: Fortress Press, 1992), pp. 97-105. See also his monumental *The Ethical Challenge of Auschwitz and Hiroshima. Apocalypse or Utopia?* (Albany: State University of New York Press, 1993).

49. J.-P. Sartre, *L'être et le néant. Essai d'ontologie phénoménologique* (Paris: Gallimard, 1949), 25th ed, pp. 85-111 (Chapter 2: *"La mauvaise foi"*), pp. 87-88.

50. S. Callahan, *In Good Conscience: Reason and Emotion in Moral Decision Making* (San Francisco: Harper & Row, 1991), pp. 143-170 (Chapter 6: "Moral Failure and Self Deception").

51. See the very renovating study of P.J. Haas, *Morality After Auschwitz: The Radical Challenge of the Nazi Ethic* (Philadelphia: Fortress Press, 1988), 1st ed., 2nd ed., 1991.

52. T. Todorov, *Au nom du peuple: témoignages sur les camps communistes.*
A translation from the Bulgarian original by M. Vrinat (Paris: Editions de
l'Aube, 1992), p. 18.

53. E. Fackenheim, *Nazi "Ethic," Nazi Weltanschauung and the Holocaust.*
A Review Essay in *The Jewish Quarterly Review* 83(1-2) (1992), pp. 167-172.

54. See F. Kafka, *Brieven aan Milena.* A translation from the German
original by W. Haas, (Amsterdam: Querido, 1974), 2nd ed.; M. Buber-
Neumann, *Milena* (Points. Actuels 95). A translation from the German original
by A. Brossat (Paris: Seuil, 1990).

55. P. Müller, *Eyewitness to Auschwitz: Three Years in the Gas Chambers*
(New York: Stein & Day, 1979), p. 46 and D.G. Roskies (ed.), *The Literature
of Destruction* (Philadelphia: The Jewish Publication Society, 1989), p. 557.

56. O. Lengyel, *Souvenirs de l'au-delà* (Climats). A translation from the
Hungarian original by G. LADISLAS, (Paris: Editions du bateau, 1946), p. 40:
"La certitude qu'en dernier ressort on est maître de sa propre vie représente la
dernière liberte."

57. Based on Ratouchinskaïa, *Grise est la couleur de l'espoir* (Paris: Plon,
1989), p. 128.

58. P. Levi, *Is dit een mens?*, pp. 44-45.

59. P. Levi, *De verdronkenen en de geredden*, pp. 119-120.

60. A. Pawelczynska, op. cit., p. 121.

61. See I. Gutman, *Zimetbaum, Mala (1922-1945),* in *Encyclopedia of the
Holocaust* (New York: Macmillan, 1990) 4 volumes, p. 1735.

62. T. Todorov, *Une tragédie française: été 44: scènes de guerre civiles. Suivi
de souvenirs d'un maire* (Histoire immédiate) (Paris: Seuil, 1994), pp. 155-156.

63. V.E. Frankl, *Man's Search for Meaning: an Introduction to Logotherapy*
(New York: Pocket Books, 1963).

64. I.J. Rosenbaum, *The Holocaust and Halakhah* (The library of Jewish law
and ethics) (New York: KTAV, 1976), pp. 47-59 (Chapter 3: "Prayer, Study,
and Martyrdom"), and G. Greenberg, *Foundations for Orthodox Jewish
Theological Response to the Holocaust: 1936-1939*, in A.L. Eckardt, *Burning*

118   *Confronting the Holocaust*

Memory. Times of Testing and Reckoning (Holocaust series) (Oxford: Pergamon Press, 1993), pp. 71-94.

65. See an example of E. Wiesel, *Night.* A translation from the French original by S. Rodway (New York: Avon Books, 1969), pp. 107-108 in P. Yancey, *Concentration Camps part II. One Lesson Stands Out: Justice Must Come from the Outside,* in *Christianity Today* 23 (5) (1979), pp. 26-30.

66. F. Fenélon, *Sursis pour l'orchestre* (Paris: Stock, 1976), pp. 172-188.

67. For the difference between *"une éthique de responsabilité"* et *"une éthique de conviction"* see T. Todorov, *Une tragédie française,* p. 149 and also J.-P. Sartre, *L'existentialisme est un humanisme* (Paris: Nagel, 1970), pp. 41-42.

68. Z. Bauman, *The Banality of the Good, Review* of T. Todorov, *Face à l'extrême* (Paris, 1991), in *Times Literary Supplement* 13 (4602) (1991), pp. 12-14.

69. See the important critic against Frankl: L.L. Langer, *Versions of Survival: the Holocaust and the Human Spirit* (Albany: State University of New York Press, 1982), p. 74:

In contradiction to those who argue that the only way of surviving was to cling to the values of civilized living despite the corrupting influence of the deathcamps, Lingens-Reiner insists that those who tried to salvage such moral luggage imposed fatal burdens on themselves.

Chapter 7

HOLOCAUST DENIAL AND THE MEDIA: MISUNDERSTANDING THE NATURE OF TRUTH

Deborah Lipstadt

Thank you, Dr. Rubenstein. I am here today to talk to you about experiences that I have had in the past two years since the publication of my book *Denying the Holocaust*. The book did strike a chord, much more than I ever imagined would be the case and in fact, I was just reminding Yehuda Bauer, a few moments ago, that he, together with Israel Gutman, were the people who approached me and urged me to write on this topic. I remember saying to both of them, "Do you really think anyone would be interested in reading about it?" And so, if you think I'm smart in having picked such a relevant topic, that story will tell you the truth.

I want to talk to you about the meaning of the truth and how truth is perceived or not perceived. How much of the world has a cloudy perception of what truth is. This is particularly true of the media which translates so much of what we do for wider audiences. While I shall speak today of Holocaust denial, please keep in mind that if this truth, the truth of the Holocaust, can be assaulted, then any truth can be assaulted. If this truth is vulnerable, any truth is vulnerable. Therefore, though I speak from the confines of the study of the Holocaust and while many of you are involved in so many ways with this field, I think it is important to remember that we speak of all types of scholarship. Moreover, rather than speaking of communication with the media, I want to speak about some of the glaring problems I observed in the media's grasp of this difficult issue.

Let me begin, however, by reading to you a letter I received shortly after the publication of *Denying the Holocaust*. It came from a gentleman in Northern California, someone I do not know, and it read as follows:

> Dear Professor Lipstadt:
>
> As I listen to your conversation on the national public radio show, Fresh Air, my mind went back to a bizarre event of some years ago. During the 1958-59 season, there appeared on tv a drama later made into the movie, Judgement at Nuremberg. From time to time, there was a momentary silence. Not part of the drama but, many of us supposed, a temporary audio failure and then a day or so later we had the explanation. Our local utility company, Pacific Gas & Electric was a co-sponsor of the production and some official there believed that references to gas chambers would give gas a bad name (and cut sales?).

By the way, this is true. Judith Doneson, who is here and who works in this area, can confirm it. To continue with the letter,

> He, therefore, ordered all such references bleeped out. So, instead of denying the holocaust, we have denying the use of gas. As Winston Churchill wrote regarding a totally different situation. One can not today even reconstruct the state of mind which would render such gestures possible.
>
>   Sincerely yours,
>
>   Edgar Andrews

I begin with that letter because it shows you how truth can be rewritten for very extraneous and, as we now recognize and would probably have recognized then, silly reasons. How much more so, *kol v'chomer* as is said in Hebrew, it can be rewritten when there is a political agenda. Particularly when this political agenda is marked by hate and prejudice. Haters are relentless. They hang around and wait for the opportunity to strike. As so many of you who have studied and written seminal works on antisemitism know, antisemitism does not go away. It increases. It decreases. But, it does not go away.

Now let me share with you another anecdote that directly relates to the media. This happened to me shortly before I finished the book when it was already well known that I was writing on this topic. I received a call from the producer of a nationally televised talk show. I grant you that talk shows are not the bastions of American intellectual thought and discernment. They were a little bit better then than they are now. They were one step above the gutter. But, I received a call from a talk show producer who said to me, Dr. Lipstadt we read in the New York Times that you are just completing a manuscript on the topic of Holocaust revisionism -- her words, not mine. I think most of you know why we don't use the word revisionism -- and we would like you to be on the show. I had learned already by that point to explicitly ask "who else will be on the show?" She said we will have some survivors of the Holocaust. I said that's excellent. They are personal witnesses. They can give personal testimony. She continued, "in addition, we will have someone who was a hidden child who now runs a Holocaust resource center." I said "that is excellent." And then she said, "I hope we will have you." Then, she paused, "and we will have some revisionists (deniers) as well."

So, I said to her, "I can't and I won't go on. I won't go on because I won't provide these people with a platform to discuss, as if we are discussing some topic on which there is a variety of opinions." I said, "second of all, I can't go on." I said I could go on a show with someone who takes a position that is diametrically opposed to what I believe in and something about which I feel quite passionately - abortion, gun control, the militia, whatever it might be. We take absolutely opposite positions. But, if I can expect and assume that they, as I, will maintain some fidelity to facts, then we can have a discussion. Now, they may interpret facts one way. I may interpret them another way. They might cite one group of statistics, I might cite another. We both might cite the same statistics and interpret them in totally opposite ways for that is what you do with statistics. But, they won't make things up at will. The problem is that deniers make things up at will.

I picked an example to give them which I thought would resonate for her. That was the example of *Anne Frank's Diary.* I chose it because it is common parlance for so many people who have very little background on the topic (as it turned out, she had taken a course on the Holocaust when she was in college). I said one of the things that deniers aim at, one of the lies they would like to prove, is that the *Diary of Anne Frank* is a fraud. Those of you who have read my book know I address that issue in the appendix. The critical edition of the *Diary of Anne Frank* goes into this matter in even greater detail. The deniers, in order to cast doubt on the veracity of the Diary, say, the Diary was written in green ball point pen and ball point pens did not come into use until the 1950s. So, how can this be a diary of the war years. Well, if you hear such claims you may be inclined to think the

Diary is, in fact, a fraud. There are, it should be noted, in the margins of the Diary, in a few places, some green annotations which were probably made by one of the early editors on the work, but the Diary itself including the ink paper and the glue used are all authentic, i.e. they are all from the mid-1940s. It has been proven by Dutch forensic experts. But, there is an easier way of proving it. But if the deniers say that the Diary was written in ball point pen which did not come into use till the 1950s then how, we might ask the deniers, can it be that the Diary was published in 1948 in the Netherlands and 1949 in France and in the early 1950s in the United States? But, if you don't know the dates of publication this argument can entrap you.

I then told the producer of the talk show that the other thing that the deniers do in order to raise questions about the Diary is to say: "There are all these references to noise in the Diary. How therefore can it be a diary about people in hiding." They point to instances where Mrs. Van Daan runs a vacuum cleaner. Or at another point, Miep Gies, the woman who was so important in hiding them, whose name we should know as well, to some degree, if not better than Anne Frank's name, brings them a sack of beans, and, the sack of beans breaks open. And Anne writes "... the noise was enough to wake the dead." The deniers say contemptuously, "Vacuum cleaners, noise enough to wake the dead; how could this be a place of hiding?"

Well, there are two ways of answering that, one is intuitively. A woman who was in hiding as a young girl in Amsterdam but who had a happier ending to her story than the Frank's family did to theirs, pointed out to me the intuitive fallacy here. I used to live in Los Angeles and in Los Angeles everybody is a frustrated screen playwriter. It does not matter if you are a professor or a plumber, an accountant, a priest, or a rabbi you've got a screenplay that, if only people in the industry were wise enough to recognize, they would see as the work of a genius. Many of these things, people are doing historical works and trying to make them very authentic. If someone were writing a diary of a family in hiding, it is very doubtful that they would put in vacuum cleaners or phrases like "noise enough to wake the dead." Just as being there lends a certain authenticity.

But, there is a better way of determining authenticity. Many of you are teachers and it does not matter what grade you teach. When you ask your students a question and they look you in the face often you say: "Don't look at me. Look in the text. Look in the book." You go back and you look in the Diary. When Mrs. Van Daan is running the vacuum cleaner, it is Sunday night. The annex in which they hid was over a warehouse which would have been locked and shuttered on a Sunday night. When Anne writes "the noise was enough to wake the dead," that is not the end of the sentence. The next phrase is "Thank God the warehouse was empty." So, what the deniers do is quote half the text. I gave the producer other examples of the deniers' tactics. Finally, at the end, she said to me in one last effort to convince me to go on the show "... you know, Dr. Lipstadt, I believe these are nefarious people. They are diabolical people. I don't believe anything they say. But, don't you think our audience has the right to hear the other side?"

Now, this was coming from someone who did not believe anything the deniers said. She recognized them as diabolic, even nefarious people. But, she nonetheless phrased it as the other side. How much more this might be the case when you are dealing with people who don't have any background. In terms of media response, what is taking place here to some degree is a reflection of what Deborah Tannen, who teaches at Georgetown University and is a specialist in communications has called the politics of confrontation. Both on the media and on the campus, public intellectual interchange has increasingly become rooted, Tannen argues, in the notion that opposition between two parties will ultimately lead to truth. When engaged in public discourse, no longer do journalists or politicians or sometimes even academics, particularly on the television circuit feel compelled to make an argument. Instead they feel compelled to have one as in having a fight. Watch the McLaughlin group. You will see the politics of confrontation. It is designed to be that way.

The culture of critique is predicated on the assumption that people enjoy watching a fight. Extreme points of view make for the best show. It does not matter if one of those points of view is rooted in utter falsehood. The lust for opposition accords the most outlandish and nonsensical notions a voice. By the way, let me anticipate the question that some of you may have. In my refusal to go on these talk shows if a denier will be on them (and I have refused), sometimes people worry if I don't go on, the deniers have the platform all to themselves. Nine times out of ten, I am not the only who refuses. Virtually every serious historian and scholar of the Holocaust, as I am sure all of you in this room would do, has refused to go on. When that happens generally the show is dropped. If they can't get someone to fight, if there are no fireworks, then there is no show. In most cases it has happened that way.

Let me return to this notion of the "other side." The Washington Post book review section, Washington Post Book World, ran a front page review of my book which was written by the eminent historian Paul Johnson. A few weeks later it printed a whole page of letters from deniers denouncing my work. Virtually the entire letters to the editor section about three weeks after the review was donated to letters from deniers. The Post then called me to ask me if I wanted to respond to these letters. They were concerned because many of their readers were upset by them. Would I respond, the person asked, to the points the deniers raised in their letters? I pointed out to them, and subsequently did write them, that Paul Johnson in his review of my book in the Washington Post Book World lauded me for refusing to debate these people. Now the Washington Post, the same paper, wanted me to engage them in debate. This was yet another example of the failure of the media to "get it."

The campus media behaved similarly. When you have someone like a Khalid Muhammad appearing on campuses, university administrators often excuse the complete lies they have to tell as a "point of view." This is the case even when all the historical "so-called facts" that they are presenting have proven to be utterly untrue. I am not suggesting that university administrators are sympathetic to a Khalid Muhammad or to a denier or even to an ad or article by a denier. I am suggesting that they often don't seem to have the guts to stand up to it. The president of a very fine university said to me not long ago that he believes that open debate is all you need. His argument was, to summarize it: Let everything be said and the truth will rise to the top. I said to him if that is the case, then can you explain the face that antisemitism and racism have persisted for so many years. If truth will always rise to the top then these and all other long standing forms of prejudice should have long ago sunk to the bottom. This basic misunderstanding about the nature of Holocaust denial permeated the campus media. When the students were presented with ads denying the Holocaust some of them justified their publications of the ads on the basis of the First Amendment. That proved to me one basic thing: they did not have a clue of what the First Amendment said. What is the first word of the First Amendment? *Congress* shall make no laws abridging freedom of the press, speech, religion, etc. The government - Congress has been defined as the government, the government can make no laws limiting what we can publish and what we can't publish. The government cannot pick and choose what will be published and what will not. However, a newspaper can pick and choose. That is what newspapers do all the time. They choose the articles they will run and reject the ones they won't run. Where they will put and where they won't put them. They do the same things with ads as well.

The former editor of the Atlanta Journal Constitution told me a very interesting story which illustrates this point. The automotive division of the advertising division of the paper had received an ad for car leasing. The people in the advertising department looked at it and were perplexed. The price offered for the lease was substantially below any other leases being offered and even when they did all the calculations the numbers would not work. The price at which the cars were being offered made no economic sense. Then they looked at the bottom of the page and in there in very small letters was this notation: this price available when you lease twenty cars or more. In other words this was a fleet lease, and as a fleet lease the price was exactly on target. The paper turned the ad down. They explained that they were not in the business of running ads which purposely mislead readers.

But some papers forget that when it comes to Holocaust denial they have this option. For example, the Duke University paper accepted the ad. The editor of the paper wrote a strong editorial saying we can not deny the deniers the right to the freedom of the press which we hold so dear. Her column was an eloquent defense of their obligation to run the ad. However, she neglected to remember that not long before that, her own paper had turned down an ad from Playboy because it was misogynist and had turned down an ad for Marlboro cigarettes because it did not want to run cigarette ads. One should give the paper some credit. For Duke University whose entire fortune and endowment is based on cigarettes, to turn down a cigarette ad - that is a "gutsy" act. But we must ask why should Playboy and Marlboro have fewer First Amendment rights than the deniers?

The media fails to understand its responsibility not to mislead its readers and certainly not to do so in the name of a confused understanding of the First Amendment. But more disturbing than the media's confusion about the First Amendment, is the confusion about what the ads really were. Repeatedly editorials in campus papers described the ads as "a point of view." For example, University of Michigan: we're "not in the business of censoring offensive ideas." In numerous papers you saw that which the deniers claimed described as an opinion, an idea even an outlandish opinion, an outlandish point of view, but as a point of view. In contrast the Harvard Crimson got it exactly right. In one of the most unequivocal responses explaining its refusal to run the ad it ran an editorial saying, "This is not an iconoclastic point of view: this is utter bullshit which has been disproven time and time again." I usually don't use language, certainly not on a podium, in front of a couple of hundred people, but in certain cases I think a quote like that deserves to be cited. But that is what most of the students who dealt with the ads didn't get and that is what much of the general press doesn't get. This is not a point of view. People like Pat Buchanan have been greatly responsible for this development. While he has never explicitly stated that he is a denier, he has been responsible for mainstreaming some of these arguments.

The most disturbing argument was contained in an editor's column in a Buffalo college newspaper. The editor ran the ad not as an ad, but as an op-ed piece because he didn't want to take money from the deniers. But he wrote as follows:

> There is enough undeniable proof as to the existence of the Nazi atrocity for the educated to understand why it shouldn't happen again. The real question is not whether it happened, but how many people don't know that it happened. If we allow this incident to become a dusty piece of history, it becomes more likely for the population as a whole to doubt its existence. However, if the Holocaust and the events leading up to it are kept fresh by dissent and debate the chances of history repeating itself are greatly reduced.

After reading that paragraph I was confused as to how he could have decided to run the ad. Then in the next paragraph he goes on to say:

> I will not stop articles like Bradley R. Smith's from being published. There are two sides to every issue and both have a place on the pages of any open minded papers editorial page. This is an exercise of how much we actually believe in our founding fathers' precious documents.

The problem, one pundit once observed, with having an open mind is that if your mind is too open your brains will fall out. I don't know who originally said that, but whoever did, understood the problem. There are not two sides to every issue and the current campus atmosphere makes it virtually a heresy to make that argument. It is politically very incorrect to stand up and say, "no there aren't two sides." Very few people in the university or the world of the media will openly make that claim. And yet few - if any - of them would say, child abuse is a good thing because it shows children in the most intimate way possible how much they are truly loved by uncle Harry.

They know that is ridiculous. But, when we speak of Holocaust denial we are talking about something with equally little credence. Yet in this arena there is a tendency to want to see two sides to this issue. I wish to make it very clear that I am not arguing against the right of deniers to say whatever they want to say. I am not arguing that they should be denied their freedom of speech. I am arguing that we are not obligated to provide them with a platform, whether it be space in a student newspaper or podium on campus or op-ed columns in general newspapers. Nor am I arguing that there is no room for discussion and debate when teaching about the Holocaust.

At a conference such as this one to make this point -- that there is room for debate when teaching about the Holocaust -- is the equivalent of bringing coals to Newcastle. You will hear talks today with different points of view. Most of us, no doubt, when we teach our courses on the Holocaust raise a myriad of questions. This past week I taught about *Judenrat*, the Jewish Council. I raised the question whether what they did was a form of collaboration or not. I feel it definitely was not. But, I wanted the students to struggle with this issue. What about Chaim Rumkowski? How do we evaluate -- not judge -- what he did. Another much debated area is the American response. Can we say America failed to do "enough?" How *can* we make that judgment? How *do* we make that judgment? When teaching about resistance there are also a myriad of questions to be considered. What constitutes resistance? How do we define resistance? Is armed resistance in the same category as artistic resistance?

There are no simple answers. But our students must leave our classrooms with more questions -- different questions -- than they walked into the classroom with. They must understand that as regards certain aspects of the Holocaust there are not absolute answers, e.g. why did one person become a killer and another refuse to become one? Why was one person willing to rescue and another not? The point is not to stifle questions. Certainly, the point is not to do what the deniers, in their most recent ads, have been accusing me of doing. In an ad attacking the museum in Washington they also attack me. If one is known by the company they keep, the deniers have put me in very good company. The ad reads,

> Deborah Lipstadt argues in her much praised Denying the Holocaust that revisionists ("deniers") should not be debated because there can not be another side to the Holocaust story. She tried to say that it is hateful to

listen to a defense of those accused of mass murder. In essence, she argues that we bury America's old civil virtues of free inquiry and open debate but to what end. But, the Deborah Lipstadts, and there is a clique of them on every campus, worked to suppress revisionist research and demand that students and faculty ape their fascist behavior. If you refuse to accept the Lipstadt clique as your intellectual Führers, you risk being branded as an anti-semite.

Free inquiry is to be encouraged. Denial of historical truth is not. Open debate about many aspects of the Holocaust is healthy, e.g., was it unique? Was it uniquely German? Outright misinterpretation and falsification of data, which is what deniers do, is not.

Why have deniers managed to confuse significant portions of the media as well as many of our students as to what and who they are? To some degree what we are dealing with is a result of the lowest common denominator of deconstructionism. I do not want to suggest in any way that deconstructionists are latent deniers. Of course not. But the atmosphere in which denial has festered and grown is one which has been shaped in measure by deconstructionism. Students understand deconstructionism to claim that any interpretation of data has some validity. If it is my opinion it must be heard. There is room for all views and all opinions, however unsupported they are by historical data. I am not suggesting when students ask how we evaluate the veracity of certain testimony or how do we know something is true that they should be shunted aside. I think if a student has had his or her judgment blurred by deniers and or revisers, it is our responsibility to address the confusion. It is crucial that students be shown how we know what we know. What scares me is I have had students come into my classroom and say, "How do we know the Diary of Anne Frank isn't bull? How do we know there really were gas chambers?" There is nothing wrong with the questions in and of themselves. But in many cases, unbeknownst to the students, these questions are informed by Holocaust deniers. How do we answer our students' questions?

We must show them the written documentation. We must demonstrate to them how testimony is evaluated for its historical accuracy and how artifacts are determined to be genuine. They also must be taught that some conclusions we once thought to be true we know are not true, e.g., the numbers of the victims at Auschwitz. They also must be taught that the intellectual process is rooted in the constant re-evaluation of previous findings based on new information. So, too, with the Holocaust. But ultimately they must understand that we debate much about it but not whether it happened. That would be the equivalent of the scholar of ancient Rome debating whether the Roman Empire ever existed or the French historian proving that there really was a French Revolution. In the academic arena there have been those who have interpreted this stance as inconsistent with the free pursuit of ideas for which the academy stands. This reflects a failure to understand both the absurdity of Holocaust denial and the nature of the academy. It reflects the moral relativism prevalent on many campus and in society at large. The misguided notion that everyone's point of view is of equal stature has created an atmosphere that not only allows Holocaust denial, but of all sorts of assaults on truth and memory, to fester and to grow.

Meanwhile the deniers claim they are not antisemites, they are only after the truth. They protest, "we are not deniers, we are revisers." But they are not revisers, because they are not revising anything, they are denying. In truth, all historians are revisers. We look for new information which will either revise or confirm our notions of history. Let me offer you an example. Much of history, certainly Jewish history, even history of the Holocaust, is the history of what happened to men. Most of the time when we talk about victims we are talking about the experience of the male victim. How does the experience of the female victim differ? Does it differ? How, when we add that into the mix, does it revise our understanding of the experience of the victims? How, when we enter in the new documentation coming out of the former Soviet Union, does it revise our understanding of what happened? That is revising.

The deniers, on the other hand, are not revising, they are simply denying. One of the tactics they have used to win not only attention but also acceptance is by dressing themselves up in sheep's clothing, i.e. they have discarded the externals of neo-Nazism. They eschew the swastika, skinheads, and leather jackets. They try to avoid inflammatory language. They hold pseudo-academic conferences - and publish pseudo-academic journals. Jewish tradition teaches "al tis-takel ba-kan-kan, ella be'mah sh'yesh bo." Don't look at the container, look at what is inside the container. What is inside the container is traditional antisemitism and neo-Nazism. Many of you remember David Duke. When David Duke was the grand wizard of the Ku Klux Klan nobody paid him any attention. When he threw away KKK garb and adopted a suit and tie we saw him on CNN, we saw him on Nightline. On these shows he was treated as a reasonable political voice. The problem was that he was saying the exact same thing that he had said before, but the packaging was different. This is what contemporary neo-Nazis and the extreme right have figured out: take that old hatred and package it in a new form and we will confuse people. Much of what we are seeing today on the campaign trail in the United States, affirms this strategy. Hannah Arendt in "Truth and politics" observed:

> Facts inform opinions and opinions inspired by different interests and passions can differ widely and still be legitimate as long as they respect factual truth. Freedom of opinion is a farce unless factual information is guaranteed and the facts themselves are not in dispute.

In any cultural debate, there is a liminal threshold between fact and opinion, but the spectrum of that debate does not include falsehood, however sincerely one may subscribe to it. One can firmly believe that Elvis Presley is alive and well and living in Minneapolis. However strong one's conviction does not make it a legitimate "other side" of the debate. In the name of free inquiry, we should not succumb to the simplistic view, as the media so often does, that every idea is of equal validity and worth.

I want to just close by making a few observations on the actual impact of Holocaust deniers. I do not want to stand here and "Shrie gevalt" or cry wolf as it is translated into English. The deniers, as of now, have had relatively little direct impact in convincing people that the Holocaust did not happen. In fact, speaking of Elvis Presley, there are probably more people in the United States who think Elvis Presley is alive and well than who believe the Holocaust did not happen. So, why the fuss? Why the concern?

Our worries are not about today. They are about a generation or two from now. For those of you with little children, grandchildren, nieces, nephews at home - little ones - when those little ones are old enough to sit in our classrooms on university campuses, when they are old enough to go to conferences like this there won't be anyone around to say "this is what happened to me, this is my story." That the absence of personal witnesses makes a crucial difference. I am reminded, and I have written about this, of two cousins of mine who grew up in Cincinnati. One is about fifteen years older than I am and one is seventeen years older than I am. There was an elderly gentleman who did odd jobs for their parents. They remember him well to this day. His name was Charlie Washington. They remember him for two reasons. He was very old and walked in a bent over fashion. I guess today we would recognize that he suffered from osteoporosis. He walked with a shuffle and, as little children, they had never seen something like this. But, more importantly, they remember Charlie Washington, because Charlie Washington had been born a slave on a plantation. And, Charlie Washington taught them slave songs. Charlie Washington had some friends that he introduced them to who also taught them songs of slaves. So, to these two cousins fifteen and seventeen years older than I, the Civil War and the history of slavery are not something from the mid-nineteenth century. For me, no matter how important I recognize them to be in the history of this country and at the root of some of the social problems that still exist in this country, as events they are from over 100 years ago. For my cousins, this is Charlie's story. And, nobody is attacking Charlie's story as not true. Take the Holocaust, which is so much more unbelievable than slavery. If you factor in the attacks on it and add our distance from the event and you can see how much more historically vulnerable it is.

I would like to close by reading to you a short quote from Camus in the Plague, which some of you may know was written in the town of Le Chambon. In the final paragraphs of the novel when the plague has been vanquished and the people are rejoicing, Camus writes about Rieux, the Plague's hero:

> ...He knew (Rieux knew) that the tale he had to tell could not be one of final victory. It could be only the record of what had to be done, and what assuredly would have to be done again in the never ending fight against terror and its relentless onslaughts, ... And, indeed as he listened to the cries of joy rising from the town, Rieux remembered that such joy is always imperiled. He knew what those jubilant crowds did not know but could have learned from books: that the plague bacillus never dies or disappears for good; that it can lie dormant for years and years in furniture and linen-chests; that it bides its time in bedrooms, cellars, trunks, and bookshelves; (...) and that perhaps the day would come when it roused up its rats again and sent them forth to die in a happy city.

In the 1930s the Germans spread a virulent new form of antisemitism that resulted in the destruction of millions. Today, those who died and those who barely survived are threatened a second time as the deniers try to destroy the world's memories of them and of their experiences. Those who are attempting to do so will continue their battle long after the last survivor has gone to her or his heavenly rest. We must fight this plague of hatred. We must remain ever vigilant for prejudice is exceedingly tenacious and truth and memory exceedingly fragile.

Thank you very much.

Chapter 8

POST HOLOCAUST JEWISH GERMAN DIALOGUE: FACE TO FACE

Hubert Locke
Abraham Peck
Gottfried Wagner

Editors' Note: The contact between Abraham J. Peck, Director of the American Jewish Archives, and Gottfried Wagner, great-grandson of Richard Wagner began at the Annual Scholars Conference in 1991 and grew into a public discourse at several Scholars' Conferences and at the 1994 Berlin "Remembering for the Future II" conference. The 1996 discussion in Minneapolis was moderated by Hubert Locke. Speakers are identified by their initials. Because of audio difficulties we could not include the Q & A period which followed the initial discussion.

[HL]: In 1992, at the annual meeting of this conference in Seattle, a most unusual event took place. The two men who are with me on the dias began a dialogue with one another. A dialogue which grows out of two very unusual personal histories.

Abraham Peck is the director of the American Jewish Archives at the Hebrew Union College in Cincinnati, where he is also lecturer in Judaic Studies. Dr. Peck is also managing editor of American Jewish Archives' principle scholarly journal in this field. He took his doctoral studies at Norwich in England and is author of some ten published volumes and an innumerable collection of scholarly articles, a number of which have been, in fact, delivered at this annual meeting. Dr. Peck is also the child of survivors. He was born in a displaced persons camp in Landsberg, the same Bavarian town which I am sure you will recognize as the site of the prison in which Adolf Hitler was incarcerated and where he wrote *Mein Kampf.*

Gottfried Wagner is a musicologist who, in addition to studying musicology, also studied philosophy and German literature. First in Munich and then in Nuremberg. Finally, writing his doctoral dissertation at the University of Vienna on the work of Kurt Weill, the Jewish composer. Dr. Wagner is also the great-grandson of the composer Richard Wagner and spent the first seven years of his life at the Villa Wahnfried, the Wagner estate in Bayreuth.

It is a matter of historical importance, I think, to both their histories and to the dialogue which they had begun, to observe that the paper on which Adolf Hitler wrote Mein Kampf in the prison in the town in which a Peck was born, the paper on which Mein Kampf was written in the Landsberg Prison was delivered to him by Gottfried Wagner's grandmother, Winnifred Wagner.

Gentlemen, we began this encounter five years ago. Let me begin by asking where are you now? What have your learned? What remains still unaddressed or unresolved?

[AP]:   You understand that it might be important for some of the individuals here who were not at that first encounter that we had at Stockton College in 1991 to know how, in fact, this all began. I will be very brief about it. Gottfried was invited and it was quite an event to have the great-grandson of Richard Wagner speak to this group about Wagner, his music and antisemitism and it was a very closed meeting in a sense, as there were not questions allowed, but really only written comments. And Gottfried, like the majority of Germans who deal with the question of German-Jewish relations in the present and the future, essentially ended by saying that he hoped that his contribution would be a step towards reconciliation, towards the German word Versöhnung. And, of course, I asked in my written question, well, you know, in our tradition we really feel that reconciliation can only be given by the victims and the victims obviously are not available or here to begin the process of it. And, I think he was quite taken aback by that. Because most Germans in any contact they have with Jews which has a positive light to it, turn the event into a *Schritt nach Versöhnung*, as they say, a step toward reconciliation. And, I think it made his view of what he was trying to do a different one. And from that point on, I think we both examined ourselves in terms of what has been the called the black box within children of survivors. It is a phrase the author Helen Epstein coined in 1979 with a book called, *Children of the Holocaust,*

I believe the first ever to deal with mostly American children of survivors. This black box contains all the emotions, all of the whirlwinds that indeed make up the life of survivors and their children. And I think in some respects what Gottfried and I have found is that we both carry a kind of black box within us. And although over the years we have opened it slowly, the ability to be together and to discuss this has allowed us to really open this black box to a much greater degree. Like Pandora's box, we are not sure what will emerge from this ultimately. But at this stage of our discussion I think we have focused on the most important thing that separates Jews and Germans right now. And that is the whole questions of *Familiengeschichte*, a family history. Because Jews and Germans can talk about many things, but when it comes to talking about their own family histories, and listening to them and understanding them, it is a very difficult and very painful step, especially, obviously, for the German side. And, I think that part of the black box has been opened fully, honestly, bluntly. I think it is really a step in a direction, not necessary towards *Versöhnung* because, again, I reject that term and I think Gottfried does, too. But, at least to understand that we have separate, very separate, but yet very related legacies that have been left to us by this event which in many respects has poisoned the psyches of our parents and certainly affected our humanity. And, what we seek is to allow some of that poison to perhaps not be passed onto our children (and we both have children). And, at the moment, this is the step and the position where we are, but where we need to go depends, of course, on others that join us in our Post-Holocaust-Dialogue-Group and allow other questions that perhaps we have not addressed to emerge as well. But, one thing I know is that from our discussions, from our encounter, we know that talking is not enough. That, indeed, acting on the consequences of both our legacies is the immediate step. Acting, any where, at any time, when that kind of poison again becomes a reality.

[GW]: Abraham already made a very important point on the word "reconciliation." This is just one of those words which I certainly have learned to re-discuss. Also, I need to make a critical self-analysis of my ideas in 1991 and right now, because I can tell you, before this first encounter with Abraham, in my life it was 1919. There is a little story which I really would like to talk about briefly. I was invited for the first time to Israel, to Tel Aviv University and I was asked to talk about Richard Wagner and, of course, when you are the great-grandson ... I mean in every Kibbutz in Israel there is software about Richard Wagner and it was not so interesting, also for my hosts and for those who came to my four lectures, to "repeat dates." They just wanted, in combination with my host, Professor Shmueli and all those who came, to address the question: Gottfried, what is your position now? There were three very essential points which have to do with what Abraham just said on the family history and also on general history and on finding a kind of a balance. So, there were three questions which are still very essential for me. One of the questions was then coming out of this Bayreuth situation, that is the Bayreuth festival and its founder, Richard Wagner, who was decisively co-responsible also for poisoning the culture climate in Germany with his antisemitic writings. So, what is your position? Also, what is your position in relation to what we just talked about also on Hitler and Landsberg, towards your family chronology and Hitler and what is now your position on German society after the Second World War, after Hitler, after the *Shoah*? These questions, of course, had a tremendous impact on me and so certainly the first start of re-thinking, also of finding myself, you know, in a situation where I just had thought, hopefully, that I could not resolve these kind of problems only in academic discussion, reading books; I need a kind of dialogue form. And, indeed, it was really thanks to Franklin Littell and Hubert Locke that I got this invitation to come to Stockton and indeed, after this encounter, I was asked even to give my rather personal impression of this historic first trip. And, from this day on, I was discussing reconciliation, yet every word that I was using I had to re-examine. What I had to learn was certainly to develop a much more, you know, critical sensitivity about using words. I also became aware of my personal nature, the need to talk. To have the personal experience again, for a third time in my life, to approach Jewish culture. Because, when it is all said and done, I am coming out of this place which is called one of the shrines of German culture. And this confrontation and this "working through" certainly has changed within the last five years. But, I can say, encouraged, by Abraham, by our group, by Franklin Littell, by Hubert Locke, I have worked through this with all its consequences. It has allowed me to finish writing a kind of autobiographical book with all its consequences, all of my personal responsibility; also, risking in a certain way to live even more in isolation on the German side -- whereas I feel rather in a beautiful way integrated in the different Jewish and other communities all over the world, I am ever more disintegrated with regard to German society. Those are some of the major points of the last five years.

[HL]: Gentlemen, you both speak of family history and the gulf, the dividing line in communication between Jewish and German people today. It strikes me that much of the conversation that does take place, between those two communities, is cast in terms of victim and victimizer. I sense in your dialogue with one another, you are moving beyond those categories. Can you talk about that? Is that a fair appraisal of where you are?

[AP]: I certainly think we are. Note, this issue is far from settled. Look, you know, when the Jews of Spain were expelled in 1492, whether it was true or not, supposedly, Rabbinic authorities placed a ban, a Rabbinic *Cherem* on Spain for 500 years and it was just lifted recently with the 500th anniversary of the expulsion. This is fifty years after the event. And I don't think that we are in any situation yet where we are ready to say we are at a point where we can say to Germans, let bygones be bygones, we are now ready to begin anew. There is too much pain and there is too much anger. And, of course, what is shocking, perhaps, is that that community that perhaps had the least involvement in the events of the Holocaust, of the *Shoah*, that is to say American Jewry is probably still the most intransigent Jewish community in the world with regard to activities and relations with Germany and things German. So, while Gottfried and I, in our own ways, move closer towards understanding who we are and what issues we need to address, that is hardly the case with the majority of Jews in this country and probably anywhere. The pain, the trauma of having a civilization, millennia destroyed, a language destroyed, a culture destroyed is not something that you suddenly put aside in your own mind, in your own daily understanding of who you are as a Jew after fifty years. And I don't think it works the same way, or any differently, I should say, on the other side. So, while we understand what our purpose really is, perhaps to be some kind of a symbol to other groups in conflict -- and there are so many of them, God knows, throughout our world -- to at least say to them, look we have been there. We understand, in the triteness of this phrase, your pain, but we also understand that there is a possibility for hope and for dialogue. If we can emerge with some kind of sign or symbol for those groups in conflict that, while there always will be pain and that, while memory is developed and interpreted by both groups in their own particular way, there is some kind of a common ground, some kind of an effort to say, ultimately, there will be a generation born that will understand fully what has gone on before in terms of working through this conflict. And that ultimately perhaps those two generations can begin some kind of a new relationship and I think that is where we want to head, but at the same time, trust me, there is so much pain, bitterness, anger, shame, guilt, repression on the part of Germans and Jews, that we have only begun to touch the surface of these issues. But, I am proud to say, at least, that I played some minor role in being able to do this and there are others who also feel this way, even though it is not a popular type of activity, I think it is one that is extremely necessary.

[HL]: Gottfried?

[GW]: And, with that, of course, actually Abraham has given the essence also of my opinion. Of course, the question also includes the issue of the resistance of being a minority and being confronted with the majority and, all of a sudden, we have sometimes turned to my own situation, even risking for certain, or again getting through periods of isolation. But, for the two of us, it is not enough just to write papers. That context does not in itself bring about change. Instead, we try out a personal dialogue. For example, one of the things we are just crying out for is not to read our papers, but to be more spontaneous. We certainly have worked very seriously on chronology and history and we are, so to speak, rather well prepared, but these moments of spontaneous reaction also help us find all the responsibilities of new ways of communication; "acting out" in that sense also means again to resist in a stronger way the fixed opinions of majorities, including also in a really sometimes doubtful way the opinion of majorities in the media. So, fighting cliches with that is really sometimes a tough work in progress.

[HL]: Let me interrupt our conversation long enough to assure those of you in the audience that you will have opportunity also to join in this conversation, but I wonder for the moment if we can explore or examine this minority theme a bit further. You both are representatives of the post-*Shoah* generation of Jews and Germans and certainly common to both experiences is the discovery of what it means to be different, to grow up, Abe, in your instance, in a home without grandparents, without aunts and uncles. In your case Gottfried, to grow up in a home with parents who refused to speak of or to confront their immediate past. These experiences, it strikes me, speak to the painful internalities of what it means to be different. What about the externalities of that experience? What does it mean, for example, to be "the other" whose experience is atypical and unpleasant; and it seems to me an appendage to that question that you both were also minorities within minorities. That is to say, you both seek in this dialogue acceptance and recognition of an idea or a responsibility which is still not widely accepted by both of your communities. Can you speak to those issues for a moment?

[AP]: When I was growing up, I had a very interesting experience as I look back on being the child of Holocaust survivors because the event essentially permeated every aspect of my family's private and public existence. I can not remember a time when I was growing up that my father did not speak of his experiences. My days and nights were filled with stories of ghettos and camps with images of sadistic SS men, camp doctors, who really in a sense were much more real to me than the shadowed figures of my murdered aunts and uncles. Who had names, but little else to tell me about how they lived and how they died. And there was in my family a very deep and uncontrolled anger that directed the lives of both my parents and into the broader American society. Like many survivors, they felt themselves the victims of a conspiracy of silence carried out by non-survivors who couldn't or wouldn't listen to their tales of starvations and beatings and gassings and crematoria. And I am certain that my father, in his efforts to tell these stories to anybody he came upon, neighbors, co-workers, teenage friends of mine who would look at me in bewilderment, as in what is he saying to us, was trying to carry out a kind of survivor mission. To tell those who hadn't looked over the abysses as he and his fellow survivors had that if they understood what awaited them when this madness would ever begin again, that they had to do something to check it. That they needed to understand that. And, when people told him to stop, they didn't understand or they didn't want to listen, they told him that Americans too had suffered because after all certain foods had been rationed in America during this time. Well, he would explode and accuse that individual with a statement that many survivors have used, "Where were you and the other Americans when my brothers and sisters were burning in the crematoria?" And, of course, he was especially incensed when American Jews complained of food shortages during their years in World War II. And, of course, I think I had my own anger and inability to fit in with part of that experience. I could not relate to my American-Jewish friends whose grandparents would pick them up from school, whose uncles and aunts would join them at the Passover seder, when our holidays were always memories of those who were no longer there and indeed of the events that were a part of my every being. In a way then, it was very fortunate that I had a chance to be angry in a community where anger was a very interesting commodity. Because in their wisdom, the people who brought us from Germany in the year of 1949, the Jewish authorities put us into the middle of an African-American community. And, I was surrounded by human beings who also shared an anger and I saw the effort of survival on the part of a people living in a racist society and so that other category, I think, was doubly reinforced by knowing that I fit in better with the anger of the African-American community than I did with the optimism of American Jewish life and therefore, during my years in high school, I joined the NAACP. In college, I participated in black liberation movements. Not as a denial of my own Jewish identity, that was still very strong. But, in a sense perhaps that, if my parents' suffering was going to mean anything, it was to allow the world to know the phrase "never again." But not in the way American Jews simply did it by using placards to say never again to us. But, indeed, what I think survivors in those early months and years understood in the mission of the survivors (and of course, Yehuda Bauer and some of his students have written about those early days of the survivors) was that it really was a mission that really said never again for anyone, anywhere. And I really never understood that until we began to look at the sources at the Yiddish writings of the newspapers and letters of the camps. But, I think, early on I felt that - and I think early on a lot of other survivor children felt that in this country because so many of them have gone into the helping professions - there is that agenda that they may not be fully aware of, but that perhaps permeates a message that was, of course, thrown out and refused to be accepted by those that I think survivors were genuinely trying to affect in those early years of their arrival in this country. But, you know, the survivors ultimately stopped talking because no one would listen. So, I think that, and certainly other status attributes affected me. I have never felt fully comfortable in an American Jewish environment because, indeed, my parents were the other and I was the other. And, I think it has directed a good part of my life.

[GW]: I faced an atypical situation as far as externalities are concerned in a completely different way: when I personally grew up in a biotechnical environment which was certainly also in the 50s again a rather eminent social meeting point for West Germans, especially for West German society, I saw myself also confronted with two positions towards the Wagner family. There were all the other Nazi Wagners which I, Gottfried, am part of and, on the other side, one is a kind of *Wunderkind*. You know, this kind of extreme position certainly wherein it is not easily to grow up, constitutes a very unbalanced approach to a child whose trust is developing. So, this I certainly did not. This was a situation in itself, let's say, rather difficult, but it became cruel, more difficult by being confronted with a film documentary at the age of nine on Nazi Germany and that film indeed was again a very public thing; I am not telling here only private family stories. The film included also my family with Adolf Hitler in Bayreuth and also at the Bayreuth Festival. From this point, this was at the age of nine years, I do not think in a relatively normal development that you, as a child, would ask your parents what was going on; first of all, of course, my father and in one of the typical, let's say this *is* typical German attitudes when it came to this point he said, no, you don't have the age. I had heard that before because there was the American officer club and I had asked what they were doing on our property. It took quite a while to finally get some answers from an adult, also a teacher, who was then called, of course, a dirty communist in my family. He was a normal decent social democrat, I think, rather conservative, and a social democrat in the fifties was certainly no danger to the starting economic boom in West German society. It is also rather interesting that, even when I personally developed more in the direction of being an active leftist, I also was not accepted by the left in German society. Oh, what is that? He is now engaged in that? What is his purpose? That means, finding yourself. I mean having a clear position about the Nazi Germany of the past. Having chosen Kurt Weill, a Jewish left liberal, as a dissertation topic, was just the kind a very clear signal: I want to go in this direction. Eventually I left Germany, but becoming accepted by the German left was certainly rather difficult. And so, overcoming these types of strange isolation certainly also brought me here, to really look for answers which I found later in Jewish communities in New York. Those parents and grandparents who at least tried to give me some answers to my question. But this took until I had come in my twenties. So, that is a little bit of the other situation.

[HL]: One final question, gentlemen. You both embarked on a journey which it is quite clear from your comments, your respective fathers would not approve. And I suppose that raises for us the question of your own responsibility as fathers. What are the stories you will pass on to your children? What are the stories that the second generation should pass on to that which is to follow? Abe, you have said that one has to avoid passing along the poison to your children. What is it that you will say to them about this history and this experience?

[AP]:   I think that, first of all, what I have tried to do with Gottfried (this is sort of a preamble to your question) is to make him understand at the most basic level my question that I think is echoed in the minds and hearts of all Jews. Do you understand what you have done? Not, indeed, carried out by some clique of fanatics acting in the name of a German nation, a phrase that eased your burden for so many years, but by ordinary men and women at the front, in the ghettos and the camps who joined for pleasure or conviction in the murder of millions. Do you understand? When that question can be asked and answered to my satisfaction, to Gottfried's and I think to the German consciences' satisfaction, then perhaps there will come a time when we can each release a kind of a communal primal scream, then I think it will be time to move on. To forge a kind of symbiosis that goes beyond what Professor Dan Diner talked about as a negative symbiosis, a victim and victimizer into a joint effort to overcome this awful burden. This awful legacy which, as I have already mentioned, twisted the psyches of my parents, their generation and poisoned, I think, both your humanity and mine. My father is 83 years old. My mother died in 1988. You are right. What I do will never be enough for him. Indeed, no amount of museums or memorials will ever change the fact that he has to go to bed at night and deal with his nightmares and his memories. But, I will tell my children the stories that I heard from my father when I was growing up and of course, as I have told you, I was a very willing and captive small audience. They were stories of how ordinary men and women became possessed by an evil that poisoned their very souls. Doctors, engineers, military leaders all devoted to cleansing the earth of lives unworthy of life. My father told me things about them. How they thought and what they felt. Things that I really still have not read or heard anywhere else. I heard of the destruction of the Sinti and Rroma camp in the Lodz ghetto. My father lived only a few hundred yards away, when the so-called gypsy camp, writhe with disease, was set ablaze. I learned at a very young age of the other victims of Nazi brutality, ideology, political prisoners, gays, communists, Russian prisoners of war. I knew them all along before they merited study. And, I think I will also pass on to my children the lessons that my father asked me to draw from his sufferings -- the place of Jews in the world, the role of Christian antisemitism and the Holocaust, those few who sought to help Jews and the many more who did not. I will never forget hearing my father tell my mother how relieved he felt coming back into our African-American neighborhood. The sight of black faces relaxed him. The sight of white police officers frightened him and brought those memories back to the fore. What can justify the suffering of my parents? The loss of my family? The "other" status among my own community? Well, I think, perhaps the realization that Gottfried and I want to achieve with this dialogue that we are now in our fifth year of and want to achieve with our group. So, Hubert, my father doesn't approve of my dialogue. He thinks it is too little and too late. But, I know that in his own life he has sought to carry forward a message not unlike the one that Gottfried and I seek to share with all of you. He was quickly disillusioned I think by a world unwilling to listen. And, I guess my prayer for myself and my children is that we do not share his fate.

[GW]: To continue the question as to what I should give, in the context of my situation, towards the next generation, towards my own son, certainly, it is extremely difficult for me because of the need to recreate myself and my own identity which is certainly the result of a very critical self-analysis. What it means to be, coming out of this family? What is being a German? What it means to be also coming from originally a Lutheran church community? These questions certainly, in my case, had to be rethought and reconstructed in a new way. But, and now comes the point, also for me the major sense out of all of this was the dialogue with Abraham. For me, having been part of this dialogue is, of course, of the greatest importance, even in re-examining and re-putting questions which are now the questions of my son. Because he is now in that very difficult situation as a result of what was going on before. My son does not even know his grandfather and probably he never will know him because there is this shadow of the past. And, how to explain that to him, now that he is eleven years. How, in that moment, can I confront him? He has just been confronted now for the first time with the Holocaust. So, doing this step by step after what happened can really split up families. It is not possible to have a normal continuity of grandfather, son and grandson and it is certainly a rather painful experience for me to note, in my explanation to my son, that this has to do with a certain thing on the other side. Also, talking about these matters, in my case, means I really do tell him things, carefully, because I don't want to provide him with a shock situation.

But, as in Abraham's situation, doing so makes me realize there is sometimes no chance for continuation. We have to concentrate with my son (who himself comes from Rumania, as you know, an adopted child) and myself to be very active, to be very concrete, even, if you know, we can not build up -- we really have to start at zero, to build up our own human orientation. And, so this is certainly a completely different situation. There is always pointing to the past and hopefully, then, to a more active future, that always active future.

[HL]:   Gentlemen, thank you both. We admire and respect you and we encourage you on a journey which is important to all of us.

Chapter 9

THE CRYSTAL OF MEMORY OR THE SMOKE OF REMEMBRANCE?

Elisabeth Maxwell

The title I have chosen for this paper is symbolic at many levels and was inspired by reading the work of the physician and biologist, Professor Henri Atlan of Paris and Jerusalem universities, for whom the words "crystal" and "smoke" contrast the logic of chemical formation and the chaos of the Holocaust. The word "crystal" alludes to the natural formation of rock crystal; it reproduces forms with perfect shapes and sharp contours and is governed by geological order. "Smoke" on the other hand, lies at the opposite end of the spectrum; it has the most indeterminate shape, infinitely varied, unpredictable and unique at any given time. It represents the arbitrary, touches the realm of the imaginary, represents chaos and, within the context of my paper, has other symbolic allusions that will become clear.

Although I married a true child of *Mitteleuropa Yiddishkeit*, it was not until years after our wedding, when our seven children no longer needed my daily care, and my husband's career allowed me to return to personal study and research, that I became fully aware of what the world had lost through the destruction of European Jewry. When in 1978 we traveled in search of my husband's roots to his native village, a *shteltl* of some 2,000 Jews, formerly in Czechoslovakia, not a single Jew was to be found. In the cemetery, there were no commemorative tombstones of the period. What had happened to all these people? All gone up in smoke? Alas! Yes, literally.

It was there that I came face to face with he appalling reality that, with the exception of two sisters and a few cousins, three generations of my husband's family had been wiped out, murdered, in Auschwitz on the orders of the German government. To rescue these innocent and unfortunate people from oblivion, people whom the world would otherwise forget, became my sacred duty, my secular Kaddish. It was my prayer for the dead, a lament in memory of a family my husband had loved, and who had died before he could tell them so. That was only the beginning of a long process of remembrance and atonement.

As a Christian, I entered what was for me a "forbidden territory," through the little door of Elie Wiesel's book, *Souls on Fire*. The story of the Baal Shem Tov and his Hasidic followers was the catalyst that led me into another world, another civilization, a new understanding of my husband and his kin, and an infinite compassion and nostalgia for his lost world. I cried with him over the loss of his family. I had entered the world of the Holocaust.

I do not need to reiterate the complex economic, sociological and political reasons which let to the foundation of the Nazi party by Hitler, nor analyze the content of *Mein Kampf*.[1] Nazi obsession with the Jews and the concept of Jews as evil rested on a long western European tradition of regarding the Jew as evil outsiders. For 1,700 years, Jews had been the objects of scorn and contempt in Europe, a socially manufactured pariah people, and the foundations of their social status were already laid down in the New Testament. Within the pages of the Gospels themselves and in later church writings, Jews are portrayed as hypocrites, evil schemers, vipers, and murderers of the Messiah.

To this religious component were added the theories of racism and eugenics en vogue since the 19th century after Darwin's work on the survival of the fittest, and that of Gobineau concerning superior and inferior races. The symbol of the Jew as quintessential evil was used to elevate the struggle between Aryan and Jew from the racial or national level to the moral plane. The exorcism of Jews from Aryan society could be conceived not only as a racial or historical need, but an ethical imperative. This reasoning opened the way for a new ethic to be established and accepted as the governing norm of a state bureaucracy. Anti-Judaism, its central concept, was the foundation for all that was to follow.

The eradication of the Jewish population from German was not a matter of spontaneous hatred or blind rage, but a carefully defined and deliberately administered social program which relied on a dedicated bureaucracy for its implementation. Legal experts were available to draw up definitions, formulate regulations and write field manuals; police officers were trained to handle the arrests; finance officials gained professional expertise in managing the complex problems of deed and title transfers. The professionalism of the modern bureaucratic state allowed the implementation of program of social segregation and genocide to appear routine, orderly and legally correct. Edgar Faure, assistant prosecutor at the international tribunal of Nuremberg, demonstrated convincingly that the German Reich had built up a veritable "criminal public service," which organized its murderous acts with an administrative machinery and efficiency that other states might use to ensure the regular functioning of government. What we observe is not a nation which had run totally amok, but on the contrary a well-regulated society operating consciously according to a particular ethic.

Furthermore, as territorial conquests took place, the whole procedure was then applied to Austria, Czechoslovakia and Poland. Similarly, deportation of the Jews was carried out throughout western Europe (where by and large all the governments cooperated) from Belgium, the Netherlands, France, Norway, as well as the Balkans, Hungary, Romania, Yugoslavia and Bulgaria. After the invasion of Russia and the acquisition of Russian territories, new policies had to be put in place to deal with the 3 million Jews concentrated in the East. When the German armies raced across the Russian border on June 22, 1941, they were accompanied by the specially organized killing units of the *Einsatzgruppen*, known euphemistically as the "special units," and some of the worst atrocities of the war were carried out there. From records of the killings kept by the German units themselves, it is estimated that 2,350,000 Jews were murdered, mostly within a few days of the arrival of the Nazis and SS forces. Forced to dig their own graves, long narrow pits, Jews were ordered to undress, pile up their clothes neatly, stand naked near the edge and were then shot down with rifles or machine guns.

Such massacres resulted from Hitler's decision taken in March 1941 and communicated to a circle of high-ranking Nazi officers, concerning the annihilation of the Jewish people, whom the Nazis considered as "non-human vermin or disease-carrying people,"[2] "germs whose very existence posed a threat to the health of the German master race."[3] Statements made at their trails by Rudolf Hoess, commandant at Auschwitz, and Adolf Eichmann, the high-ranking officer in charge of deportation, prove that in July and August 1941, Heinrich Himmler and Heydrich had received the "go ahead" from Hitler himself. This is further substantiated by a letter from Himmler to Gauleiter Greiser, in whose area the infamous Lodz ghetto was situated. The letter began with the words: "The Führer wishes the Altreich and the Protectorate to be cleared of and freed from Jews from West to East as soon as possible."[4]

The plan to exterminate the Jewish people was detailed at the Wannsee conference, called by Goering on January 20, 1942 and chaired by Heydrich. The fifteen men who gathered around the table of the elegant villa for their 85-minute meeting (interrupted on several occasions by light refreshments and drinks) included high-level functionaries from the SS, the SD, the Gestapo, the Ministry of the Interior, the Ministry of Justice, the Foreign Office, the party Chancellery, the Reich Chancellery and Ministry of the Occupied Territories. They decided there on the orders of Himmler, who transmitted the "wishes of the Führer," to perpetrate the genocide of the Jewish people. Under the mask of geniality, old-boy friendship and *gemütlich* atmosphere, the most chilling discussion imaginable took place, sealing the fate of millions of Jews. Although they later tried to destroy all traces of the written evidence of this meeting, one copy of the Wannsee Conference protocol survived. It represents inescapable evidence of the bureaucratic mass murder of an entire people.

The American scholar, Peter Haas,[5] who researched the bureaucratic aspect of the Holocaust in depth, believes that

> sometime in 1941 or 1942 an important psychological barrier was crossed. The exact time and place cannot be defined. The change did not hit everyone at the same time. But the *Einsatzgruppen* indicate that something had radically altered, and that the unthinkable was now fully conceivable as a policy. A whole civilization, virtually a whole continent, was enmeshed in a new ethic of racial warfare.

As the French film director Claude Lanzmann wrote,

> Between the conditions that allowed the extermination and the actual extermination, there is a solution of continuity, a hiatus, a leap, there is an abyss.[6]

It was then that the descent into the abyss started, and the commandment "Thou shalt not kill" became in the new Nazi ethic "Thou shalt kill."

Undeniable proof of atrocities is to be found in the Nuremberg trial exhibits and transcripts, the trial transcripts of Adolf Eichmann, the working diaries of Hans Frank, General Governor of the central part of occupied Poland, and of Joseph Bühler, head of the General Government of Poland. These diaries and transcripts give clear evidence that the leaders fully understood what they were doing. Like most of the influential SS officers tried at Nuremberg, Joseph Goebbels acknowledged in his journal that what they were undertaking was the indiscriminate killing of the Jews. Himmler himself was especially explicit in several confidential talks preserved in the shorthand records of his secretaries. He was obliged to explain his position clearly:

> The following question has been asked of us: What is to be done with the women and children? There also, I have found an obvious solution: I did not feel that I have the right to exterminate the men and let the children grow up to avenge themselves on our children and our descendants. It is become necessary to make the grave decision to cause this people to disappear from the earth.

And he added, "Keep that to yourselves."[7]

The documentary sources, including both official archives and private records, are very comprehensive. Nazi antisemitism was no secret. The Nazis' early persecution (from 1933 to 1939) was conducted openly and fully reported in the German and foreign press. There are also the published texts of Nazi laws and decrees, legal and business records, as well as books, magazines, leaflets and films disseminated by the Nazis. A huge quantity of German documents provide proof that the Final Solution was a goal of the Nazi war machine. Further evidence is to be found in the testimonies of Gauleiters (heads of Nazi administrative districts), in the memoirs and statements of Rudolf Hoess, as well as in the transcripts of genocide trials held before Polish Courts: those of some 50 SS officers from Auschwitz, hangmen from the remnants of the Warsaw and Lodz ghettos or concentration and death camp commanders; or similarly in Hoess's testimony of Himmler's orders regarding the construction of gas chambers. Numerous Nazi propaganda films have survived, as well as public and private photographic records and personal diaries and letters written by German soldiers and officers. The industrial drawings and specifications for the crematoria at Auschwitz are also available, along with orders for spare parts and demands for repairs, complaints of malfunctioning and subsequent replies. Multiple transport documents remain, specifying the quantity of the "cargo" and the number of "pieces" transported, together with receipts for the completed deliveries and return of the empty cattle cars. In his film, *Shoah*, Lanzman describes these documents known as *Fahrplananordnung* as he holds one in his hand.

From these archives there emerges an indisputable account of a remorseless systematic plan to annihilate an entire people. Sources of this kind offer crystal-clear evidence of the facts of the Holocaust. But should we be content with this kind of documentation alone? Where does the "smoke of remembrance" come in?

Some eight years ago, I was invited to speak at a conference in Paris, shortly after the trial in Lyon of Klaus Barbie, the man commonly called the "Butcher of Lyon." It was the first French trial for crimes against humanity. This was the year when France had at long last made its *mea culpa* and tried to look with some honesty at its murky past under Nazi occupation. Shortly before the trial started, then prime minister Jacques Chirac took the decision that all French schoolchildren would be given a one-hour lesson on the Holocaust. It was also at this period that Lanzmann's film was given its first showing. Kept on ice for two years because no television channel had the courage to show it, it was finally forced into the light of day. It was the combination of these three factors which finally highlighted all the work that was being done on the Holocaust: the steady research of French scholars, the courageous work of people like Serge and Beate Klarsfeld to unearth the truth, and public discussions on the ambivalent attitude of Vichy France. Conferences were then organized, articles appeared more often in the press, books began to be published on the subject in greater numbers, and a past which was already 50 years old was given a new lease of life; perhaps for the last time, the shroud of history was torn away from Nazi crimes. The Holocaust had been reimposed on the conscience of a nation.

It was one of these ensuing conferences that I was asked to address and its title was particularly appropriate: *De la Génération du Souvenir à la Génération de la Mémoire* (From the Generation of Remembrance to the Generation of Memory). The French language has two words to translate the concept of memory: one is "le souvenir," the remembrance of what one has experienced; the other is "la mémoire," the remembrance of what one has read or learned. As far as the Holocaust is concerned, the generation of "le souvenir" will very soon have passed away and only the generations of "la mémoire" will remain. This is precisely the reason why I am concerned about our responsibility as educators and what message we will pass on to future generations who will only know of the Holocaust through what they have read in print or seen in films or on television. It is our duty to pass on a history which is as close to reality as possible, a history strong enough to resist the undermining attempts of the deniers or disinformers.

The unmasking of civilization by the events of 1933 to 1945 are among the most painful features of that time for those of us who live after that period. We can no longer regard ourselves as cultured and civilized because in our time these things were done at Auschwitz. As Christian Meier said, "It was a completely new type of crime against the rank and file of mankind."[8]

All historical consciousness should start from the premise that no attempt be made to deny or merely suppress what has taken place. As Alexander Donat, a well-known survivor, wrote in his book, *The Holocaust Kingdom*, "everything depends on who transmits and who writes the history of this period,"[9] and it is therefore an obligation to listen to the survivors themselves. It is not sufficient to base our knowledge on written evidence; we must question the victims, the bystanders and perpetrators. It is offensive in the extreme to have the deniers claim that the "tales" of the survivors must be discarded as unreliable. Should we simply ignore any oral tradition when such has served us so well for thousands of years as a cornerstone of civilization's advance?

The gathering of oral evidence, however, has not been an easy task. For many years after the war, people would just not listen to the victims; they either felt ashamed or simply did not want to hear such nauseating tales. For their part, the survivors wanted to forget the trauma that had shattered their lives, forget about death and get on with living. They tried to rebuild their lives and by and large succeeded; above all, they tried to protect their children from all knowledge of the horrors they had to endure. It took their grandchildren to start them talking again, and now, alas, in most cases, in the words of George Clare, "we waited too long. It is too late now to search for lost parents."[10]

For many years, the world refused to believe a massacre was in progress and just after the war, when the full tragedy emerged, survivors' accounts were greeted with incredulity. The historian Isaac Schiffer perceived this malaise clearly while he was still in Majdanek and asked himself:

> Who will listen to our tales? No one will believe us because our curse is that of the whole civilized world. It will be our thankless task to prove to a world which refuses to hear that we are Abel, the murdered brother.[11]

Why is it so vitally important to collect these testimonies before time runs out? Are we right to assume that we can still gather information from the sometimes hazy recollections of people who are now getting quite old? It is a tragic fact that only the smoke which rose from crematoria chimneys or the blood which oozed from eastern pits could tell us the ultimate agony of millions of people. Yet it is an affront to common sense to deny the importance of the cumulative effect and cross-verifiable consistency of the personal testimonies and contemporaneous documents emanating from survivors and their rescuers. They are clearly invaluable in helping to buttress the hard facts presented by the official documents. The oral testimonies of the victims constitute the crucial ammunition needed to defeat present and future falsifiers of memory and therefore of history. With the passing of time, memory may play tricks on us, and we may lose some of the accuracy of details and dates; we may confuse some parts of the story. But nothing will ever erase from survivors' recollections the horrors that they endured: for many of them event he smallest detail is as vivid and painful as it was fifty years ago.

How can we tolerate today the perverse use of semantics to minimize or even obfuscate into a misty past the reality of a crime that will not go away? The falsification of history starts with vocabulary, a method the Nazis used extensively to lull their victims into a false sense of security, allowing their own nationals to pretend they did not really know the meaning of words like "resettlement," "special treatment," "cleansing," "final solution," "cargo" or "pieces." If we allow memory to tamper with the past, we are not only becoming partners in crime, helping to kill the dead a second time, but we are also allowing the ideologies of the repressors of memory to go on unchallenged. We are therefore becoming collaborators in the falsification of history by giving way to an unavowed desire to forget a disturbing past.

We have an obligation to hear what each survivor has to say and thus we may help to recreate an oral tradition which is no longer to be found in Europe. For it is not a matter of the history of distant, little-known countries in a remote past, or events happening in far-flung Siberia or the Kalahari desert. For the European of the 20th century and the Allies who came to our rescue, we are discussing our own time, our lives, our countries; it is our history.

Lanzmann tried to penetrate this *royaume de l'ombre,* this ghostly kingdom, by using the dimension of *le souvenir,* the memory of those who had actually lived through the events, and he tried to integrate this special kind of memory into the tradition historical discourse. In *Shoah* he made us listen to the testimonies of the bystanders and perpetrators along with the victims. This film is truly history made captive. Thirty years from now, that *souvenir* dimension will be lost and no one will be able to say "I was there."

The same motivation is at the heart of Steven Spielberg's initiative to collect survivors' testimonies through his "Shoah Visual History Foundation." Founded on the profits of *Schindler's List*, the foundation's stated aim is to create a visual and oral database of the testimonies of 50,000 survivors within the next two years.

The victims themselves also provided evidence in the form of eye-witness accounts and diaries, some of which were fond buried long after the death of their writers. The Warsaw historian Emmanuel Ringelblum, for instance, gathered together a major source of documentation, for he aimed to record every aspect of Jewish life at the time of its destruction by the Nazis. These documents were found hidden in milk churns and buried in a Warsaw cellar, although one churn is still missing.

Confirming evidence comes also in testimonies from non-Jews who took part in the killing process, but took the risk of recording events as a form of protest. The best known example of this is perhaps the account of Kurt Gerstein, an SS officer and Christian, who witnessed the deaths of thousands in Belzec and Treblinka after he was made responsible for obtaining supplies of Zyklon B Gas and for finding methods of improving the techniques. He wanted to stop the genocide, but at the time he was largely disbelieved.

It is our duty as scholars and educators to ensure the best teaching possible based on the solid, unimpeachable, crystal-sharp, crystal-clear evidence available to us and to illustrate what the laws, cold bureaucratic orders, regulations, accounting, field manuals, factory rules and end-products actually meant in terms of human suffering, by listening to the repercussion of these inescapable facts on the victims they targeted. This we can only do by collecting and reading the accumulated testimonies of survivors. We can no longer afford to be bystanders as history begins to repeat itself: it is a risk which none of us can take. We have to take action, beginning with a program or information and education which will reach the widest possible audience. As Yehuda Bauer concluded in his inaugural lecture at the London conference on Wannsee: "We live at a time when Wannsee meetings are possible. The Holocaust can be a warning or it can be a precedent. It should be the former."

It was the French writer Charles Péguy who said that for every man and every event there is a precise moment in time when the bell tolls to signify that reality has frozen into history. Once history has taken over from memory, there may be no way of correcting any detail in the accepted record that has been falsified. It follows therefore that the longer we can delay the moment when the Holocaust definitely falls into the category of historical events, the more time is still available to ensure that its memory is preserved as closely as possible to actual events. If our generation can ensure that as much of the story is preserved as possible within our century, then we will have fulfilled our duty, even belatedly. In the centuries ahead, the myth-makers will evolve a version of the tradition which will be tolerable but not altogether erroneous, a tale so dense, so fascinating chilling and unfathomably rich that in 3,000 years from now, our descendants will carry the odyssey of our Jewish European heroes to the stars.

Notes

1. Adolf Hitler, *Mein Kampf* (Boston: Houghton, Mifflin Company, 1971). Translated by Ralph Mannheim.

2. *Hitler's Secret Conversations 1941-1944* (New York: Octagon Books, 1976).

3. *Auschwitz: Yesterday's Racism* (Materials for Teachers). Published by the London Auschwitz Committee, P.O. Box 248, London E1 5BN (undated).

4. Himmler to Greiser, September 18, 1941, cited by Peter Witte in "The Decisions Concerning the Final Solution to the Jewish Question: Deportation to Lodz and Mass Murder in chelmno" in *Holocaust and Genocide Studies*, Vol 9, Number 3, Winter 1995.

5. Peter J. Haas, *Morality after Auschwitz, The Radical Challenge of the Nazi Ethic,* (Philadelphia: Fortress Press, 1992), p. 90.

6. Claude Lanzmann *Au sujet de Shoah* in *De l'Holocauste à Holocauste ou comment s'en débarrasser* (Paris: Editions Belin 1990), pp. 314-15.

7. Himmler to Greiser, op. cit.

8. Christian Meir, *Yad Vashem Studies*, vol XIX Jerusalem 1988, p. 95.

9. Cited by Geoffrey H. Hartman in Marcia Littell (ed.), *The Holocaust Forty Years After,* Symposium Studies (Lewiston: Mellen Press, 1989), vol 22 p. 55.

10. George Clare, *Last Waltz in Vienna,* published by Pan Books Ltd, London 1982, p. 253.

11. Cited by Charlotte Wardi in *Le Génocide dans la Fiction Romanesque*, Paris, PUF, 1988, p. 22 (my translation).

Chapter 10

CAMP MUSIC AND CAMP SONGS: SZYMON LAKS AND ALEKSANDER KULISIEWICZ

David H. Hirsch

In 1948, a compact book entitled *Musiques d'un autre monde* was published in Paris. The author, Szymon Laks, described his experiences as a Jewish musician in a Nazi concentration camp. He provided a detailed account of the conditions and structure of the Auschwitz-Birkenau complex, because, as he noted,

> ... This is not a book about *music*. It is a book about *music in a Nazi concentration camp*. One could also say: about *music in a distorting mirror*" (author's emphasis).[1]

Laks tells how his musical talents and training enabled him to secure a privileged position in the camp hierarchy, a position that eventually led, against all odds, to his survival in the camp.[2]

The English version of the book, which did not appear till 1989, contains some added material and takes up issues that arose after the original book had appeared. The original book addressed the paradox of how it was possible that the people of Bach and Beethoven, who were genuine lovers of great music, could also be the inventors and executors of the death camps. The later English version addresses two new questions: Did music in the camps provide spiritual uplift? Did the music created by the prisoners constitute a form of resistance and defense? To both these questions Laks answers an emphatic, "No!" and argues that for him and other Jewish musicians, music and music-making in the German concentration camps gave neither pleasure nor fulfillment, but became simply one more method of surviving.

Originally, Laks challenged the belief that music, one of the great achievements of European (and especially German) culture, still elevated the human soul and cultivated a spirit of universal empathy in the camp environment. In Auschwitz, Laks discovered that educated, highly cultured men who responded with great sensitivity to the sublimity of serious music, had no problem conducting themselves as sadistic killers. Laks wondered how it happened that "... music -- that most sublime expression of the human spirit -- also became entangled in the hellish enterprise of the extermination of millions of people and even took an active part in this extermination?" (p. 5).

Erich Kahler called attention to a similar enigma in a now much neglected book, *The Tower and the Abyss,* when he referred to

> ... a novel kind of schizophrenia which, in a rudimentary or potential form, is present everywhere in our modern civilization, but has grown to extremes only in the Nazi situation.[3]

Kahler spoke of the

> ... executives, ... doctors and university professors [who,] ... after having done their gruesome work, ... partook of all the modes and manners of our modern civilization without even the slightest sense of the flagrant contrast between the two aspects of their lives (p. 75).

Even in the final stage of the extermination process, Jews condemned to death by a Jew-hating ideology were permitted to live a little longer if they possessed musical talent. Such talented Jews were temporarily kept from the gas because of their ability to entertain the camp elite. Though Laks does not refer to a new kind of schizophrenia, as Kahler does, he seems to be describing exactly that in the following observation:

> When an SS man listened to music, especially of the kind he really liked, he somehow became strangely similar to a human being. His voice lost its typical harshness, he suddenly acquired an easy manner, and one could talk with him almost as one equal to another. Sometimes one got the impression that some melody stirred in him the memory of his dear ones, a girl-friend who he had not seen for a long time, and then his eyes got misty with something that gave the illusion of human tears. At such moments the hope stirred in us that maybe everything was not lost after all. Could people who love music to this extent, people who can cry when they hear it, be at the same time capable of committing so many

atrocities on the rest of humanity? There are realities in which one cannot believe. And yet ... (p. 70)

"And yet ...," it was indeed true that the SS men could be moved by music, and still not be deflected from their cruel tasks. Worse, perhaps, there were SS men who were musical virtuosos and mass killers, as was the case with *Rottenführer*, Pery Broad. "In a certain sense," Laks writes, Broad

> ... was a prodigy. He was not quite twenty-two years old, ... yet he had already risen to the position of chief of the Political Bureau (*Politische Abteilung*) at Birkenau (pp. 79-80).

Laks informs the reader that Broad's instrument was the accordion, for which Laks "... had always had contempt ..." But

> here in the person of Broad I met a genuine artist, a virtuoso of the highest class, in both group and solo performances. Under his long aristocratic fingers, nimbly darting over the keys and registers, with the simultaneous moving of the bellows back and forth, the accordion I had held in contempt was instantly rehabilitated into the great family of musical instruments.

A frequent visiter to the orchestra's barracks, Broad once

> ... disappeared from our horizon for much longer than previously. It concerned a trifle: the burning of a few thousand Gypsies and then the same number of Czechs (p. 82).

Laks seems to conclude that in the deepest sense, musicianship, in the camp, turned out to be little more than a certain technical ability, and music itself a mere diversion for the torturers and a life-saving reed to hang onto for the Jews. For the VIP's music was a form of entertainment, and for "the class of paupers," music "... had a disheartening ... effect ... and deepened still further their chronic state of physical and mental prostration" (p. 118).

The English version, Laks explains, has "... been enriched with still other disclosures, documents, and testimonies that have been sent to me over the years" (p. 6). Between the publication of the French and English editions, Laks had read essays by Polish musicologists and survivors expressing a point of view quite different from his own. As a consequence, Laks added materials to the English edition which were intended to refute a claim made by various Polish ex-prisoners who were also musicians, namely that music in the camps served a constructive and uplifting purpose for the prisoners. Laks cites an issue of *Przeglad Lekarski* [*The Medical Review*] (1977, no. 1), which published a number of essays arguing that music in the camps was a form of resistance.   Laks, who was a player in the orchestra, a *Notenschreiber* (music transcriber), and for a time, the *Kapellmeister* of the Auschwitz II orchestra, is outraged by this claim. From the issue of *Przeglad Lekarski* mentioned above, he cites the following words by Adam Kopcysnki, orchestra director in Auschwitz I:

> Thanks to its power and suggestiveness, music strengthened in the camp listeners what was most important -- their true nature. Perhaps that is why many certainly tried instinctively to make a certain cult of this most beautiful of the arts, which precisely there in camp conditions could be, and certainly was, medicine for the sick soul of the prisoners. (p. 117)

Laks declares that it is hard for him

> ... to believe this bombastic claptrap came from the mouth of a professional musician who was a prisoner in a real Hitlerite concentration camp and saw there more or less the same things I saw in Birkenau (p. 117).

In February 1974, Laks had met Aleksander Kulisiewicz, author of one of the articles from which he quotes. Laks writes that

> ... Kulisiewicz, a former prisoner at the Sachsenhausen concentration camp, came from Poland to see me in Paris. ... I had heard a lot about him, namely, that he was very active in collecting songs, tunes, poetry, and camp music in general in all of its aspects. ... He had devoted all of his efforts after the war to the history of the songs of the resistance movement in the concentration camps (p. 11).

But Laks had very little use for the kind of music Kulisiewicz was collecting. "I have gathered information," he wrote,

> from friends and acquaintances all over the world, former prisoners of various concentration camps. Nearly all of them maintain that the songs that originated in the camps were vulgar, in local dialects, or even trashy and had nothing in common with raising people's fortitude, and that the

songs and tunes that could be regarded as manifestations of the resistance movement were written *after the war*. (p. 119; author's emphasis)

A very harsh judgment indeed, but since I am neither a musician nor a camp survivor, it would be foolhardy for me to try to adjudicate between Laks and Kulisiewicz, though it is curious that two men who both seem to be painstakingly honest and totally authentic can disagree so completely on what are, at the very least, parallel experiences.

Kulisiewicz was, in his own right, an extraordinary human being. Born in Krakow in 1918, he aspired to become a musical performer. In October 1939, however, soon after Germany had invaded Poland, he was picked up in a Gestapo dragnet and incarcerated in the Sachsenhausen concentration camp near Berlin, where he remained until liberated on May 2, 1945. As a prisoner,

Alex helped organize and himself performed in numerous illegal poetry readings and sings. When an informer denounced him to the authorities as a "nightingale" SS doctors employed "scientific" means to try and shut him up. Three times they injected him with diphtheria bacilli to destroy his hearing and three times comrades managed to smuggle in the antidote. Finally the doctors gave up. "Let the dog sing," they laughed.[4]

For a brief period in 1944, Kulisiewicz worked in the SS canine training center (SS *Hundenzwinger Kommando*), where he contracted an infection of animal origin and nearly lost his sight. In addition to collecting songs, he composed 54 camp songs, 15 of which included both the words and music. In June of 1945, following his liberation, he spent more than three weeks dictating camp songs he had memorized, a total of 716 typed pages. At the time, he was a patient in the tubercular clinic in Krakow, and dictated the songs from a hospital bed. The doctors thought Alex was mad.[5] After his recovery, Kulisiewicz performed the camp songs around the world.

On at least one matter, Kulisiewicz and Laks agree: this is music from another world. More precisely, Kulisiewicz refers to his repertory as songs from Hell. He has explained his commitment to performing the songs in a radio program, "*Lieder Aus Der Hölle*," for Radio Bern (Switzerland), in March and November of 1970.

... When I sing my songs from the Nazi concentration camps, I ask the public not to applaud. These are songs from the other world -- completely degenerate, a product of the pandemonium created by the SS state. The most horrible songs were written in the camps, truthful songs never heard before, anywhere. It is not possible to applaud the singing of songs with such morbid subject matter.

Many people sing to become famous. I don't seek fame. Every singer feels satisfaction during his performance, and wants to show off his well trained voice. I can't sing beautifully. Every time I sing, I am back in this accursed concentration camp. I not only have to reproduce in sound all the horror portrayed by the songs, but once again I have to experience what it was like to exist in a concentration camp.

I must not be an actor. There is a fine line dividing documentary retrospection from the singer's theatrical art, and too much art runs the danger of declining into empty mannerism. One might say, in German, "*So ein gutter Schauspieler!*" ("What a fine actor!"). But then, no one would believe in the authenticity of the performance.

Singing these painful songs is my duty. I don't sing to earn money, or to make a career, or out of revenge. I sing to keep alive the memory of millions of murdered companions whose voices were forever silenced in the camps. They are always with me, in every European concert hall, in each radio studio, or on television. That is why I never feel stage fright.[6]

The lyrics of some of these songs are so revolting as to make listening to them not only painful, but almost unbearable. But they are, after all, songs, and the bare lyrics do not do them justice. Not only are the words inseparable from music, but the songs are inseparable from the singer, whose raspy voice is a legacy of his captors' efforts to silence him by injecting him with diphtheria bacilli. Kulisiewicz's rendition of the songs projects a sense of total authenticity that no one seems likely to match. A listener cannot help noticing incongruities between the music and the lyrics. In the "Lullaby for Birkenau," for example, the horrible disgusting meaning of the words contrasts sharply with the tenderness of the music.

Sung by Kulisiewicz, the songs become a unique form of Holocaust testimony. In the present climate of deconstructionist literary theories, Holocaust scholars, both historians and literary commentators, tend to focus on the fallibility of memory, on history as narrative or pure rhetoric, and on the unreliability of methods of telling and commemorating. But Kulisiewicz's songs are the equivalent of imperative statements, which are not subject to true-or-false criteria. They are cries from the depths that simply *are*, and that cannot be manipulated out of existence by equivocating theories intended to establish "indeterminacy" and the uncertainty of all witness and historical accounts.

As an example of this straightforward urgency, I would like to discuss the song, "Birkenau," a denunciation of the camp order. The lyrics, reproduced below, have been translated by Roslyn Hirsch from the recording *Piesni Obozowe*, made in Poland in 1981. The translation was made directly from the recording, without benefit of a written text.[7]

BIRKENAU

Accursed scrap of earth,
Where people are nothing but numbers
Where base brother oppresses brother,
Where bony death stretches out his palm,
Where everything is drenched in blood and tears,
Where you wake up screaming in the watches of the night.

If one should ask,
"Where,
"Oh where is Hell?"
You can surely answer,
"Birkenau, accursed Birkenau."

Bathed in blood and tears,
Birkenau, forgotten by God,
Godforsaken hellhole, Birkenau,
Thorny path,
Where millions of victims lie
In a common grave.
Birkenau, evil kingdom,
Where there is no God.
This is Birkenau.

Crematoria consuming human carcasses,
Pestilential stench of human flesh,
Chimneys belching reddish smoke,
This is the journey's end,
The end of all suffering.

And you, my friend,
Will be a handful of ashes,
Swept away by the prairie wind.
But it doesn't matter.
You're one of many
Forgotten by this beastly world.

Birkenau, accursed Birkenau,
Drenched in blood and tears,
Forgotten by God.
Birkenau, thorny path,
Where millions of victims lie
In a common grave,
Kingdom
Without God.
This is Birkenau.

Written in Birkenau in 1943, by an unknown author, "Birkenau"
represents the fierceness of a new moral order that reduced human
beings first to anonymity and then nothingness.   The song's title,
"Birkenau," is a word of horror for anyone at all familiar with the
referent, and both the title and song parody the convention of musical
compositions celebrating -- and often sentimentalizing -- a place or a
geographical phenomenon, such as "The Beautiful Blue Danube," or
"The Tales of the Vienna Woods," or, "Chicago," etc. Such songs are
filled with nostalgia, glorify the places they celebrate, and instill in the
listener a desire to be there.

"Birkenau" reverses these conventions. It is a song denouncing the
place it sings about, expressing despair rather than joy. As Kulisiewicz
says, "... This is a song ... from the other world, ... a most horrible song
... full of truth." This parodic tribute to a place begins with an unusual
apostrophe: "Accursed scrap of earth." The next line develops the
condition of accursedness: "Where people are nothing but numbers."
In an ordinary poem this would sound like a metaphor calling for
interpretation; but with reference to Auschwitz-Birkenau the statement
is simply descriptive: people with numbers tattooed on their arms is the
working-out in history, in the physical world, of the philosophical
principle of the Nietzschean "Overman," which led, with a hefty
admixture of Darwinian survivalism, to the principle of the super race.
Non-Aryans are subhuman, non-people: mere numbers.

In the world of the "Overman," "base brother oppresses brother." We
wonder,   which   nameless   faceless   victim   wrote   this   scorching

commentary on the new order that has overturned two thousand years of Judeo-Christian ethics, turned those ethics inside out, and created a world in which the principle of social order has become, not "I am my brother's keeper" but "base brother oppressing brother?" Was it a man or woman who wrote the song? A child or an adult? Gentile or Jew? Believer or non-believer?

And who, in this factory of death, is the kindest brother of all? The Angel of Death: the "bony brother" who stretches out his palm in true brotherhood, offering the only relief available to the victims of the new order, where death has become preferable to a life of unbearable suffering. Whereas the phrase, "people are nothing but numbers" sounded like a metaphor but was merely description, here we have true metaphor, an imagistic use of language that conveys a new reality poetically, making us see and feel at the same time what the anonymous author is trying to tell us: "bony death" is a mocking image of the camp inmates -- the musselmen who, starved and wracked by dysentery, are now become walking skeletons: truly bony death.

The last two lines of this verse mingle metaphor and direct speech. "Everything is drenched in blood and tears." Is this literal truth or metaphor? And the terror. The night terror of those to whom "bony death" has not yet stretched out his palm, reminiscent of the unanswered questions of William Blake's prophetic lyric: "Tyger, tyger burning bright/In the forests of the night/... When thy heart began to beat/What dread hand, and what dread feet?"

And then a refrain in which the hitherto unnamed scrap of accursed earth is given both a real and a metaphorical identity: "If someone should ask, 'Where, oh where is Hell?' You can answer, 'Accursed Birkenau.'" A refrain to celebrate the place the song commemorates.

The next verse, invokes the sub-refrain of blood and tears, now accompanied by the deceptively benign verb, "bathed." The author of this song was perhaps not a theologian, but in the next lines he raises questions that theologians studying the Holocaust have pondered for the last fifty years. Birkenau is a Godforsaken hellhole, an "evil kingdom ... where millions of victims lie in a mass grave. ... A kingdom where there is no God, This is Birkenau." A kingdom without a king. Is this not, perhaps, the author's definition of Hell, "a world without God?" The anonymous author seems to be saying that where God does not exist, there Hell does.

The next verse can only be called the poetry of horror: a shocking metaphor in which the death-camp machinery is personified as if in an echo from an old medieval poem with a fire-breathing dragon. But the dragon is modern technology: gas chambers and crematoria to dispose of human victims. The anonymous author embodies this reality in the revolting image of the "crematoria consuming stinking human carcasses;" but even the death machinery cannot digest this putrid diet, so it "belches reddish smoke." For the victims in the new order of super beings, "this is the end of all suffering."

An ambivalent verse precedes the final refrain: "And you, my friends, will be a handful of ashes,/Swept by the prairie wind." Is the author comforting the victims with the thought of annihilation, or is he presenting them with the bleakness of their future: ashes swept over the universe? In Shelley's "Ode to the West Wind," the West Wind is a destroyer and preserver, because while it brings death it is also a harbinger of life. It is part of the natural cycle of life and death, and hence the speaker invokes the wind to "Drive my dead thoughts over the universe/Like withered leaves to quicken a new birth." But it is questionable whether these ashes of humans belched by chimneys will bring forth new life. Swept away by the prairie wind, they will be forgotten by the beastly world, as those who are about to be converted into ashes are forgotten in the present.

For lack of space, I cannot reproduce lyrics of protest songs, with their gallows humor, as in the song "Auschwitzlager," by Tadeusz Kanski: "There goes Adolf/With his hand/Three meters up his ass, Scratching." Nor is it possible to reproduce the frightful lullabies which replace restorative sleep with all-encompassing death. These songs might help to explain the nature of the disagreement between Laks and Kulisiewicz.

It may be that the differences between Laks and Kulisiewicz must be traced to the fact that Laks was a Jew and Kulisiewicz was not. Without minimizing either the suffering or the noble character of Kulisiewicz himself, it must be said that for Jews, who were at the bottom of the food chain in the Nazi camps, hope was not possible. For Laks, sentenced to death for being a Jew, each moment of life was a momentary reprieve that could instantly be repealed. Every moment of life he could gain by taking advantage of his privileged position in the orchestra was just that, only a moment with no promise of hope. Moreover, like all the Jews in the camp he had no family or people or home to return to even if he did survive.

Kulisiewicz also lived on the margins of death for five years, but he was not totally without hope, and he could live in the expectation of returning to a family, a home, a reinvigorated nation. Hence, the lyrics, "But We'll hang on/Survive Auschwitz/And go cavorting home."

It should also be said that Laks still considered music a sublime spiritual phenomenon. His assertion that camp music was "vulgar, in local dialects, or even trashy," was probably accurate, but in Kulisiewicz's view, those elements were not negatives, but rather sources of power. No less than Jewish survivors, Kulisiewicz dedicated his post-camp life to commemorating the victims.[8] In a 1978 letter to a Mr. Graves, Kulisiewicz wrote,

> My performing [these concentration camp songs] even though I am not Jewish is of deep and particular significance.... My songs preserve the memory of people who were eternally joined together by having been common victims of the most terrifying human disaster, the Nazi concentration camp.[9]

Notes

1. Szymon Laks, *Music From Another World* (Evanston, Ill.: Northwestern University Press, 1989), p. 7. Further references will appear in text.

2. On the question of camp hierarchy and the importance of securing a privileged position in the camp as a condition of survival, see Primo Levi, "The Gray Zone," in *The Drowned and the Saved* (New York: Random House, 1989), pp. 39-45, et. passim.

3. Erich Kahler, *The Tower and the Abyss* (New York: G. Braziller, 1957), p. 68.

4. Peter Wortsman, "Aleksander Kulisiewicz: A Singer From Hell," *Sing Out! The Folk Magazine* (25:3, 1977), 15.

5. Aleksander Kulisiewicz, paraphrased from "Artistic Biography," in a letter to Rod Eglash of the Milwaukee Jewish Community Center, received December 15, 1978, p. 2. Unpublished materials were sent to the author by Krzystof Kulisiewicz.

6. *Ibid.*, p.5.

7. *Piesni Obozowe*, Polskie Nagrania: Muza, SX1715. The recording contains 16 songs. Some of the information that follows is taken from notes on the record jacket. The Kulisiewicz archive is now deposited in the U.S. Holocaust

Memorial Museum, but we have not yet had an opportunity to examine these materials.

8. See Aleksander Kulisiewicz, "Polish Camp Songs, 1939-1945," in Modern Language Studies, XVI (Winter, 1986), 3-9.

9. Materials sent to author by Krzystof Kulisiewcicz.

Chapter 11

CLOSING REMARKS

Hubert Locke

Editors' Note: Professor Locke's response to his introduction has been deleted. The mention of the analysis of the genocide of the Romani people refers to the plenary address given at the conference by Ian Hancock included in this volume. The reference to a fourth bomb and Dr. Locke's subsequent comments refer to a series of four bombings in Israel in the week prior to, and during the conference. The bombings, which caused substantial loss of life, were to play a major role in the 1996 elections in Israel.

Friends and colleagues, two weeks ago, as I began to think about these closing comments I thought that it would be appropriate perhaps to speak briefly regarding three distinct and I hoped not unrelated matters. The first, is the role of this scholars' conference in the evolution of Holocaust scholarship and studies. I wanted to point to the virtual explosion that all of you are aware of in research and scholarship focused on the destruction of European Jewry under the Nazi Third Reich and I would have said then that it would be remiss not to take note of the role that this annual meeting of scholars has played in this remarkable development. At the time of the first meeting of this conference in 1970, there was a paucity of scholarly effort and virtually nothing in the way of courses of study devoted to the *Shoah* in any American college or university. To the extent that a virtual handful of publications in the late 1960s and early 1970s has become a veritable tidal wave of scholarship in the last quarter century, this conference has had a major role in bringing that development to fruition. I would risk failure to make mention of many major examples that should be cited, but I think of the profound theological questions raised first by Richard Rubenstein's *Death of God* assertions early in these gatherings, as well as the new dimensions in Christian-Jewish dialogue, theological dialogue, raised by the efforts now headed by Zev Garber, by Jim Moore, and by Henry Knight. I think of the work of John Pawlikowski in bringing about a reassessment of the place of Poland and the Poles in the grand scheme of Nazi slaughter, helping to place in context such volatile issues of those which have been examined by our colleague, Harry James Cargas and Zev Garber regarding the Edith Stein controversy and that surrounding the Carmelite Convent at Auschwitz. In each of these and in many other important areas, this conference has emerged as an extraordinary influential intellectual center for the discussion and the debate of *Shoah* scholarship.

Two weeks ago, I also wanted to say a word about what Franklin Littell, were he here, would call the imperative of Holocaust and *Kirchenkampf*. That is to say, with respect to the *Kirchenkampf* or the Church Struggle in Nazi Germany, we have moved from the rough insights of the immediate post war period in which a few German church leaders appeared to emerge from the calamity of the twelve years of the Reich in somewhat heroic dimension, while the churches themselves, both Protestant and Catholic, were seen in a far less commendatory light -- we have moved from that position to the much more nuanced understanding of the role of churches and their leaders that have come about thanks to the work of John Conway, of William Helmreich, of Robert Ericksen who is here at this meeting this year, and to others, to the much greater detailed picture of the church struggle that is provided by the studies of Victoria Barnett, Theodore Thomas' work on "The Role of Women in the Church Struggle" and the studies of Burton Nelson and J. Patrick Kelly on Bonhoeffer, the studies of Doris Bergen and others. And, here, again, colleagues, it has been in this conference that many of these more nuanced studies and detailed pictures of what is a far more than simple story of failure on the part of the churches have emerged. Increasingly, as the Church Struggle is seen in the context of the times and the circumstances in which it took place, it has become a complex account of an intense moral and human struggle which, I believe, thanks to these meetings we are able to appreciate far more today than we could and did a quarter century ago.

I would have wanted to add a word to remind us again of the insistent claim of this conference of scholars which no one has articulated more clearly or more forcefully than dear Franklin Littell that the *Shoah* and the *Kirchenkampf* be examined together as intertwined and interrelated themes. It is this which has marked this annual meeting and which has set it apart from all other meetings about the Holocaust, against the temptation to isolate and extract from the totality that was the German Third Reich a particular horror or a particular outrage that one might want to emphasize - the *Shoah* and the Church Struggle. The destruction of the Jewish community of Europe and the struggle of the churches in Nazi Germany are reminders, that in most instances, isolation and segmentation have led to distortion, both of the record of the Third Reich and of the experience within that era with which one is concerned. We saw this distortion in its most gross form in the stance of the DDR up until its collapse. From the perspective of the East German government, the Nazi experience was a sustained and almost exclusive assault on Marxist socialism. Monuments were recast, concentration camps were reconfigured and the history taught to children in the schools was revised to tell a story of oppression and persecution of Marxist stalwarts. It was as if nothing else of major significance had occurred.

This temptation to isolate and extract, as you know, has occurred in other areas as well. One of the more recent efforts seeks to segment out the role of women during the Third Reich and concludes that German women were innocent of the crimes of National Socialism and instead were the victims of a sexist, racist, male regime which reduced women to the status of mere objects. In opposition to these distorting developments, the combined study, which this conference pursues, links the examination of one of national socialism's major public policies with an examination of the way in which the Nazi government went about its attempts to mobilize the German populace in support of its policies. The study of *Shoah* and Church Struggle forces a look at one of the objectives the Nazi government coveted most - the eradication of Jewish people from the life of German and by extension, European society - and its successes, as well as its failures as it sought to bend the will of one institution and its adherence in compliance with its policies.

Two week ago, I also wanted to say a word about I would have termed, a new dialogue for the bystander. It is readily apparent that where the *Shoah* is concerned, the passage of time presents us with two inescapable problems. The first is the frequently noted irreplaceable loss of survivors for whose testimonies we shall have to increasingly rely upon their archival records. The second problem, frequently discussed, is the increasing number of persons who are not only distant in time, but who also consider themselves distant psychologically from the *Shoah* as well. This involves growing numbers of Americans for whom the *Shoah* is a matter of casual interest, but not of compelling concern. Perhaps far more important it describes the stance of growing numbers of young Germans who do not identify with the notion of victimizer, who do not accept any burden of personal responsibility as we discussed this morning in the Peck/Wagner dialogue; who do not accept burdens of personal responsibility for the history and behavior of their nation one-half century ago; who are not skinheads or Neo-Nazis or *Shoah* deniers, but who simply refuse to take seriously the idea that they have any particular role or unique duty with respect to the *Shoah* and its message.

I believe there is an imperative to develop (along side the pioneering discussion that has been launched by Abraham Peck and Gottfried Wagner, as well as the probing theological inquiry in which Moore and Knight and Garber and others are engaged) a new dialogue, and if I had time I would have tried to speak to what I think some of the dimensions of that dialogue would be.

Let me say to you, that ten days ago, I thought all these things were important to say to you, as a way of emphasizing and underscoring the relevance of your work to one of the most insistent questions of the century. I think they are still important to say, but oh, my friends how dwarfed they become by the events of the last ten days.

Two years ago, in March 1994, at the close of the International Conference "Remembering for the Future II" in Berlin, I had the opportunity to say that the scholars who work in this field we call "Holocaust Studies," are captives of a memory that entwines itself around us and that has become an inextricable part of our existence. We are among those for whom history has been radically altered. We closed the Berlin conference with a formal statement which, because we were in Berlin, we had the immodesty to term an *Erklärung* - a declaration. We noted that declarations are something which professors and scholars normally do not make. We are much more comfortable in our work and in our professional lives when we can take a slice of life or human experience, physically or sociologically or politically or economically or psychologically, and put it under our intellectual microscopes or capture a piece of history and put it under a bell jar and examine it from every possible angle. But we are professors and scholars in this meeting who understand ourselves to be under the shadow of Auschwitz. That shadow compels us to concern ourselves not only with the past, but with the present. In the context of this 26th Annual Meeting, for many of us over the course of the past two and a half days, that has come to mean two things. First, those of you who were present on Monday at noon, heard a remarkable, an astute analysis of the genocide of the Romani people during the era of the Third Reich. Professor Yehuda Bauer is foremost among those who attest to how neglected the study of the Romani genocide has been among scholars and in the larger context, how pervasive is the continued and continual persecution and oppression of the Romani people in our time. This situation presents an internal challenge to us in the context of this conference, a challenge to place the Romani genocide more visibly on our agenda of examination and inquiry, as well as to speak against the continued persecution of the Romani people. Professor Bauer has prepared a statement expressing both these concerns and Yehuda, I should like to invite you now to present that.

[Yehuda Bauer]

I thought it would be appropriate for those of us who feel like it, who think the way that I feel, to make a statement, basically to ourselves to start with; not as a form of decision by any conference, but as an expression of concern by those scholars here who, as I say, feel like that. This is beyond the conservancy that I eluded to in my opening remarks on Sunday evening. This is a real problem and so I suggested that those of us who feel like it, as I say, would wish to sign such a statement. And it says,

Fifty years after the end of World War II, one of the most terrible genocidal acts of the Nazi regime, the mass destruction of the Romani (Gypsy people) is still being ignored. Their continued vilification, discrimination and persecution on racist grounds reminiscent of Nazi attitudes has not ceased, especially in the countries of eastern Europe. It the sense of the following scholars who participated at the 26th Annual Scholars Conference on the Holocaust and the Churches, that it is appropriate for democratic governments, religious organizations, academic and civil bodies to call upon governments and political parties in the countries mentioned to act forcefully against anti-Romani policies which if continued may well create another political genocidal situation.

[Hubert Locke]: Thank you, Yehuda.

Now ladies and gentlemen, yesterday morning the conference committee, which advises on the planning of this annual meeting, met and after some painful discussion, reasserted what has been a twenty-six year tradition at this national meeting (as distinct from the international meeting which took place in Berlin), a tradition that we would not issue any public statements at the close of our statements. Even as we deliberated yesterday morning, a fourth bomb exploded on the streets of Tel Aviv and the death toll mounted. As the day progressed, as we walked these corridors, as we listened to one another's papers and sat next to each other in our discussion sessions and shared meals together, it became increasingly clear that we could not keep silent. The statement's pronouncements are, to be sure, feeble responses to the enormity of the tragedy that has taken place in Israel. But a statement at the least saves us from the sin of silence and at best it offers and extends a small, wholly inadequate, but nevertheless fervent expression of solidarity with the people and the nation who are in the midst of such horrendous circumstances. The following statement which is the work also of professor Bauer and professor Garber and dean Jan Colijn has been prepared for your consideration:

> The series of terrorist outrages that hit Israel in the last few days are yet another proof that the dangers discussed at the 26th Annual Scholars Conference on the Holocaust the Churches are still with us. The murderers and those who sent them are motivated by antisemitic and anti-democratic ideology which is directed against Israel, against any type of peace agreement in the Middle-East and against their own Palestinian people. The following scholars, participating at the 26th Annual Scholars' Conference on the Holocaust and the Churches, call upon the civilized world to aid all those who will take action to stop the murderers from achieving their goals. We call upon people of moral conscience and good will to condemn the cowardly acts of terrorism in the streets of Jerusalem and the land of Zion. For out of Zion comes forth the Torah: choose life, peacemakers, not death.

To keep faith with those scholars who are not here, who have already departed this meeting, we dare not issue these two statements in the name of the conference, but we invite any and all in this room who wish to sign these statements which will be forwarded to appropriate journals and publications and will be printed in the newsletter of this conference. It remains for me only to salute warmly, fervently and prayerfully each of you as colleagues and friends, to wish you well in your work over the course of the coming year and, Deo valente, to look forward to our meeting again next year in Tampa at the University of South Florida. Thank you very much.

Contributors

Paul R. Bartrop teaches in the Jewish Studies Department at Bialik College, Melbourne, Australia. In 1996 he was Visiting Professor in the Department of Political Science at Virginia Commonwealth University, Richmond (VA). His published works include *Australia and the Holocaust, 1933-45* (Scholarly Publishing, 1994) and (ed.) *False Havens: The British Empire and the Holocaust* (University Press of America, 1995). In addition, he has published numerous scholarly articles in journals and books. Dr. Bartrop was President of the Australian Association for Jewish Studies.

Yehuda Bauer is the Jona M. Machover Professor of Holocaust Studies (Emeritus) at Hebrew University, Jerusalem and the Director of the International Institute of Holocaust studies at Yad Vashem. He is the Chair of the International Committee of the Vidal Sassoon International Center for the Study of Antisemitism (Hebrew University), and the immediate past Chair of that Center. He was for ten years the chief editor of the *Journal of Holocaust and Genocide Studies*, and is a member of the Academic Research Committee of the United States Holocaust Memorial Museum. His most recent books are *Out of the Ashes* (Pergamon Press, 1989), and *Jews for Sale?* (Yale University Press, 1995). Born in 1926 in Prague, he emigrated to Palestine in 1939, studied at Cardiff College-University of Wales, and received his Ph.D. at Hebrew University. He has published 12 books in English, and some 80 articles and chapters in books.

G. Jan Colijn is Dean of General Studies at The Richard Stockton College of New Jersey. Among his responsibilities falls the supervision of the College's Holocaust Resource Center. He chaired the 21st Annual Scholars Conference on the Holocaust and the Churches and served as Chairman, American Committee of "Remembering for the Future II." His editorial work includes *From Prejudice to Destruction: Western Civilization in the Shadow of Auschwitz,* Lit Verlag, 1995, and *The Netherlands and Nazi Genocide* (Mellen Press, 1992) and *The Holocaust: Remembering for the Future* (Special Edition of the Annals of the American Academy of Political and Social Science, November, 1996).

Ian Hancock is Main Representative for the Romani people in the United Nations Economic and Social Council (Category II), and to UNICEF and UN-DPI. He is President of the International Rroma Federation, Inc., co-founder of the Romani Jewish Alliance, Inc., and a member of the Project on Ethnic Relations Romani Advisory Council (Princeton). Between 1985-1987 he was Special Advisor on Romani-related Affairs to Elie Wiesel, then Chair of the U.S. Holocaust Memorial Council. He has served as a member of the U.S. Department of State's diplomatic team at the Warsaw meeting of the Organization for Security and Cooperation in Europe. He is Professor of English and Linguistics at The University of Texas at Austin.

David H. Hirsch is Professor, emeritus of English and Judaic Studies at Brown University. In 1966-67 he taught at Bar-Ilan University, in Ramat-Gan, Israel. Some relevant publications include, *Auschwitz: True Tales from a Grostesque Land,* translation from Polish of a typescript in the Yad Vashem archive, by Sara Przytyk, with Roslyn Hirsch; afterword, with Eli Pfefferkorn (University of North Carolina Press, 1985); *The Deconstruction of Literature: Criticism After Auschwitz* (University of New England Press, 1991); Isaiah Spiegel, "Bread," *Midstream* XXX (Dec., 1984), 15-18 (translation from Yiddish); Spiegel, "The Sampolne Rebbe," translation, *Tikkun,* May/June, 1995, pp. 24-26.

Deborah E. Lipstadt is Dorot Professor of Modern Jewish and Holocaust Studies at Emory University. Her widely acclaimed book *Denying The Holocaust: The Growing Assault on Truth and Memory* (Free Press/Macmillan, 1993) became a best seller and received the 1994 National Jewish Book Award. Dr. Lipstadt was a historical consultant to the United States Holocaust Memorial Museum where she helped design the section dedicated to the American Response to the Holocaust. In 1994 she was appointed by President Clinton to serve on the United States Holocaust Memorial Council. She is a member of the

Council's Executive Committee and chairs the museum's Education Committee. She serves on the State Department Advisory Committee on Religious Freedom Abroad.

Marcia Sachs Littell is Executive Director of The Annual Scholars' Conference on the Holocaust and the Philadelphia Center on the Holocaust, Genocide and Human Rights. She teaches at Temple University. Among her publications are *Liturgies on the Holocaust: An Interfaith Anthology* (Trinity Press, 1996), *The Holocaust: Forty Years After* (Mellen Press, 1989), *Holocaust Education: A Resource Book for Teachers and Professional Leaders* (Mellen Press, 1985) and *Remembrance and Recollection* (University Press of America, 1996).

Hubert G. Locke is the John and Marguerite Corbally Professor of Public Service and Dean emeritus of the Graduate School of Public Affairs, University of Washington, Seattle. He is Co-founder of the Annual Scholars' Conference on the Holocaust and the Churches and Director of the William O. Douglas Institute and Associate Editor of *Holocaust and Genocide Studies*. He has written and edited numerous books which include, *The German Church Struggle and the Holocaust, The Church Confronts The Nazis, Exile in the Father Land, Remembrance and Recollection* (1996) and *Holocaust and Church Struggle: Religion, Power and the Politics of Resistance* (University Press of America, 1996).

Jürgen Manemann, is the assistant of Prof. Jürgen Werbick (Institute of Foundational Theology at the University of Münster), writing a habilitation-dissertation: "The Uncertainty of Modernity: Carl Schmitt and the New Political Theology." He is the author of *"Weil es nicht nur Geschichte ist." Die Begründung der Notwendigkeit einer fragmentarischen Historiographie des Nationalsozialismus aus politisch-theologischer Sicht* (LIT Verlag, 1995), and editor of *Jahrbuch Neue Politische Theologie. Bd. 1: Demokratiefähigkeit* (LIT Verlag, 1995).

Elisabeth Maxwell was born and grew up in France, but has spent all of her adult life in England. She holds a Ph.D. in Modern Languages from Oxford University and began studying the Holocaust as a result of genealogical research on her husband's family tree. Dr. Maxwell chaired the first major international conference on Holocaust Studies in England, "Remembering for the Future," in 1988. Former vice-president of the ICCJ, Honorary Doctor of Temple University and

Honorary Fellow of Tel Aviv University, she lectures widely on the Holocaust in Europe and the USA and recently published her memoirs, *A Mind of My Own* (Harper Collins 1994).

John T. Pawlikowski is Professor of Social Ethics at the Catholic Theological Union in Chicago. He is a member of the Executive committee of the U.S. Holocaust Memorial Council. He serves as Chair of the Committee on Church Relations and is a member of its Committee on Conscience and Academic Committee. He is also a member of the U.S. Catholic Bishops' Advisory Committee for Catholic-Jewish Relations and Co-Chairs the National Polish-American/Jewish-American Council. He has authored ten volumes including *The Challenge of the Holocaust for Christian Theology* and *Jesus and the Theology of Israel*.

Abraham J. Peck is the Director of the American Jewish Archives, Cincinnati, Ohio and co-founder of the Greater Cincinnati Interfaith Holocaust Memorial Foundation. He served as special advisor to the chairman of the United States Holocaust Memorial Museum and has published ten books on topics dealing with German antisemitism, the Holocaust and American Jewish history and life.

Didier Pollefeyt holds a bachelor's degree in Philosophy, a Licentiate Degree in Religious Studies and a master's and doctorate in Theology. He has written two studies respectively on the Jewish post-Holocaust thinking of Rubenstein and Fackenheim, both of which were awarded a prize of encouragement of the *Foundation Auschwitz* (Brussels, 1989 & 1992). Since 1991 he worked as Doctoral Researcher of the National Fund for Scientific Research (N.F.W.O.) at the Faculty of Theology of the Catholic University Louvain. In 1993 his work "Religious Teaching of the Holocaust" was awarded the Belgian "Prize of Peace."

Gottfried Helferich Wagner, born in Bayreuth, is the great grandson of Richard Wagner. He studied musicology (under Professor Wessely, Vienna) German Philology (under Professor Zeman, Vienna), philosophy (under Professor Klein, Vienna) and piano, counterpoint and harmony (under Professor Kojetinsky, Graz, Bayreuth) and singing (E. Schartel, Nuremberg Conservatory). Since 1990, he has made rapprochement with children of survivors and children of perpetrators central to his life's work.